Claude Julien

D1326974

Suicide of the Democracies

Translated by J. A. Underwood

CALDER & BOYARS

First published in Great Britain in 1975
by Calder & Boyars Ltd
18 Brewer Street London W1R 4AS

Originally published in France in 1972
as *Le Suicide des Democraties* by
Editions Bernard Grasset, Paris

Typeset by Gloucester Typesetting Co. Ltd and printed by
Ebenezer Baylis & Son Ltd, The Trinity Press,
Worcester

CONTENTS

PREFACE TO THE
ENGLISH EDITION

It is extraordinary when the diagnosis put forward in a book is so resoundingly confirmed by events. The author would be tempted to sit back and take pleasure in having been proved exactly right if there were not so much hanging on the outcome of the debate. Debate? But what makes one so uneasy is that, despite the mass of facts already on record, there is no debate, only discussions devoted to adjusting details, and no getting down to the fundamental difficulties that beset *all* democratic societies. The Western democracies are in too much of a shambles to go on with minor repairs. If they are to be saved, new forms of government and new ways of consulting the people have to be invented which are more suitable to the demands of industrial societies; otherwise both Europe and North America will remain attached to a democratic ritual that is devoid of meaning and out of touch with reality, while the real decisions will be the product of mechanisms alien to the democratic spirit.

This book is a warning. It endeavours to demonstrate that, with the complicity of public opinion, political parties and the mass media, the West has allowed democratic life to grow anaemic. Numerous causes have conspired to this tragic result, but the most important of these can be reduced to the fact that Western societies have let their economic objectives get ahead of their political objectives. Without altogether losing sight of their desire to reinforce fundamental liberties, to assure an equitable justice and to promote equality among citizens, they have, with an eye trained on the curve of GNP, given priority to developing the forces of production, and to various techniques aimed at further expansion. Generally speaking, they have reached their goal, or are very close. But, at the same time, they have seen their democratic vitality stagnate or even regress. For economic expansion is not synonymous with democracy, and it can even be achieved—as has happened in Brazil—by dictatorial means. A full and satisfied consumer is not for that a free citizen.

Reducing socio-economic inequalities has been the dream of every industrial society but, as the first chapter of this book shows, expansion only makes inequality more pronounced when its fruits are unequally distributed. In fact, the figures quoted in support of this argument are already, within months, out of date, largely because the inflation which has hit the whole of Western Europe and North America penalizes the poor much more heavily than the leisured classes. With the rate of inflation at 8 to 10 per cent, salary adjustments cannot hope to compensate for rises in the price of goods absolutely indispensable to ordinary life. 'Poverty areas' like those analyzed in the following pages are still larger in 1973, and the situation can only get worse in 1974. The figures will not be known for two or three years, but they will show that the democracies have come no closer to their goal of narrowing the gap between rich and poor. An eventual slowdown of economic activity, following on the energy crisis, will make that gap even wider. Our societies are less democratic today than they were yesterday, and they run a high risk of being even less so tomorrow if an economic tailspin provokes more widespread unemployment.

The second chapter shows that democratic institutions are breaking down in those gigantic urban complexes which are so far from being able to perform the functions of cities that they no longer deserve the name. For the most part, 'urbanized areas' coincide with 'poverty areas' and render the contrasts between misery and luxury all the more glaring. It seems that citizens have become so used to slow but inexorable decay that they are no longer aware of it. Yet as the buying power of the poor shrinks, the dramatic conflicts which rack the vast urban areas have become still harsher.

In the final analysis, however, none of this goes to the heart of the problem. The aggravation of social inequalities damages the democratic principle, but it is not enough to kill it. It can even stimulate it to the degree that it stirs a greater number of citizens to intervene more actively in public life. Many poor people get personally involved in the life of society as active citizens responsible for its development, whereas too many of the affluent are so locked up in their cushioned isolation that they become parasites whose thirst for power has nothing to do with concern for their fellow citizens. The real drama is that the procedure for selecting public officials is so far from complying with the demands of democracy and that decision making continues to escape real democratic control. And these are the two points that have been so thoroughly reinforced by the events that have taken place since this book was written.

Chapter III points out how universal suffrage has been perverted by the money spent on long-drawn-out election campaigns, and by the lack of courage displayed by parties and candidates who avoid all real debate on vital issues when they go after the citizen's vote. Various politico-financial scandals and numerous cases of corruption are cited in this book; they have been given wider publicity since the first edition was published. Other disturbing facts have been revealed since then, like the sorry complaisance of a German Opposition Deputy who, for money, let Chancellor Brandt escape defeat in a crucial vote of confidence.

It is in the United States, however, that the most serious violation of democracy has been committed. Triumphally re-elected at the moment when the French edition of this book appeared, President Richard Nixon hit a record low in the popularity polls several months later. What explains such a reversal of public opinion in a democratic regime? Optimists will say that the Watergate scandal argues on behalf of democracy, which is the only system that would allow press and parliament publicly to denounce the illegal machinations of a Chief of State. This argument should certainly not be discounted, but it leaves the essential problem untouched, namely that universal suffrage has brought to power a man who did not deserve it, a man who had held on to power for months while the voters and their representatives had made it clear that he no longer enjoyed their confidence. In England during this same period, personalities who were implicated in much less serious compromises at least had the elegance and loyalty to hand in their resignations.

What is most upsetting is not that the Republican Party had Democratic Campaign Headquarters broken into and sabotaged their opponent's election campaign nor, for that matter, that these tactics were superfluous to ensure electoral victory; what must not be overlooked in any examination of the workings of American democracy is:

(1) that them incumbent president had given himself, with the help of techniques borrowed from the advertising industry, an entirely false image. There is no such thing as the 'new Nixon' who had been made respectable and responsible by the exercise of power. The Americans elected in 1968, and re-elected in 1972, a Nixon whose spirit, ideas and

methods were directly traceable to the young demagogue who began his political career twenty years earlier with a dishonest campaign in California and who was accused of embezzling funds in 1952. Since then, he had perfected and carried to the highest degree of efficiency methods which are unacceptable in a democracy; thanks to the development of television he had been able to deceive a greater number of voters. The law punishes the industrialist or merchant who uses false advertising to sell his product; it does not sanction politicians and parties who use it to sell candidates and their programmes.

(2) that a man who got into power by deceiving his fellow citizens with a false image continued to mislead them while in office. He deceived them not only with regard to Watergate and the notorious tapes of his conversations, but also by firing Special Prosecutor Archibald Cox after having solemnly promised him every latitude in inquiring into the affair.

(3) that the President had recourse, in the exercise of his functions, to means forbidden by laws, as in the instance of attempting to bribe the judge in the Ellsberg case by offering him the directorship of the FBI.

(4) that Mr. Nixon surrounded himself with collaborators whom no one could suppose worthy of the confidence of a Chief of State. He twice chose as his vice-president Mr. Spiro Agnew, who has since been forced to resign in the face of evidence that he had peddled influence while serving as governor of Maryland and of indications that he continued to do so after assuming a position one step from the presidency. Two members of the Nixon Cabinet, Maurice Stans and John Mitchell (who was also the President's campaign manager) have been indicted, as are other men who directly advised the President on affairs of State. This has threatened not only the reputation of an individual president but the very trustworthiness of democratic institutions.

These are still not grounds enough for placing the United States in a grave constitutional crisis. But to this list of violations of elementary public morality (and an item could be appended on the financing of two private residences in California and Florida) Mr Richard Nixon has added the infringement of constitutional principles and the misuse of democratic institutions. He deceived the Congress and citizens by illegally ordering the bombing of Cambodia. He juggled the federal budget by, on the one hand, financing projects opposed by Congress and, on the other, by impounding funds appropriated for programmes he refused to execute. There is nor surer way to destroy democracy than to upset the balance of powers. This offence against the very essence of democracy cannot be eradicated by the simple act of resignation.

Who today would dare to maintain that the balance of powers is more scrupulously respected in Europe than in the United States? President Georges Pompidou discussed the matter in a television interview on 24 October 1973—he was calling for a reduction of the presidential term to five years—and managed to speak only of the balance between executive and legislative power, without ever mentioning the judiciary which is, in France, dangerously subordinated to the executive. In Italy, the unbalance is organized, as it was in France under the Fourth Republic, to the advantage of a legislature which is very often paralyzed by the instability of parliamentary coalitions. In England, many voices—and they are cited in this book—have been raised in protest against the government's attitude toward the House of Commons.

This constitutional problem has crippled the ability of institutions to function democratically; it is aggravated by the lack of authentic debate on questions affecting the future of the nation. Without debate, there is no democracy, and too many democratic countries are satisfied with the appearances of debate, on the excuse that the issues are too complex to be understood by the ordinary voter. For example, the entire West is in the grip of an energy crisis. This is not just due to the conflict in the Middle East; even if the Arab countries had not made a political weapon of reduced oil shipments, Europe and America would very shortly have been confronted by an energy crisis for the very simple reason—and no expert will deny this—that the consumption of energy in the West had reached such a rate of growth that it was urgent to develop new energy sources or to stabilize energy consumption. This presupposes a radical transformation of the current economic model. But this central problem has never been taken up seriously by the parties in an election campaign. What this means is that the techno-structures and the governments now in power make major decisions quite apart from any real democratic consultation.

The great electoral debates in Europe and in the United States have likewise sidestepped the question of relations with Israel and with the Arab countries, despite its being at the heart of a drama which could unleash a world crisis. This issue, like the fight against inflation, has been brushed off with passing allusions that are too vague to disturb any potential voter. Pious phrases are no substitute for democratic debate.

So we are left in 1975 with the spectacle of countries that like to think of themselves as democratic, but which never offer voters the possibility of choosing between candidates who stand on clearly defined positions. Election campaigns get more and more expensive, so that parties get more and more wrapped up in serious compromises that diminish even further the possibility of rational debate so necessary to a healthy democracy. Whatever anyone may claim, the ideal purpose of a political party is not merely to seize power but to accede to power with a clear mandate from the voters to carry out a clearly specified programme.

The European countries may not have had any scandals as serious as Watergate, but they can hardly doze off in self-satisfaction. They should know that Watergate sprang from elements well-known to Europe: inadequate communication between electors and elected; substitution of the will to power for the will to serve the public welfare; inadequate controls on the role of money in public life; superficial and, in the end, useless debates on the most important problems facing the country. Unless they act quickly, the Western democracies risk falling before the first crisis. Unfortunately, it seems that both voters and those voted into office have, by their passivity, already accepted this form of suicide.

C.J.

INTRODUCTION

The Promises and the Reality

For a number of years now governments in both Western Europe and North America have been promising reforms of a more or less bold nature designed to usher in a 'new society'. They do so in response to a certain feeling of expectancy, to certain sometimes ill-defined but nevertheless deeply felt aspirations on the part of the people at large. The latter indeed have daily to face problems of which they perhaps see the ideal solution but not the practical means of putting it into effect. They feel powerless in the face of the difficulties of everyday existence, multiplied as these are by giantism of urban concentrations, by modern forms of production, and by the unwieldiness of the bureaucracies that be. Such frustration may seem incomprehensible in wealthy societies enjoying a high standard of living, an advanced degree of scientific and economic development, and very considerable human and material resources. It is none the less real, and the mass media aggravate it by giving wide publicity to the image of a highly desirable future made possible by the progress of science, technology, and the mind of man.

Between the hope thus nourished and the reality of experience, the contrast is brutal. Governments and opposition parties vie with one another in promising remedies while extremists of either camp regard the evil as inherent in the very system itself. The public for its part protests occasionally but with no great conviction. When all is said and done, its attitude to the obstacles it comes up against is more resigned than angry. Such despondency is the opposite of reassuring: it is akin to the kind of despair that can end in rebellion.

Are such dissatisfaction and discontent justified? Not for a moment can Western man escape the ambiguity of his situation: he may see himself as the victim of injustice and of assaults upon his dignity or freedom, powerless to make good his rights, beguiled with promises that are never kept—but nothing will let him forget that he belongs to a tiny, highly privileged minority in a world in which two thousand million human beings live in misery or under regimes that allow them no rights whatever. Cultivating this ambiguity, the mass media, while conjuring up for him the wonderful future to which he can look forward, treat him to a hefty, daily dose of brutal or pitiable images of a world where violence, destitution, death, and contempt are the rule. If he looks at the world around him Western man may react with a blush of shame at his privileged position. If for the sake of his intellectual comfort he chooses to ignore that world and think only of himself he remains, for all his privileges, dissatisfied.

However enviable his lot, he naturally hopes it will go on getting better and better. No doubt it lies in his make-up to do so. But on top of that Western man lives in societies that have taught him that his highest aspirations lie within the realm of possibility, and the progress made over the last few decades convinces him that this is no vain hope.

Such progress has been the fruit of governments defined summarily as democratic and capitalist. Democracy and capitalism foster in the individual the conviction that he is master of his own destiny: in casting his vote he personally determines the broad political orientation of his country; by his labour and enterprise he determines the prosperity and vigour of his society. Such, at any rate, is the theory, broadly speaking. The people is sovereign. Satisfied and content, it is beholden to none but itself. Dissatisfied and discontented, it has none but itself to blame.

In reality, however, the picture is rather different. Freedom of enterprise is subject to certain necessary restraints laid down by the state as emanation of the popular will. Through social and economic legislation, through public investment and government contracts with private industry, through taxation and credit, through defining rates of exchange, and in a thousand other ways the state is continually intervening in the economy. It does so in the name of the public interest and on the strength of the powers vested in it by a majority of the citizens. So how can those citizens complain about their standard of living, about housing or transport conditions, the inadequacy of educational or medical facilities, town-planning decisions, lack of cultural activities or leisure to enjoy them, and so on? The sovereign is disgruntled, feels it has been had. By whom? By its elected representatives? By the administration? By the system?

Authoritative voices on both sides of the Atlantic claim that the 'system' is to a greater or lesser extent paralyzed, that society is 'jammed'. Opposition forces take up the cry, and even governments are inclined to agree. Aware of their successes, the societies of the West are also conscious of their faults. Delays and injustices, binding and grinding in all spheres of social activity prove that the democratic machine is not running as smoothly as it would and should.

Is it possible to uncover the roots of the evil? Countries as different as France and the United States, Italy and Canada are up against the same difficulties. A comparative study of the most serious problems facing the democracies of western Europe and North America ought to throw some light on the subject. Despite differences in constitutional structure, electoral system, population, economic development, national tradition, and financial or military strength, all these countries belong to the same sector of civilization—namely that governed by regimes both democratic and capitalist. Whether small or great, endowed with stable governments backed by a solid majority or with weak coalition governments, centralized or highly decentralized in structure, with or without ethnically and linguistically homogeneous populations, all the countries of the West are a prey to the same sickness.

What appears to be at issue, then, is a Western system whose political regimes are based on universal suffrage and whose economic regimes are founded on freedom of enterprise within the limits laid down by segislation. Other countries no doubt face the same problems but under altogether different economic and political conditions. Class conflicts, social inequality, injustice, actual violations of the law, and so on are also rife in under-developed countries with regimes of a more or less authoritarian nature, but these countries do not enjoy the same material resources nor their inhabitants the same political powers to put matters right. The development of urban concentrations preoccupies not only the West but also the socialist countries and the countries of the Third World, but such solutions as they may variously arrive at will not proceed from the same principles. Criticism of modern methods of production and the organization of labour is not exclusive to the West, but the means available to the German, the Soviet, and the Brazilian worker for changing his society are in no way comparable.

Without forgetting the universal character of certain problems currently facing the West, then, it will be useful to grasp their specific character and the specific conditions obtaining in the countries on both sides of the Atlantic that base their existence on liberal democracy and controlled capitalism. A reminder that Indonesians, Poles, or Argentinians

2

are up against similar or even more serious difficulties is not going to be much help to workers at Renault, Fiat, or Ford, students in Rome, Berkeley, or Nanterre, southern-Italian peasants, Breton farmers, or Californian fruit-growers. The thing to do is to define possible solutions, and these will not be the same for wage-earners in Belgium and Hungary, blacks in Chicago and Dakar, voters in France and Rumania, or TV viewers in New York and Leningrad.

The Western democracies can of course be evaluated in relation to the under-developed countries or the socialist countries: such a comparison will throw into relief the prosperity and freedom that they guarantee to their nationals. They can also be judged on their own account, in relation to the ideal they profess: this will bring out their defects and shortcomings, the things that nourish the sickness. Conservatives can counter the most justified of criticisms by quoting the West's successes, while progressives will stress the gap that exists between the dream and the reality. Dialogue becomes impossible. Good sense, however, suggests a double obligation on the Western democracies: they owe it to themselves to come as close as possible to the goals they have freely set themselves; with regard to the less developed, their wealth imposes a duty of solidarity.

It is in this context that the democracies of the West are here passed rapidly under review. Many aspects of the problem have deliberately been shelved, leaving only such questions as are essential to the phenomenon of Western democracy. Has it fulfilled its principal promises, as expressed in simple terms that are passing steadily out of use in the forum of political debate—justice, liberty, equality, fraternity? Every scrap of progress in these four spheres strengthens democracy both in its institutions and in the minds of its citizens. Every violation of these basic principles undermines the very foundations of democratic society.

Such a review, as well as being inevitably incomplete, cannot be anything but provisional. For all their many chronic 'blockages', there is nothing static about the societies of the West. They are changing all the time with the evolution of men's minds—a slow enough process, perhaps—and with the introduction of technological innovations— often a rapid one. The difference between these two rhythms gives rise to unavoidable distortions. One Western country, the first to enter the technological era, has evolved more rapidly than the rest: the United States. Looking at American society today, Western Europe can get some idea of the problems it will be up against in a few years' time. In this comparative study of the societies of Western Europe and North

America it is thus the latter that is most fully documented: whether it is a question of social inequality (chapter one), urbanization (chapter two), the workings of political institutions (chapter three), economic concepts and structures (chapter four), or civil rights (chapter five), the United States offers as it were a magnified version of what is happening in Europe. In various degrees and at various levels of intensity all the Western democracies suffer from a sickness that would appear to be approaching its culminating point in the United States. Comparison of these situations may make diagnosis easier and point to the treatment required.

Some possible remedies are mentioned during the course of the argument. Clearly these will not be sufficient in themselves. The first thing to do is to spot the dangers. Most of them, as we shall see, stem from the fact that the Western democracies have abandoned certain of their most ambitious objectives. It seemed the right time to recall these objectives by contrasting them with the reality obtaining in the various countries of Europe and America. To rediscover the democracies' ultimate purpose is to give them a chance of flourishing. To let that purpose become overshadowed is to admit that they are bound for suicide.

C.J.
June 1972

CHAPTER ONE

A Dream Betrayed - Equality

- The privileges of the West
- Poverty amid plenty
- Destitution is profitable
- The pariahs of capitalism
- Accumulated inequalities

The dazzling success of the West has been sung in every key. The industrialized countries on both sides of the Atlantic comprise a bare 15 per cent of the population of the world—an extraordinarily privileged minority on a planet where more than two thousand million human beings are under-nourished, under-educated, ill-housed, and ill-equipped.

The evidence of discontent or crisis can blind no one to the triumphant achievements of Western Europe and North America. This success can be gauged by a variety of simple indices of which the simplest and most convincing is drawn not from production figures but from demographic statistics: Westerners are born into conditions of existence that give them a life expectancy of 70 years in Italy and the United States, 71 years in Great Britain, France, West Germany, Switzerland, and Belgium, 72 years in Canada, 73 years in Norway and 74 years in Holland, the record being held by Sweden with 77 years. The Soviet Union (70 years) and Japan (71 years) are in the same bracket.

In general terms life expectancy in the industrialized countries of the West has increased by some twenty years since the beginning of the century. This is in brutal contrast to the countries of the Third World, where it is no more than 25 years for men in Gabon and 31 years for women in Upper Volta. In the former Belgian Congo it stands at a bare 39 years, in Indonesia at 44 years, in Morocco and South Africa at 47 years, in Bolivia, India, and Nigeria at 50 years, in Pakistan at 51 years, in Egypt at 53 years, and in the Philippines at 58 years.

Success and diversity

Better food and better sanitary conditions give the Westerner more protection against illness and a chance of living longer. While the industrialized nations naturally promote massive medical research into the ailments characteristic of their level of development (cardiac and nervous diseases, cancer, etc.), the Third World is seriously under-equipped as far as the most elementary sanitary services are concerned. The number of doctors and hospital beds at the disposal of the population offers another index of the success of the West:

	Number of inhabitants to	
	1 *doctor*	1 *hospital bed*
Industrialized Countries		
Great Britain	977	101
France	900	86
West Germany	650	93
Italy	570	100
Belgium	—	359
Holland	860	238
Norway	741	100
Sweden	890	62
United States	670	120
Canada	892	90
Third World		
India	4,860	1,710
Brazil	1,810	298
Morocco	12,000	660
Indonesia	23,000	1,200
Nigeria	36,500	1,780
Pakistan	6,600	3,120

These figures bring out a paradox: among the industralized countries, the level of public health facilities is not a function of prosperity. For example the wealthiest country—the United States—does not have the highest life expectancy, and as far as hospital beds are concerned it is less well off than Canada, Sweden, France, and even Italy. It has less doctors in relation to its population than West Germany, though it has for years been practising a policy of importing large numbers of medical personnel, mainly from the English-speaking countries; an average of 1,200 foreign doctors emigrate to the United States each year. Nevertheless, as against the rest of the world the industrialized countries constitute a pretty homogeneous whole. Yet they regard their own health services as inadequate: in Europe hospitals are often antiquated, and the United States had to increase its public health budget from $1,700 million in 1965–6 to $13,000 million in 1970–71 and to $18,000 million in 1972–3.

Differences in standard of living among the industrialized nations are equally pronounced. Average annual per capita income is more than three times higher in the United States than it is in Italy. But however large the gaps, they look tiny in the context of the world as a whole. If the average Italian lives only a third as well as the American, he is twelve times better off than the Indonesian and seventeen times better

Average per capita income (in dollars)

Industrialized countries

United States	3,680
Sweden	2,665
Canada	2,087
Norway	1,800
West Germany	1,753
France	1,738
Belgium	1,700
Holland	1,610
Great Britain	1,560
Italy	1,116

Third World

South Africa	521
Brazil	350
Morocco	168
Egypt	166
Bolivia	165
Philippines	126
Indonesia	95
Pakistan	89
India	73
Nigeria	63

2*

off than the Nigerian. Certain Westerners, then, while feeling themselves privileged in comparison with the inhabitants of the Third
World, at the same time see themselves as the 'rejects' of an affluence
distributed unequally among the industrialized countries.

All terms of comparison bring out in the same way both the privileged character of the industrialized nations of the West and the very
considerable differences that exist between them. These differences,
whether due to the size of a particular country, its degree of technological evolution, its national traditions, or some quite other reason,
can be illustrated by means of a few simple figures regarding the structure of the economy: the contribution of agriculture to the gross
national product varies from 4 per cent in West Germany and 6 per
cent in the United States to 18 per cent in Italy—but it stands at 32 per
cent in the Philippines, 47 per cent in Indonesia, for all its wealth of
mineral resources, 49 per cent in India, and 56 per cent in Nigeria.
Nuances between the rich nations tend to become blurred in any
comparison with the rest of the world.

Because of the disparities between them the industrialized countries
have occasionally experienced and will continue to experience tensions
and crises. Their common membership in a small and privileged club,
however, ensures their continued solidarity. In spite of appreciable
differences of level and vastly different degrees of economic power,
they all draw their prosperity from the same sources: it is the fruit of
an economic system and a political system that are mutually inseparable.

The differences arise out of the degree of industrialization achieved,
the way in which industry and agriculture are conceived and organized,
the distribution of purchasing power and of social or fiscal burdens, the
financing of investments, the structure of external trade, the extent of
competition, and so on—in a word, all the criteria by which Western
capitalism can be defined. Such capitalism can differ considerably in
appearance from country to country: Great Britain and France have
resorted to a greater or lesser degree of nationalization, a course that
the United States has rejected, and the extent of state intervention in the
economy varies from one country to another. But these nuances, however considerable, do not really alter the distinctive character of the
industrialized countries: be their nationalized sector large or small, they
are all wedded to freedom of enterprise within a context in which the
public authority can, by means of taxation, credit, and budgetary
measures, steer the economy, stimulate certain activities, suggest goals,
fix rules, or lay down norms.

Between the feudalism that is still rife in certain under-developed countries and the various forms of socialism practised in four continents, the industrialized West remains homogeneous in its diversity. Granted that a worker's average weekly wage is $132 in the United States and only $55 in Great Britain, his average monthly income $444 in Canada and only $250 in West Germany. Nevertheless all these countries provide their workers with a standard of living higher than that which they would enjoy under other regimes. The countries of the West feel themselves to be—and indeed are—fused into a single capitalist whole.

The political differences between them are no less great, but they all fall within a certain definition of liberal democracy. The two-party system works differently in Great Britain than in the United States; the West German, American, and Canadian federations differ in their distribution of powers between central and local government; general elections are variously organized; relations between executive and legislative branches are not subject to the same laws; and so one could go on. This diversity of constitutional machinery, however, serves only to illustrate a common allegiance to a single conception of democracy as expressed in differing national contexts.

This wide variety of political systems and economic structures is inherent in the very aspirations of the West. Far from being an accident of history it is part of the logic of a system based on a desire for freedom and progress within a context of respect for the law. It is not something that is tolerated as a necessary evil: it is the concrete expression from country to country of that fluidity and flexibility without which neither capitalism nor liberal democracy could exist.

This is why, in their diversity, the industrialized countries affirm their solidarity by means of alliances and agreements covering all spheres of human activity. They are driven to it by necessity: it is among themselves that they do four-fifths of their business, and it is only by a common effort that they can ensure their defence—as France recognized when it decided to remain a member of NATO, even after withdrawing its forces from the organization.

The industrialized countries of the West know that what unites them is stronger than what divides them, and they never forget it even in the heat of their fiercest debates. But they are all a prey to the same misgiving: they all question the value of the society they have created, for the picture that they actually present is too far removed from the hopes they have themselves aroused.

Areas of poverty

The contrast between rich and poor countries is a brutal one and despite widespread indifference will come increasingly to constitute a threat to the 'haves'. Added to this danger from without, however, there is a danger from within. The prosperity prevailing in the West is itself very unevenly distributed, not only from country to country but within each national community. The industrialized societies of the West have something else in common besides their enviable general level of affluence—their areas of poverty.

If the average person is three times as wealthy in the United States as he is in Italy, the threshold of poverty likewise varies from one country to another. Whether black or white, the poor American living in a destitute rural area or in the slums of one of the great cities has, in absolute terms, a higher income than his European counterpart. But he also lives in a society in which rents, food, clothing, and above all medical care are all more expensive.

On both sides of the Atlantic these areas of poverty can be defined more or less as follows: the unemployed whom economic expansion has failed to provide with a job, certain categories of workers having no professional qualification, small farmers or traders whose businesses cannot keep up with modern needs, old people with inadequate pensions or social security, the physically or mentally handicapped, and lastly certain ethnic groups constituting the sub-proletariat of post-industrial society.

The affluent societies are unwilling to face up to the vast areas of poverty and sometimes of destitution that expose both the crying injustices and the absurd waste inherent in their expansion. Such expansion is the fruit of an economic system that has proved itself and of a political regime with which it is closely bound up. Can that system and that regime be called democratic when they tolerate such grave inequalities—so much poverty beside so much luxury? Or is that poverty merely an accident, an imperfection that is doubtless deplorable but that can easily be put right thanks to the very dynamism of the capitalist system and to the democratic character of a regime based on freedom of criticism and debate?

The fact is that in the century of speed and efficiency the societies of the West are slow to discern their faults and even slower to correct them. The following remark by the authors of an excellent study of poverty in Great Britain can be applied to the West as a whole:

The period since the end of the Second World War was interpreted as one of more or less uninterrupted and continuing economic growth, with the new wealth being distributed increasingly equitably throughout the population. The age-old malaise of poverty, far from being an endemic problem facing a mass of the population, was felt to be a slight social hangover: a problem affecting tiny groups of people who, through their incompetence or fecklessness, were failing to share in the new affluence.[1]

If luxury is sometimes loud, poverty is as a rule discreet. So the British remained in the dark for a long time regarding the numerical importance of these 'small groups of people' condemned to live on the fringe of the general prosperity. Their surprise was considerable when Brian Abel-Smith and Peter Townsend published the results of an inquiry that has since become a classic.[2] Their investigations led them to this astounding conclusion: Great Britain, in 1960, had seven and a half million poor, that is to say 14 per cent of the total population. But what was most disturbing was that the areas of poverty were not shrinking in proportion as economic expansion continued. On the contrary, they were growing larger: the proportion of poor people to the total population had doubled between 1953 and 1960, and it had further increased between 1960 and 1965. Was this kind of parallelism between economic expansion and the development of areas of poverty compatible with a civilization that called itself democratic? To answer this it was first necessary to push the inquiry further.

Who were these mysterious poor whose very existence passed unnoticed as far as the majority of Britons were concerned? Abel-Smith and Townsend broke down the seven and a half million total as follows:

——3,000,000 people living in families where the father was working full-time;

——2,500,000 living in families where the father had reached retiring age;

——750,000 living in fatherless families;

——750,000 with one parent sick or disabled;

——500,000 where the father was out of work.

Commenting on these figures five years later, Coates and Silburn were able to write: 'The most important single cause of poverty is not indolence, nor fecundity, nor sickness, nor even unemployment, nor villainy of any kind but is, quite simply, low wages.'[3] Throughout the

West, in a context of unprecedented affluence, economic expansion has failed to eliminate low wages. Perhaps it even needs them, no amount of automation having succeeded in abolishing jobs that, since they require no special skills, are the least well paid.

Of these seven and a half million British living in poverty, more than two million are children under fifteen. For them the future is even darker than the present is for their parents. In a country such as Great Britain, where education is relatively less democratized than in certain Continental countries or in the United States, these children have virtually no hope of acquiring the education that is so much more necessary today than it was when their parents were adolescents.

Great Britain, thanks to its Labour governments, has a highly developed system of social security, which many Americans have been denouncing for a quarter of a century as crypto-socialism. Yet this system has failed to eliminate poverty. In fact, 'while between 1948–60 the real value of the scales was increased by about a quarter, real disposable income per head increased by twice that rate. Thus, far from being over-generous the National Assistance Board scales were demonstrably over-stringent.'[4]

These allowances are useful. Thanks to them the poor have become a little less poor. They are not enough, however, for they have not enabled the people drawing them to escape from poverty. Democracy is not a charitable institution setting out merely to alleviate social ills. Determined to eliminate them, it seeks to be an instrument of justice. Faced by the permanence of injustice, it is prompted by a defensive reflex to make much of the measures by which it has reduced the extent of the evil. But what are its terms of reference? It draws them from the past in order to prove—and no one disputes this—that the poor of today are less poor than those of a generation ago. But poverty cannot be measured in terms of past epochs and distant lands. Poverty is defined in the context of the present situation in a particular country by comparing people's actual condition and the aspirations society nurtures in them.

Poverty is a social phenomenon. It cannot be gauged by a simple calculation of available resources and the cost of bodily subsistence. Like all social problems it depends on the given society's general degree of evolution: a bathroom was a luxury eighty years ago, a washing-machine thirty years ago. The characteristics of present-day poverty would have defined a decent if modest existence at the beginning of the century. Adam Smith hit the nail on the head when he wrote, 'by necessaries I understand, not only the commodities which are indispensably necessary for the support of life, but whatever the custom of the country renders it indecent for creditable people, even of the lowest order, to be without'.[5]

Analysing the faults and failings of the affluent society in the United States, John K. Galbraith arrived at a similar definition:

> People are poverty-stricken when their income, even if it is adequate for survival, falls markedly below that of the community. Then they cannot have what the larger community regards as the minimum necessary for decency; and they cannot wholly escape, therefore, the judgement of the larger community that they are indecent. They are degraded, for, in the literal sense, they live outside the grades or categories which the community regards as acceptable.[6]

Seen from this point of view poverty is nothing short of scandalous, for it is society that sets the norms for a decent minimum and it is society that lets a large number of people live below that minimum. The scandal is all the greater for the fact that the society in question calls itself democratic. Until the contrary is shown to be the case democracy implies a ceaseless struggle for social justice and, if its dreams do not run to Utopian egalitarianism, it rejects such excessive inequalities as are degrading to man. John K. Galbraith has not really thought the thing through to its logical conclusion when he describes people who live below the 'acceptable minimum' as being 'degraded': what is in point of fact degraded is the democratic spirit to which society pays lip-service.

The British trade unions recently established that 'About 2·5 million males and about 5 million females, including juveniles and part-time workers, habitually earn less than £15 a week, whilst 1·5 million adult male full-time workers take home less than £15 a week.'[7] In France the number of wage-earners on SMIG ('Salaire Minimum Interprofessionel Garanti', the guaranteed minimum wage of between 682 and 792 F. a month according to whether a 40 or 44 hour week is worked) has decreased slightly and now stands at between five and six hundred thousand. But they are far from representing the sum total of the poor—the old people, smallholders, foreign workers, and so on that populate the 'poor France'[8] that a rich France prefers to ignore.

Altogether, in 1972, some ten million French households have an income of less than 1,500 F. a month. For most of them their pay rises do no more than keep pace with rising prices, i.e. their purchasing power remains essentially the same: they have no share in the fruits of the country's economic growth.

Not only do the poorest and weakest draw the lowest wages and the smallest pensions but they are hit much harder than anyone else by inflation. They have to swallow the hard realities of unequal development twice over. Under the present system they have no chance whatever of escaping from the vicious circle of poverty.[9]

The gap is widening between a privileged minority and a mass of people allowed no part in expansion. Between the two a substantial slice of the population enjoys a greater or lesser degree of affluence. It is this slice that sets the tone of society as a whole: the entire machinery of production and distribution as well as all the resources of publicity urge it to look up towards what it has little chance of attaining rather than down to where poverty and destitution nourish despair in the form of uncomfortable and sometimes insanitary housing conditions, illness, difficulties of social integration, and so on.

Foreign workers

Are these areas of poverty mere 'blots' on the face of societies enjoying a state of rapid growth? The fate of the foreign worker in the majority of countries suggests a different explanation. Whatever their growth-rate, all the societies of the West have large-scale unemployment. Like the blacks, Mexicans, and Puerto Ricans in the United States, the immigrant workers of Europe are the first to get the sack. In the Thionville region during 1971 numbers of them were laid off one or more days a week and others were repatriated. 'It's their job to be sacrificed,' said one employer. 'That's partly why we took them on. In a crisis they count less than our nationals.'[10]

Immigrant workers in France, for example, play an indispensable role—the only reason, indeed, for their being there. Their situation throws a particular light on that of the lowest paid French workers. According to the Ministry of Labour there are 3,200,000 aliens living in France of whom some 1,500,000 are wage earners.[11] They are divided up as follows:

	1972	1964
Algerians	750,000	520,000
Portuguese	685,000	100,000
Spaniards	650,000	517,000
Italians	590,000	688,000
Moroccans	170,000	60,000
Tunisians	95,000	40,000
Yugoslavs	65,000	17,000

More than 195,000 foreign workers entered France in 1969, then in 1970 the figure rose to a record 212,785, dropping back to 177,377 in 1971. Of this latter figure 72·5 per cent were manual or skilled workers prepared to accept jobs that nationals no longer wanted but that are nevertheless indispensable to the country's economic growth.

How do these foreign workers live? To take one example among thousands, in a building in the 18th *arrondissement* of Paris

a hundred and twenty African workers are crowded twenty or thirty to a room—tiny, windowless rooms with neither tables nor chairs. The heating is antiquated, the rain comes in everywhere, the sanitary arrangements—two water closets and four cold-water taps— leave a great deal to be desired, and the bedding is never changed. Briefly, an appalling slum. Moreover the landlord, who has been collecting 75 F. per person per month since 1968, has paid neither gas, nor electricity, nor water bills since 1969, with the result that these are continually being cut off.[12]

The proportion of foreign workers to the total working population of France increased from 6·88 per cent in 1962 to 7·61 per cent in 1968, and it has further increased since that date. But the majority of them are concentrated in the Paris region and in the south-eastern, Rhône-Alpes region. In the Rhône *département*, for example, they constitute 15 per cent of the working population. When the foreign workers at the Pennaroya works in Lyon went on strike at the beginning of 1972, the management conceded that they had grounds for complaint and that their conditions of accommodation in particular were 'open to criticism'. They even added, 'Furthermore, we have never ourselves regarded these as satisfactory.' But it needed a strike to make the firm think about improving conditions that were described as follows:

These Algerians, Moroccans, and Tunisians are living in poky little courts adjoining the factory, with five or seven beds to a room placed so close together you could barely get a broom between them, in a stuffy atmosphere with the grey of their blankets matching the greyness of the narrow windows that they sometimes cannot open on account of the fumes and noise from the sheds in which lead, bronze, and aluminium are being cast round the clock.[13]

In their common declaration of 21 December 1971, the CGT and the CFDT, the two big French trade-union organizations, could hardly do less than recall that 'the particular situation of the immigrant workers . . . is made intolerable by the widespread social and union discrimination they come under, by their deplorable living conditions, especially as regards housing, and by the pressures and repression of which they are frequently the victims.'

This is precisely what the government has said. The Prime Minister himself promised in 1970 that the slums would be gone by the end of 1971. The slums are still there, while the construction of acceptable housing drags on and on. Subversion lies not in denunciation of the scandal but in the very fact of its existence. Nor is the scandal primarily the government's doing. Indeed modern companies are coming increasingly if belatedly to recognize that their role cannot be confined strictly to the economic sphere. Were they to content themselves with producing and selling, the recruitment of labour under no matter what conditions would have a certain logic about it. But their fate is intimately bound up with that of the democratic society in which they live and develop and that safeguards their freedom. Democracy cannot resign itself to slums, insanitary housing conditions, poverty wages, and inhuman working conditions. If, neglecting these democratic imperatives, companies were to content themselves with producing as cheaply as possible, they would in effect be unloading on the state the task of making up for their shortcomings and rectifying their omissions. This would be tantamount to admitting the legitimacy of an increase in the kind of state intervention to which they are in principle opposed. They would be asking the community to shoulder part of their own responsibilities and the tax-payer to finance the process. This of course would involve certain guarantees. Are companies prepared to provide them?

The French government for its part has turned its attention to controlling the immigration of foreign workers. Agreements to this effect with the Algerian or Portuguese authorities cannot constitute more than a first step. The CGT and the CFDT are quite right in charging the government's plans with 'serious omissions as far as reception, social rights, and education are concerned, and telling denials as regards the right of immigrant workers to union representation'.[14]

The problem is the same all over Europe. In West Germany, where one worker in ten is an alien, only 20 per cent of them belong to a union. Yet the personnel manager of Daimler-Benz has said, 'Without the foreign workers German industry would not be where it is today.' Whether foreign workers constitute one in twenty of the wage-earning population as in Belgium and Sweden or one in four as in Switzerland, they are everywhere treated less well than nationals and to a greater or lesser extent kept on the fringe of society.

The cracks in a wealthy, democratic society can be seen in the countless violations of law of which foreign workers are the victims. In France the Law Association observed on 4 March 1972 that, as far as the penal code is concerned, immigrants are subject to texts that are meaningless to them. It added that the decrees and regulations governing rents are 'blithely by-passed' and that foreign workers encounter discrimination before the courts and in prison. Just as blacks in the United States are the chief victims of crime and delinquency, in France the victims of crimes committed by aliens are usually other aliens.

Throughout the West, because of the age curve, a large proportion of the poor contingent—national or immigrant—is made up of children. Of these it is of course the immigrant children that, for reasons of language and social and cultural adaptation, are at the greatest disadvantage. In France some 700,000 of them are of school age. For these 700,000 there are 250 'initiation classes'—obviously a totally inadequate number.

Taken as a whole, immigrant workers are the poor among the poor. Badly paid and badly housed, they are the victims of all kinds of discrimination. Is it merely because they are aliens that they are treated thus? If they were granted the host country's nationality—which most of them do not want—would this as it were magically ensure that their most basic human rights were respected? The answer is clearly no: they are exploited because their ignorance of language and the law as well as an element of racialism make them the more easily exploitable. Together with the less well qualified and less well organized of the national workers they are the appointed victims of a capitalist system that limits its narrow conception of progress to the economic sphere and of a political regime that is too ready to abandon its democratic aspirations.

Injustice and democracy

Democracy can brook no compromise with the kinds of injustice that afflict certain categories of wage-earners, whether national or immigrant. It stands condemned whenever it resigns itself to social inequalities that run counter to its ideal. No doubt the institutions of the Western democracies have failed to adapt to fresh problems. No doubt their structures are too cumbersome, too inefficient. But it is easier to modernize and renovate institutions and structures than it is to re-awaken the democratic faith and sense of justice of a whole people. The attention the unions have recently been paying to the problems of immigrant workers in France and the gesture of a number of young farmers in supplying striking foreign workers with food are encouraging signs. But is not this awakening long overdue?

The time-lag is too long between the moment when a problem arises and the moment when certain sections of opinion become aware of it. The poor—national and alien alike—are the forgotten ones of our affluent societies. More than their poverty it is this fact of their being forgotten that points to the crisis the societies of the West are passing through. It is above all a crisis of the democratic spirit.

This democratic spirit appears to be as dormant in the majority of citizens as it is in the men responsible for the smooth running of society's institutions. Concern for the general interest and for fundamental justice has been sacrificed to corporate interests backed by powerful pressure groups. Woe betide the weak and ill-organized who lack the means of making themselves heard. Their only recourse lies in violence and illegality. Whereupon society sits up and starts thinking of reforming its institutions or even inventing new ones. But in doing so it misses the main point, as summed up by Jacques Fauvet in these few lines that express the self-doubt of Western societies:

> To change present-day society, change its spirit more than its structures, to understand those who reject it, to make social relationships more just and above all human relationships more fraternal. If it were merely a question of politics, the actors and the roles are there, many and various. But since it is a crisis of civilization?[15]

A civilization is in a state of crisis when it is failing to live up to its aspirations. Its own momentum will no doubt keep it going. But suddenly that very momentum will reveal fresh challenges that, in its lethargy, it is slow to discern and slow to meet. The crisis having become apparent, a minority rises up in anger while the vast bulk of a contented society, not liking to be disturbed, draws itself in. Democracy once implied an egalitarian ideal that was what first gave it life. It has allowed it to atrophy.

Is it already too late? Tocqueville rightly observed that, if the French and American democracies were both attached to an ideal of liberty and equality, the French democracy tended to stress its libertarian aspect and the American its egalitarian aspiration. The American democracy, however, is itself going through a crisis that is all the more serious for the fact that America is the wealthiest country and the one that was most attached to an egalitarianism it is unable to bring about.

The fact is that one-fifth of American families shares 3·2 per cent of the national income while at the other end of the scale a further fifth hogs 45·8 per cent. At the top of the pyramid, 1 per cent of American families shares 6·8 per cent of the national income, that is to say twice as big a slice of the cake as the bottom 20 per cent of families must make do with.

The democracy most concerned for equality has thus arrived at social inequalities that are all the greater for the society's being more prosperous. If—as is too often said without the implicit conclusions being drawn—America is essentially the 'model' of the West as a whole, Europe must, in its own interests, find out who the poor in the United States are, where they come from, and what kind of future lies in store for them.

Poverty in America

The gap between America's prosperity and that of Europe is pretty much the same as between a poor American and a poor European. The middle class is richer in America than in Europe; a poor man is less poor in America than in Europe. President Nixon was right when he told a congress of American trade-unionists on 19 November 1971: 'Remember: The poor in America would be rich in 90 per cent of the world today.' True—but no president of the United States has been able to forget, even if only for electoral reasons, that certain privations are harder to bear in the society that holds all the records for wealth and luxury.

A citizen of the United States is officially regarded as poor if his income is less than $1,600 per annum. That is twenty-five times the income of a Nigerian, twenty-two times that of an Indian. But neither the Nigerian nor the Indian has any say in the choice between the various candidates for the White House, nor is he steeped daily in the environment typical of an affluent society.

At first glance an American pauper would cut a pretty prosperous figure even in Western Europe. For him to qualify for assistance and social subsidies his resources must be below the 'threshold of poverty', but that threshold ($1,600) is higher than the average annual income of the Italian ($1,116) and the Briton ($1,560) and approximately on a level with that of the Dutchman ($1,610). Such figures are of course deceptive. They would mean that France and West Germany, the two countries of the Common Market with the highest per capita income ($1,738 and $1,753 respectively), had only just emerged from poverty. But no one in America contests the official definition of poverty: it corresponds to a socio-economic reality in which it is not possible to live a decent life on less than $133 a month.

The problem of poverty in America is not of course new. One need go no further back than forty years to find Franklin D. Roosevelt drawing attention to the fact that a third of the population of America was 'ill clad, ill fed and ill housed'. But that was during the great economic crisis with millions out of work, a daily crop of bankruptcies, 'hunger marches', and soup kitchens.

The paradox is that America has rediscovered the tragedies of poverty in the very moment of abandoning itself to the intoxication of unprecedented wealth. The United States' gross national product, expressed in constant dollars, more than doubled between 1945 and 1970, reaching a per capita level ($5,712) more than three times as high as that of Western Europe ($1,708). Even in its euphoria American society was certainly not unaware of the fact that it had its poorer members, but it thought primarily in terms of blacks and Puerto Ricans. While generally agreeing that no one could remain indifferent to the latter's fate, it continued to think and write to the effect that the problem was a complex one because the blacks and Puerto Ricans were 'different'. It became concerned about the lot of the ethnic minorities, but these then raised their heads and began actively to claim their rights. Attention became concentrated on the poverty of the people whose skin was a different colour.

The storm burst in 1962 when Michael Harrington published his book on 'Poverty in the United States'.[16] He showed that there were fifty million poor people in America. Since a fair number of blacks had achieved a standard of relative prosperity, this figure meant—and this was the real shock—that more than thirty million whites out of 165 million were living in a state of poverty. They included a lot of young people, peasants, physically and mentally handicapped, unemployed, and old people—all living on the fringes of affluence, staring with eyes empty of hope at the unattainable promises of shop windows and advertisers' bill-boards. Fifty million out of a total population of two hundred million were no longer the 'third' of Franklin D. Roosevelt's times but a quarter, and America had just elected a young president of forty-four upon whom it had thrust all its hopes. These poor people were no doubt less poor than those of the pre-war period. But America was now enjoying a period of full expansion. Consequently the difference between this and the earlier poverty was one not only of degree but of nature. The poor of the New Deal era were the victims of a system that had gone bust; the poor of the sixties were the victims of a prosperity that, carried away by its own momentum, had never even suspected their existence.

John F. Kennedy got hold of Harrington's book and launched a campaign against poverty that was pursued by Lyndon B. Johnson. Moved and concerned, the entire country began to take an interest in the problem. The government pledged vast resources for this 'war on poverty', and little by little public concern and interest began to fall off: the State was taking care of the matter, and the public could trust it to do a good job. The government's efforts, however, did not succeed in wiping out poverty. In 1969 Richard Nixon resumed, with certain corrections of detail, the offensive launched by his predecessors. Other problems have preoccupied public opinion—unrest in the universities, drugs, de-escalation and withdrawal in Vietnam, the monetary crisis, relations with China, and so on—but an important slice of the federal budget has regularly, year by year, been devoted to the war on poverty.

The measures needing to be taken have been burdened right from the outset by problems of definition: what is the lowest acceptable income, below which a person is poor? There had to be a 'threshold', but was the person whose annual income stood at ten or fifteen dollars above that figure really less poor? Michael Harrington's estimate was that there were some fifty million poor in the United States; official statistics made the total only forty million.

Between 1959 and 1969 the United States succeeded in reducing the number of the poor from 39,500,000 to 24,300,000, that is to say from 22 to 12 per cent of the total population. A four-person family is regarded as poor if it has an annual income of less than $3,300 living in the city and less than $2,300 living on a farm. An eight-person family, to qualify as poor, must have less than $5,400 in the city and less than $3,800 on a farm.

In the United States as in Great Britain and France the chief cause of poverty is low wages. One poor person in three lives in a family whose head works all the year round and one in four in a family whose head has had seasonal employment. In other words more than half the poor people in the United States live in families that have a wage-packet coming into the house. This, in view of the social legislation in force, means that they can only benefit very marginally from assistance programmes. The lowest-paid workers have become the sacrificial victims of an affluence unequalled in any other country on earth.

In one-third of American families the wife is earning a salary. Theoretically her contribution to the family budget constitutes a means of crossing the threshold of poverty. In fact this possibility is only open to women who possess some professional qualifications and are not house-bound by young children. But of course it is precisely at the least-privileged levels of society that education and professional training —for men as well as for women—are most neglected and child-care facilities most inadequate. In the four-person families with an annual income of between $1,000 and $2,000, i.e. very much below the threshold of poverty, only 14 per cent of the mothers have a job. By contrast, in a well-to-do class in which annual family incomes run between $15,000 and $20,000, more than 53 per cent of mothers are earning a salary. The organization of female employment is geared to the mechanisms that create poverty.

Thus an entire socio-economic structure makes it possible for well-to-do families to increase their incomes while the poorest families are left virtually without any hope of improving their standard of living.

Ethnic minorities

Of the 24,300,000 poor counted in 1969 whites were the most numerous (16,700,000), yet they represented only 10 per cent of the white population. The Negro, Indian, and Puerto Rican poor, numbering 7,600,000, constituted 31 per cent of the total non-white population. The 23,000,000 Negroes, 1,500,000 Puerto Ricans, 5,000,000 Mexicans, and 700,000 Indians constitute poverty's favourite haunt.

Since 1947 incomes of blacks have risen faster (122·4 per cent) than those of whites. In absolute figures, however, in terms of dollars, the gap *continues to increase* (see page 173). Expansion makes the inequalities even greater. Statistically the average black family comprises 4·35 persons and has an annual income of $5,359, whereas the average white family comprises only 3·59 persons and has an income of $8,936. Puerto Ricans, two-thirds of whom live in the New York region, are for reasons of language even worse off than the blacks.

The situation of the 700,000 Indians is by far the most tragic. Some 500,000 of them live on reservations. Half the Indian families have an income of less than $2,000 a year, and three-quarters of them do not reach the $3,000 mark. Among them unemployment stands at ten times the national average, and the incidence of tuberculosis is seven times the national average. Fifty thousand Indian families live in shacks or in the wrecks of abandoned cars. Forty-two per cent of Indian children drop out before completing their four years' high school.

Compared with the 23,000,000 blacks—ubiquitous, organized, quick to claim their rights, sowing panic with every riot—the Indians, possibly because there are so few of them, cause scarcely a ripple on the surface of America's social conscience. Unlike the blacks, they have not succeeded in making their mark through top-ranking personalities—politicians, lawyers, writers, actors, musicians, singers, churchmen, sportsmen, and so on. Perhaps it is this failure more than any other criterion that indicates the sorry state they are in. Government efforts on their behalf are both limited and ineffective: social, medical, and educational aid programmes slowly improve their material conditions without touching the root of the problem.

America could by straight gifts extend its prosperity to the Indians, who constitute a bare ·25 per cent of its population. It does not do so. Even if it did, the question would remain whether the very principle of reservations is consonant with human dignity. The majority of Indians, however, neither wish to leave the reservations, nor are they likely to find a place in a society in which they would merely be swelling the ranks of the unemployed. The government for its part has no real Indian policy. Powerless in the face of the problem, it also feels legally bound to respect treaties that have nevertheless been repeatedly violated since the West began to be opened up.

The case of Mexicans in the United States is not unlike that of the immigrant workers in Europe: both groups have only recently succeeded in drawing attention to their lot. Yet there were nearly four million Mexicans in the United States in 1960, and their numbers increase by more than a million every ten years. Their family incomes are usually slightly above those of blacks in the south-western states, but they live crowded into hovels in districts that very often have neither main drainage, nor street-lighting, nor pavements. Their infant mortality rate and the incidence of tuberculosis and accident are several times the national average. Great efforts have been made to organize medical services, yet their expectation of life is some fifteen years below the average for the country.

It was not until 1970—more than thirty years after *The Grapes of Wrath*—that the Mexican Americans finally succeeded, under the leadership of the several times imprisoned Cesar Chavez, in organizing an agricultural workers' union. They were then able to launch a successful campaign on a national scale to boycott California grapes. Faced with this pressure, the growers resigned themselves to meeting demands that were after all no more than basic. The boycott would not have succeeded without the co-operation and support of the central union body, the AFL-CIO, and of the Roman Catholic bishops.

Be that as it may, the affair assumed enormous proportions, so that during the summer of 1970 Americans were very much less pre-occupied with the war in Vietnam, strategic defence problems, or the crisis affecting the international monetary system than they were with the boycott of California grapes and the imprisonment of Cesar Chavez.

The press, the novel, and the cinema had been telling the public at large about the lot of the Mexican agricultural workers for decades. Yet they continued to vegetate miserably amid the universal indifference of a society seduced by its own affluence. The wealthiest societies are the most pitiless with regard to the poverty they daily rub shoulders with; and yet it is they that benefit from the labour of this underpaid proletariat living on the fringe of society and doing the jobs the 'ordinary' man will no longer touch.

In 1930 there were 1,300,000 Mexicans in the United States—enough to do the menial jobs, too few to influence the decisions of society. Increasing prosperity prompted a growing number of Americans to turn down arduous and ill-paid jobs, so that management began look-ing round for cheap foreign labour. Illegal immigration (the number of workers to have entered the United States illegally is reckoned at three million) combined with immigration through official channels to send the number of Mexican workers soaring. Driven by a narrow corporatism, for a long time the unions took no interest in this fringe group. But then came a day when the immigrants discovered they

were numerous enough to make themselves heard; they were sufficiently 'integrated' to realize the extent of their repression. Finally, after
a delay by which American society stands accused, they burst upon the
public scene.

Sixteen million poor whites

The most delicate problem, which stems from the structures of a highly
industrialized society, is the existence of 16,700,000 poor whites, representing rather more than two-thirds of the total number of poor people
in America. For these are not victims of racial prejudice but the natural
detritus of capitalist, democratic society.

There were 28,500,000 of these poor whites in 1959. The efforts of
the Kennedy, Johnson, and Nixon administrations have made it possible for 11,800,000 of them to better their lot, thanks to allowances. In
his budget for 1972–3 President Nixon proposed to continue along the
same lines by devoting $110,900 million, i.e. 45 per cent of total
expenditure, to the social budget, which represented an increase of
$10,000 million on the previous budgetary year and which provided
for a 5 per cent rise in welfare allowances.

In a total population of 207 million the United States has 20 million
people over 65. Five million of these qualify as needy. For them
President Nixon has set aside $50,000 million, i.e. $16,000 million
more than in 1969–70. Furthermore welfare reforms will increase their
incomes by $5,500 million. The health budget has been increased by
$1,700 million, and here again the chief beneficiaries are the old.
Altogether, with state expenditure standing at $220,800 million, aid
to needy old people accounts for more than a quarter of the federal
budget—a colossal figure, revealing a serious lack of social balance.

This choice of budgetary priorities represents an electoral calculation in so far as it is generally accepted that old people constitute for
the most part potential Republican voters. It is natural that the State
should intervene on their behalf, but is it realistic to spend more on
some five million needy old people than on the nine million children
under sixteen belonging to poor families? These children are not of
course of voting age, and their parents, people of very moderate education, belong to that startlingly large group of some 47 million citizens
(39 per cent of the electorate), who cannot be bothered to exercise
their democratic prerogative. But it is absurd that electoral considerations should dissuade the American government from tackling the

problem of poverty at its source—namely in the education and training of the young.

The fact is that the greater part of these children will not complete their four years' high school and only a tiny number of them will go to college. Lacking any professional training, in a few years these young people will be needy adults and in a few more years needy old people, and the federal government will be obliged to keep up and even to increase the vast subsidies that are today set aside for the aged. As far as the great majority of these poor youngsters are concerned, it is a vicious circle: only a few will escape, and these few—as rare as they are spectacular—will confirm society's good opinion of its own 'flexibility' and of the 'opportunities' it offers to anyone wanting to 'rise in the social scale'.

By concentrating mainly on the aged (who vote) and not on the young (who do not yet have the vote), the campaign against poverty has solved nothing. Indeed the American government estimated that in 1959 there were eleven million poor *under 18*. Ten years later it had nine million poor *under 16*. Thus the situation of young people, instead of improving or at least remaining the same, appears to have got worse. In 1965 White House economic advisers noted that 'the estimated number of children in poverty rises by more than one-third, from eleven million to fifteen million. That means that one-fourth of the nation's children live in families that are poor.'[17]

Since no adult education programme can be as effective as training at school age, the real problem, in the United States as in Europe, lies in the cost of a child and his or her education.

Inequality by education

A few years ago the Institute of Life Insurance estimated that the education of an American child up to the age of 18 cost $23,835 for a family with an annual income of $6,600. In January 1972 a federal commission reckoned the cost of educating a child up to the age of 18 at $35,000—the richest families of course spending very much more (between $40,000 and $75,000) by sending their child to college and to one of the more prestigious universities, at which a single year's studies can cost more than $4,000 instead of the $1,500 or so that is the average at a state university. Choice of educational establishment is often decisive for the child's future: in 1966 holders of doctorates had incomes 42 per cent higher than those of holders of bachelor's degrees obtained after four years of college; moreover, graduates of a college of middling reputation were earning $7,881 instead of the $11,678 that graduates of a well-known college were getting.

The population of the United States comprises rather more than 50 million families, of which 22 million have either no children as yet or children over 18. The 28 million families with one or more dependent children are divided up as follows:

—— 1 child .... 9,140,000 families
—— 2 children .... 8,552,000 ——
—— 3 children .... 5,298,000 ——
—— 4 children and over .... 5,182,000 ——

Average annual family income is at its maximum—between $14,000 and $15,000—in four states: Alaska, Connecticut, Illinois, and Michigan. In the whole country 12 million families—less than one in four—had an income of more than $15,000 in 1970. After income tax a family earning $15,500 keeps $12,500 and a family earning $10,000 keeps $8,500. Such families represent a fairly privileged mean situated well above the threshold of poverty—fixed at $3,300 for a couple with two children. When those two children reach college age, however, the cost of their education is taking up more than half the family's post-tax income. The rest is barely enough to live on (food and clothing) by the time the rent (several hundred dollars a month) or the mortgage payments on a house have been paid, to say nothing of insurance, the car, and the family's health bills.

With education costing what it does the situation is hopeless for the nine million under-16s living in poor families. As a result of divorce or death almost half these families are headed by the mother. They are also victims of the way the school system is organized: side by side with racial segregation there is another, economic segregation into districts, and the American school system is essentially financed by local rates. Poverty is thus subject to an absolute law: a poor district has a poor school—poor in terms of buildings and equipment, poor in terms of the pedagogic standard of teachers that are less well paid than those in wealthy districts, and poor in terms of the general level of the pupils, who fail to find at home the kind of cultural climate they need to support them and bring them out.

This situation will continue as long as education is left in the hands of local authorities rather than of the central government. Despite its

concern for fairness and efficiency, American society has been led by its
mistrust of state intervention to tolerate a school system that fosters
inequality in the classroom and later on in the working environment.
But this kind of socio-economic discrimination is also rife in countries
like France where in spite of a centralized educational system very few
sons of workers and peasants have access to higher education. Assuming
that France will one day reach the level of affluence of the United
States, access to culture is not going to become automatically more
democratic.

In the United States as in Europe, those who do not have access to a
good education will later be filling the lowest paid jobs, or signing on at
the labour exchange, or living on allowances. Many of them at any rate
will be a charge on society. President Johnson was right when he said:

> The poverty of other people is already a mounting burden. We
> are now paying $4 million a year for public assistance. We are now
> paying $8 billion a year for police and health and fire departments.
> The costs are high and they are going higher. Unless we attack the
> causes of poverty. . . . We must teach skills to those who have no
> skills. It costs money to do this. But if the nine million families
> who are poor can earn minimum incomes of $3000 a year, personal
> income in the nation will climb more than $11 billion per year.[18]

The United States has not attacked 'the causes of poverty', and in a
few years the 'burden' represented by the social sector in public expenditure has become even more 'mounting'. It will become yet more so in
future because of the progressive modification of the age pyramid.
Various factors, not all of them economic, are contributing to this
change.

Two statistics give an indication of what is happening. There were
one million marriages in the United States in 1960 and 2,146,000
marriages in 1969, this increase being the natural consequence of the
post-war 'baby boom'. But the birth rate, which stood at 23·7 per
thousand in 1960, had fallen to 17·7 per thousand by 1968.

The lesson is clear: children are expensive, the middle class knows
this, so the middle class limits the number it bears. The gap between the
number of children in poor families and the number of children in
rich families is progessively widening. By the same token the gap
between the two broad social strata—those who are raising their standard of living and those who are stagnating in poverty—is also widening. Looking at it another way, we are witnessing a repetition within

American society of the phenomenon that, on a world scale, separates the industrialized countries from the countries of the Third World. There is one decisive difference, however: whereas the federal government provides for a social budget of $110,000 million, economic aid to foreign countries represents a bare $1,500 million. Well-organized charity begins at home. The conception of aid to under-developed countries, of dubious efficacy anyway, has been seriously called into question.[19] One day the government will come to see that the seventy times greater aid it gives its own needy citizens is itself ill-conceived.

The beneficiaries of poverty

In the case of social aid as in the case of all action programmes, the waste of public funds is not everybody's loss, being naturally accompanied by embezzlement and fraud, even if these words sometimes cover perfectly 'legal' operations.

In the United States fraud assumes a wide variety of forms. In certain cities as well as in isolated villages the local authorities have always diverted a big slice of social funds for the benefit of their families or friends whether in the form of subsidies or through the creation of fictitious municipal posts. But certain systems in particular legally organize fraud. The Department of Agriculture, for example, administers the aid funds for 14 million poor people living on farms or in rural developments. These poor people are old farmers who have not been able to take out any old-age insurance or put aside any savings, agricultural workers who find employment for only part of the year and are not protected by labour legislation, particularly as regards minimum wages, and farm labourers living in shacks. The number of farms under cultivation has fallen from six to less than three million over the last twenty years, whereas social aid funds have quadrupled, reaching $7,400 million in 1970. But these funds are utilized on the basis of laws pushed through by the 'farm bloc', the wealthy farmers' pressure group in Congress. Most of the credits concerned have been assigned to the agricultural price support programme and to various subsidies. The lion's share has thus found its way into the pockets of the wealthiest farmers.

At the bottom end of the scale, approximately one million farmers living below the threshold of poverty receive less than $400 a year from the federal government. At the other end of the scale, 8,500 prosperous farmers have received $25,000 each by way of 'relief'. The record is held by James G. Boswell, who owns vast estates in Arizona and California and who received more than $4 million. What has happened to the 'war on poverty' when the federal administration behaves so parsimoniously towards the poor and so open-handedly towards the rich? The present system in fact only serves to deepen existing inequalities.

It would be tempting to assume that injustice of so absurd a kind and on so monumental a scale could only exist in the country where monumentality is the norm. In fact this is not the case. Over the last quarter of a century the French have grown accustomed to regulations and provisions that fly no less blatantly in the face of equity and common sense. Yet it is hardly normal that all the socially insured—the richest and the poorest alike—should have the same right to family allowances and reimbursement of medical, pharmaceutical, and surgical costs. This equality as regards reimbursement stands in contradiction to the inequality introduced into the system of contributions by the establishment of a 'ceiling' above which the top slice of the biggest incomes is not subject to social deductions. To correct this aberration it would be necessary to abolish the 'ceiling' for social deductions on the one hand, and on the other hand to co-ordinate social allowances with taxable income, which would reintroduce a measure of justice by increasing fiscal pressure on the highest incomes.

Moreover the current system in France gives disguised subsidies to some of the country's wealthiest firms, namely the pharmaceutical laboratories. No system of price controls any more than the 'visa' procedure for launching new medicaments has succeeded in preventing the laboratories from making enormous profits that contribute to the social security deficit. Price controls are easily ducked by bringing out a 'new' medicament with a formula very slightly different from that of the product it is to replace on the market. Being a 'new' product, it can be priced very much higher than the old one.

In France as in the United States and Great Britain, social aid provides a means of helping families in need. But the very conception of that aid results in channelling a considerable portion of public fund, into the pockets of wealthy people who are not in need at all. Coalitions of interest defend and perpetuate a system that is none the less aberrant. In the United States the 'farm bloc' has secured the co-operation of rural legislators who, by virtue of the seniority rule, serve as life chairmen of the relevant House and Senate committees. In France the way agricultural prices are fixed makes it possible for the biggest producers, who get a better yield and a better return on their outlay, to make bigger profits. The 'lobbies' are no less effective in the one country than in the other. The pharmaceutical lobby in France has likewise, under the Fourth and Fifth Republics, acquired political backing that has never let it down.

Money and political power

The prosperity of the West has completely transformed the conditions under which several hundred million people live. If Europe chooses to follow the example of the United States it must realize, on the basis of its own experience and of the results obtained by its very much more developed 'model', that growth is clearly not in itself enough to abolish areas of poverty that are a heavy burden in social, economic, and political terms. It must take a closer look at the real cost of American affluence.

The Americans have long regarded the problem as being one not of 'sharing the cake' in a more equitable manner among the rich, the less rich, and the poor; they have cultivated the idea that one need only make the cake bigger for everyone to have his share. Their own experience, however, has led them to envisage various ways of effecting a new distribution of income and to devote an enormous part of their social resources to a 'social budget' that increases from year to year.

The expansion of the West thus poses a double problem:

Economic structures on the one hand maintain areas of poverty that are too widespread for the public authorities to ignore them. In certain cases not only do the mechanics of growth tolerate these areas of poverty by leaving large numbers of individuals beyond the fringe of affluence but they actively create them: modernization and expansion are ruthless towards the weak, whether small industrial or agricultural businesses or individuals. 'Inequality,' writes Paul-Marie de La Gorce, 'is springing up where it did not exist before and becoming more pronounced where it did exist before; it is raising new barriers between men, admitting some to progress they perhaps no longer hoped to achieve, the others to a kind of economic dissidence, to exile at the very heart of affluence.'[20] This is the law of a type of progress that men have insisted on conceiving and measuring in essentially economic terms. Is that law in itself absurd? It at least brings out the need for compensatory intervention.

Political structures, on the other hand, intervene to provide precisely

3

the necessary correctives. Such at least is, in principle, one of their chief functions. In fact political intervention has not succeeded in eliminating the most serious inequalities. It has applied brakes and restraints without which those inequalities would be even more glaring than they are. But it is always behind economic progress, coming after the event to do what most urgently needs to be done about repairing the human and social damage caused by upheavals in the process of production. The industrialized societies of the West have in common a wide variety of systems designed to minimize or remove the principal injustices arising out of capitalist development. These systems are the fruit of democratic regimes that, by means of trade union action, appeals to public opinion, and universal suffrage, have made the public authorities provide relief for the most disadvantaged. Such democratic intervention, however, is always behind capitalist progress, stopping with a greater or lesser degree of effectiveness and dispatch the gaps it failed to see coming.

Why this lag that causes so much misery? Because the public authorities concern themselves more with economic growth than with the spread of social justice? Because businessmen and technocrats have more say in government affairs than the small wage-earner? Because the ties of private interest are stronger than the democratic community? Because the familiar democratic forms are not adapted to the problems of modern capitalist society? Because democratic awareness has itself become blunted?

Whatever the reason, in every country in the West, never mind what the official speeches may say, the compensatory measures taken are subject to one and the same error of conception. They are seen as *social* aid, whereas the causes of poverty are primarily *economic*.

Areas of poverty are not an inevitable residual phenomenon whose victims must be given relief. They are the direct consequence of a pattern of development that ignores or sacrifices a human potential it considers marginal. But why should societies so set on efficiency be less efficient on the human level than they are on the level of production? In the name of what definition of progress can they give the 'economic' priority over the 'social'?

The 'crisis of civilization' is apparent every time someone, in order to carry through a decision leading to some kind of human betterment, feels obliged to justify it in terms of the economic advantages that will follow in its wake, arguing that productivity will increase if the workers are working in cleaner, brighter, better ventilated, and less noisy surroundings, if their rhythm is made more flexible, if their 'human relationships' are warmer, and if they have a picture of the end result to which their particular little job contributes. A civilization worthy of the name would find such improvements on the human level sufficient in themselves without needing to bring out the boost in output that would result. Yet even the promise of increased productivity is insufficient to persuade those responsible that they must humanize working conditions. To make them do so the state has belatedly to impose sanctions for non-observance of the norms governing hygiene, safety, and wages and the trade unions have to remain constantly on the alert. It is an ever-lasting battle to ensure that man is not sacrificed to the 'imperatives' of production, to put the machinery of production at the service of man.

Low wages, inhuman working conditions, bad housing—could it be that certain sectors of society have an interest in creating or main-taining areas of poverty the existence of which guarantees them higher profits and the social burden of which falls not on them alone but on the whole community?

In North America as in Western Europe these areas of poverty are politically tolerable up to the point where a particular group of 'rejects' becomes organized and takes the initiative. The least privileged sectors are not necessarily the most dynamic—far from it. Their role is a revelatory one: their very existence shows that something is wrong in the machinery of production, that something in the apparatus of democracy is out of true.

Upheavals and revolts among the victims of economic growth throw fresh light on certain other problems to which the industrialized West has remained blind and intensify their human relevance. The poor and the exploited are not the only victims: others have become more and more accustomed to a kind of evolution that has gradually—but at what cost?—made it possible for them to consume more and more without achieving the more human life-style they have a right to expect.

In particular, without their having ever been democratically con-sulted on the matter, people are being forced by this same conception of economic growth to spend their days in conditions that many regard as inhuman. Industrialization necessarily involves a certain amount of urban concentration—but what form is this to take?

The problems arising out of certain forms of urban concentration affect not only a 'marginal' population but people who rightly regard themselves as the beneficiaries of an affluent society. Among the 'privileged' who have achieved a decent standard of living there are many who in another way pay a high price for our present forms of economic growth. Their discontent too calls into question a basic feature of Western civilization—a certain conception of progress, a certain relinquishment of democratic control over economic decisions that dictate the very quality of society.

References

1 Ken Coates and Richard Silburn, *Poverty: The Forgotten Englishman*, Penguin Books, 1970, p. 13.
2 Brian Abel-Smith and Peter Townsend, *The Poor and the Poorest*, Bell, London, 1965.
3 Ken Coates and Richard Silburn, *op. cit.*, p. 50.
4 *Idem*, p. 31.
5 Adam Smith, *The Wealth of Nations*.
6 John K. Galbraith, *The Affluent Society*, Hamish Hamilton, 1958, p. 252.
7 *TUC Report*, 1968, p. 577.
8 Paul-Marie de La Gorce, *La France pauvre*, Bernard Grasset, Paris, 1965.
9 Prof. Christian Goux, 'Indice unique, indice inique', *Le Monde de l'Economie*, 14 March 1972.
10 'La Crise de l'emploi en Lorraine', *Le Monde*, 14 December 1971.
11 *Bilan de l'immigration en 1971*, Notes du Ministère du Travail, de l'Emploi et de la Population, 14–20 February 1972.
12 *Bulletin municipal officiel de Paris*, 27 February 1972, statement by M. Jean Gajer, councillor of the city of Paris.
13 Jean-Marc Théolleyre, *Le Monde*, 19 February 1972.
14 *Le Monde*, 5 February 1972.
15 Jacques Fauvet, 'Ordre et contradiction', *Le Monde*, 14 March 1972.
16 Michael Harrington, *The Other America: Poverty in the United States*, Macmillan, New York, 1962.
17 Quoted by Michael Harrington in *Dissent*, Autumn 1965.
18 Lyndon B. Johnson, *My Hope for America*, Random House, 1964.
19 Tibor Mende, *De l'aide à la recolonisation: Les leçons d'un échec*, Editions du Seuil, 1972.
20 *La France pauvre*, *op. cit.*, p. 284.

CHAPTER TWO

Man and the City

- The insolvent megalopolis
- The public authority and private interests
- The city-dweller and the developer
- The absence of democracy
- Scandal and corruption
- Progress and profits

Notwithstanding their very different demographic conditions, North America and Western Europe have only succeeded in becoming industrialized at the expense of an anarchical process of urban concentration. Industrialization is the key to their prosperity, uncontrolled urban concentration the price they have paid for it. What is at issue here is not the growth of the big cities of the West but the disorderly character of their development—as caricatured by the major capitals of the Third World.

Most of the problems facing the societies of the West are aggravated by this chaotic process of concentration. Crowding people together into confined spaces presents society with difficulties of three kinds:

It diminishes the quality of life: Increasingly widespread agreement on this point is still insufficient to reverse the trend. The process of concentration continues, and certain governments even contemplate deliberately speeding it up rather than slowing it down. Yet in its present form the big city no longer offers the attractions that once lent it great prestige and gave it an irreplaceable role in the life of the country. In a few years' time the towns and cities of Europe will find themselves in the impasse that America is vainly trying to escape.

The high cost of urban concentration acts as a brake on economic development: Since industrial expansion is associated historically with the growth of towns, a confusion of cause and effect sometimes leads people to conclude that acceleration of the process of urban concentration will stimulate economic progress. They forget that concentration comes expensive, leading as it does to big increases in the costs of building land, floor space, staff, production, and all services. The cost of theoretically conceivable solutions is even higher. A conference of American mayors and top town-planning experts held early in 1970 concluded that the sixties had been disastrous for America's towns and cities—in fact the

rot goes back very much further—and that the seventies would probably be even worse. The federal authorities estimated at that time that
an attempt to save America's cities would cost something like $100,000
million, and no one supposes for a moment that any government could
ever raise that kind of money. In ten or fifteen years the major cities of
Europe will be in a similarly critical situation.

Urban concentration paralyses political life: Towns and cities are the
seats of governments—national or local—handling large-scale budgets.
They are also the favourite places for holding mammoth political
demonstrations. All of which can be misleading. In fact the clumsiness
and inefficiency of powerful administrations and the size and occasionally the violence of demonstrations against them are evidence of one
and the same malaise: beyond a certain point urban concentration by
its very giantism eludes the democratic controls on which the societies
of the West are based. The problem, already perceptible in Europe, is
very much more marked in America.

The high cost of concentration

The human, economic, and political consequences of urban concentration cannot be said to have taken the West by surprise. As early as
1938 Lewis Mumford analysed the blind forces leading big cities into
an impasse. He issued a warning that America was to take note of
thirty years later—too late—and that Europe does not appear to have
heard yet. Seeing further than businessmen, administrators who sometimes combine a private interest with a blind eye, and experts stuck
within the narrow confines of their special subject, Mumford declared
in *The Culture of Cities*[1] that society must entirely rebuild its cities. This
was on the eve of the Second World War and America had other
problems to contend with. But with the return of peace and prosperity
the United States remained helpless before the most complex problem
facing modern socieites. Indeed it is easier—and less expensive—to send
men to the moon than it is to solve the urban crisis.

Thanks to the prosperity it has enjoyed since 1945 America has had
the material means of rebuilding its cities as Lewis Mumford advocated
long ago, or at least of changing them for the better. It has not done so.
Mere negligence? An accident of history? What follows, as we shall see,
suggests a different answer because within the logic of capitalism overly
powerful interests were at stake. The fact remains that, in a context of
unprecedented prosperity, the urban crisis has got steadily worse.

In this respect the example of New York is among the most typical. It illustrates clearly the problems facing the West as a whole.

In spite of having laid off large numbers of municipal employees, New York announces an annual deficit of $300 million on a budget of some $5,000 million. The city has 3·3 policemen per thousand inhabitants (national average 2·2) and this proportion will have to be increased, for New York holds the record for criminality among the 26 cities that, although they contain only a sixth of the total population, account for half the crimes committed in the United States.

With regard to reading ability, New York's schoolchildren were ten months behind the national average in 1969, fourteen months behind in 1970, and the gap is still widening. Yet expenditure on public education in New York stands at $1,028 per pupil per year as against $560 in Cincinnati, $552 in Cleveland, and $620 in Detroit.

New York has one hospital bed to 200 inhabitants as opposed to 1:120 for the country as a whole. Infant mortality conforms to the national average (20 per thousand) among the white population but stands at almost double that (38·4 per thousand) among the non-white population, i.e. the poorest sector. Yet the city has one doctor to 400 inhabitants where the national proportion is 1:620.

The total per capita tax load stands at $274 in New York; in New Orleans (600, 000 inhabitants) it is $73, in Miami (340,000 inhabitants) $113.

Whether in terms of public health, the quality of education, or security of persons and property, the situation of the New Yorker is both less advantageous and more burdensome financially than that of the inhabitant of America's less populous industrial cities.

In New York as in all the major cities of Europe and America, increasing population density puts up land prices and rents. The municipality, like the private sector, has to allow for this in paying its staff (administrative personnel, teachers, firemen, policemen, etc.). By the same token the costs of road upkeep, garbage disposal, street lighting, and public transport are also pushed up. As the demand for water and electricity increases, supplies have to be brought in from further and further away—at the cost of major installations. Big cities send cinema, restaurant, and garage prices soaring. From the economic point of view they are an aberration.

A high degree of urban concentration puts a heavy burden on the social budget—for two reasons: firstly, the majority of the poor in the United States are city-dwellers: secondly, since the cost of living is

3*

higher in the city than in the country, the 'threshold of poverty' is
40 per cent higher for an urban family than for a rural family of the
same number of persons (see page 39). Thus five states alone absorb the
lion's share of welfare funds, namely the states with the highest population density: New York, California, Illinois, Pennsylvania, and Ohio.
The number of New Yorkers on welfare increased by a quarter of a
million in the seventeen-year period from 1948 to 1965, then by another
quarter million in the two-year period 1966-7, and by a further quarter
million during 1968-9. In less than ten years the average allowance
being paid out in New York to families with dependent children has
increased by 56 per cent from $178 to $277. Everything costs more in
the city, even—no, especially—poverty.

And while the cost of living increases, the pleasures of living decrease.
Pollution, noise, traffic problems, time wasted in travelling, and so on
weigh more and more heavily on the city-dweller's daily existence,
adding to his fatigue and robbing him of his rest. All the available
statistical evidence points to the same lowering of the quality of human
life, notwithstanding public and private expenditure on a scale far
greater than in smaller cities and towns. What is more, things are
getting steadily worse.

The suburban mirage

The population of New York actually increased by 1·1 per cent
between 1960 and 1970. Since over the same period the total population
of the United States increased by 13 per cent, this figure may appear
ridiculously insignificant. But if the increase within the administrative
limits of the city was a mere 85,796, the population of 'Greater New ·
York' increased by 715,000, i.e. by 6·2 per cent.[2] The city is growing
simultaneously with the metropolitan area that surrounds it like a
gangue. Altogether it is the number of people living in areas of high
density that is steadily on the increase.

Since the Second World War demographers, sociologists, and
planners have been living in the hope that a new and more human life
style would emerge as a result of the steady flux of city-dwellers moving
out into green and pleasant suburbs. The attraction of the suburbs has
indeed gradually become irresistible to everyone suffering from the
discomforts of the city. But if there still are one or two green and pleasant
suburbs left, the majority of them are beginning to present the same
disadvantages as the city. Added to which there is of course the daily

misery of travelling to the city and back by means of overcrowded transport systems. The more families the flight to the suburbs attracts, the less that flight offers in terms of an escape from the tensions of the city.

Looked at on a national scale, this flight has not reduced the urban population. Quite the contrary: the population figures have gone up both for the bigger towns and cities and for their suburbs. Areas of high urban concentration have thus gained 18 million inhabitants in six years:

	1960	1970
Population of major towns and cities	59,400,000	62,200,000
Population of their suburbs	59,000,000	74,200,000
Total urban population	118,400,000	136,400,000

The desire on the part of privileged social categories to flee from the centres of overcrowded cities is not in itself sufficient to account for this movement. It needed a complex of administrative decisions to make it possible. In an era when 'public housing' was virtually non-existent the railroad contributed to the development of cities. Subsequently, however, two further elements were to lead to very much more rapid expansion: on the one hand the spread of the private car with its corollary, the construction of roads by the public authorities; on the other hand subsidised housing.

The stratagems designed to reduce urban congestion have, quite apart from increasing it, cost more than the congestion itself. As early as 1955 Lewis Mumford denounced 'the reckless subsidized building of superhighways' on the grounds that they have obviously 'pumped more cars into the city and populated nearby open spaces that should have been permanently preserved.' Mumford added the common sense observation that highway construction 'increases random movement without creating a new pattern of urban settlement' and is chiefly effective in 'extending the congestion of midtown New York to outlying areas.'[3]

When France launched a big programme of motorway construction in the sixties, America's experience had already amply shown that such a programme, far from solving the problem of urban congestion, would only make it worse. But apparently French experts allowed themselves to be dazzled by the great works of art that had been built in America—gigantic 'clover-leaf' intersections on three or four levels, bridges, tunnels, etc. Looked at from the purely technical point of view these works of art figure as a veritable symbol of progress, despite the fact that they are always inadequate in relation to the number of cars on the road as well as increasing both the size and the congestion of the towns and cities they are meant to serve.

The result is what Lewis Mumford called 'the gluey crawl of the Sunday driver'. What he said of America in 1955 applies to Western Europe today: "So the suburbanite who twenty years ago had the country at his doorstep must also pile his family into the car and seek it farther away . . . In the suburb as in the crowded city, land values have risen as living values have gone down."[4]

If the suburbs no longer offer the advantages originally expected of them it is essentially because the car and urban motorways have reduced the remaining free space in the most populous areas. In the United States a car carries an average of 1·5 passengers. A bus carries as many passengers as 34 cars with less traffic congestion, greater speed, and reduced atmospheric pollution. It has further been estimated that the railway's 'efficiency quotient' is twenty times that of the road since the railway occupies only a quarter of the surface area and can carry five times as many passengers.

The public authorities, however, responsive to the pressures of the car industry and of an ill-informed public opinion, continue to sink vast if always insufficient budgets into the construction of roads and motorways. In the United States the number of passengers using suburban trains fell from 9,782 million in 1935 to 6,491 million in 1968. The railway companies are insolvent, the deficit being made up by the federal government, i.e. by the taxpayer. Yet the United States continues to put 8·2 million cars on the road annually, and Western Europe more than 9 million.

Motorway construction has further congested and polluted the bigger towns and cities and their enormous suburbs. It makes no appreciable difference to the accident rate. Countries like West Germany and the United States, well equipped with motorways, have respectively 28·3 and 26·7 road deaths per 100,000 inhabitants; France, with a less developed motorways network, has 25·6.

Car production, however, is seen as a gauge of industrial dynamism, and motorway construction as a measure of progress. The result, as Lewis Mumford pointed out, is 'to concentrate an ever heavier load of weekday traffic upon the highways pointed toward New York and to add an ever larger part of the suburban population to the hordes escaping from New York on weekends.'

Notwithstanding the disastrous results of the American experiment, Europe has embarked on the process that Lewis Mumford summed up twenty years ago as follows:

> Metropolitan congestion and physical frustration; suburban escape; population pressure; overcrowding; extravagant highway building to promote further channels of escape at greater distance from the once so admirable centre; finally, intensified congestion both in the original center and in the suburb, which wipes out the social assets of the city and the rural assets of the country.

The use made of the private car and the laying-out of motorways spell death to the urban and suburban environment. Aware that if the car is efficient on the open road it is very much less so in town, Mumford considered that the only way to preserve the advantages of motorized traffic was to create an extensive road network at the same time as new urban centres surrounded and protected by broad and permanent belts of green countryside. This is more or less what Great Britain has done. Mumford particularly advocated the acquisition by the state of vast tracts of land, so-called 'strategic buffers' that would force the new urbanized areas to take shape at some distance from the major cities instead of hemming them in with a ring of dense suburbs doomed to a process of proletarianization. The idea was to create a situation whereby 'the creeping blight of realty speculation might have been controlled.'

The actions of speculators, however, have actually been encouraged by the public authorities. Government housing and road-building subsidies, while failing to provide adequate protective controls, have prompted developers and motorway builders to look, on a larger scale, for the maximum profit by sacrificing the interests of city-dwellers. The questions Mumford asked face every one of the major cities of Europe today, with the possible exception of London: 'What will have been lost? Only New York's greatest natural asset—an accessible rural resort . . . What will have been gained? Ask the highway engineers and the realty operators.'

Public authorities incapable of looking ahead, planners not up to exploiting the possibilities opened up by modern technology, and financial consortium, developers, and building firms greedy for quick profits have pooled their efforts to asphyxiate our cities, their vast suburbs, and their ever more numerous populations. Yet half a century has passed since Clarence S. Stein and Henry Wright glimpsed the marvellous possibilities opened up by progress. They suggested creating independent industrial centres spread over very much larger areas than today's urbanized zones and linked by a network of roads and railways. It is a truism that industry and habitat follow means of communication. Motorways that were supposed to relieve the congestion of towns and cities have only congested them more, as well as making them bigger in every case where they are not surrounded by a broad, at least ten or twenty mile wide protected green belt. When the state fails to take this elementary precaution, its decision to finance or subsidize motorways pushes up land prices, lines the pockets of developers and builders, suffocates cities and their suburbs, penalizes the non-urban taxpayer, and lowers the quality of life for the city-dwellers on whose behalf it claims to have laid out the vast budgets involved.

Whether concealed or admitted, there is a *de facto* complicity between the public authorities and the speculators. 'Meanwhile,' said Mumford, 'the present processes and plans keep on working automatically and we go on, like so many busy beavers in flood areas, building new suburbs that will be inundated, only to build the same kind of suburbs a few years later a little farther away.'

And so it has vanished into thin air—the mirage of those green and pleasant suburbs that might have become active, autonomous centres linked to the city whose impulses they would continue to receive while yet leading a life of their own. By the same token the city itself is decaying because the weakness of the state and the desire for big, quick profits have inhibited any proper consideration of the function of suburbs. This is no accident: the industrialized West is powered by the profit motive and requires the state to confine its interventions to a minimum, except when it is a question of palliating with public funds the shortcomings of private capital.

Social segregation

The law of profit is unrelenting. Approximately one million well-to-do whites left New York for the suburbs between 1960 and 1970, but the excess of births over deaths meant that the white population decreased by only 617,000. During the same period 435,840 non-whites with low incomes moved into New York, an immigration that, together with the excess of births over deaths, increased the non-white population of the city by 702,903. New York thus gained more than 85,000 inhabitants.

The role played by the non-white population in the United States fosters in many Europeans the illusion that urbanization is not subject to the same laws on both sides of the Atlantic. They forget that the phenomenon is more economic than racial. Black migrations make it easier to follow the movements of an economically underprivileged section of the population that hopes to find better-paid work in the big cities. Independently of the colour of their skin, however, it is the well-to-do families that leave the city, and only the poorest—or the richest, who can afford the high rents asked for comfortable apartments —that remain. New York is becoming proletarian.

One result is that the fiscal resources of New York and other big cities are tending to get smaller. At the same time municipal costs are increasing even faster than the population.

In Paris, province-to-city and city-to-suburb migration patterns are slightly different. Excess of births over deaths increases the population of the Paris region by an average of 67,000 annually. In the same period 81,000 people leave for the provinces, making 14,000 inhabitants less. But then 141,000 provincials arrive in Paris, resulting in a net gain of 127,000 inhabitants. Thus the population of the Paris region is increasing by between 1·2 and 1·3 million every ten years, whereas for the metropolitan area of New York the increase is only 715,000. Quite something to be proud of—Paris beating New York!

At the same time there is a process of social segregation at work between Paris and its suburbs, but in the opposite direction to that of New York. A prey to developers, the region around the capital is becoming rapidly urbanized: there are plans for a million inhabitants near Palaiseau, another million on the edge of the Forêt de Sénart, 600,000 in the Montmorency valley, the same number in the Chevreuse valley, and other 'new towns' besides. The last 'green' suburbs are to be sacrificed and will inevitably become proletarianized in the space of a few years.

The term 'suburb' covers both Sarcelles—for slender purses—as well as the smarter Parly II. Social discrimination is already a fact of the new suburbs, just as it is in America. At the same time urban renewal programmes are changing the composition of the population of inner Paris. M. Chalandon, Minister of Housing, says we must avoid 'increasing social segregation in the matter of where people live', seeing this as an 'unacceptable trend'.[5] Yet this is just what is happening. The proportion of workers to the active population of Paris has dropped from 30 per cent to 26 per cent in fifteen years, while that of middle and upper management personnel has increased from 18 per cent to 23 per cent. Migration is thus moving in opposite directions in New York and Paris. Both forms of social segregation, however, are equally anti-democratic.

Since Paris has not allowed certain quarters to decay as New York has done, a well-to-do family may find it advantageous to move into the city. Since the layer of atmospheric pollution extends over a radius of some thirteen miles, it hardly causes greater inconvenience in Paris itself than in the nearer suburbs. On the other hand less time is lost in travelling, and on the whole the capital offers its inhabitants better schools than do the majority of the suburbs, in which moreover transport facilities for schoolchildren are sometimes inadequate.

At any rate the problem of the city on its own can no longer be considered independently. As such it is insoluble, for reasons both economic and political. Our towns and cities have become engulfed in urban complexes that are becoming ever larger; the solution can only lie in a radical re-examination of the social, economic, and political concepts that have brought the industrialized West its prosperity but also given it these vast, overpopulated areas in which urban civilization is slowly dying.

These areas spill over the boundaries of traditional administrative units. The urban area of New York, for example, extends into three states and comes under more than a thousand local governments. Some modification of administrative structures could in the long run adapt the forms of power to the needs of large-scale planning. Such is the role of the 'District of Paris'.

But will this new organization succeed in planning the process of urbanization along more human, more efficient, more democratic, and less burdensome lines? Will it be able to improve housing and traffic conditions, leisure and other amenities, and cut down pollution? Does it offer a chance of reducing in the country as a whole the human, economic, and political inequalities that are the mark of the affluent societies of the West? Does it not penalize the provinces by making them foot the enormous bill for intensified urbanization?

The answers to these questions will in large measure determine the success or failure of the industrialized West.

The useless model

At the outset urbanization policy faced very much more favourable conditions in the United States than in Western Europe: no old towns with narrow streets, wide open spaces, and a low population density. Today, with only 23 inhabitants to the square kilometre, the United States has a population density one quarter that of France, one tenth that of West Germany, and one eighteenth that of Holland.[6] But what counts is the fact that in the United States 70 per cent of the population is crowded into only 2 per cent of the country's territory. What this amounts to is that 142 million Americans live at a density of 756 inhabitants to the square kilometre, which is nearly two and a half times that of Belgium.

Is the situation any better in Europe? The city of Paris has 25,000 inhabitants to the square kilometre, that is to say twice as many as New York and three times as many as London. All three being surrounded by suburbs growing denser all the time, and administrative divisions varying from country to country, the important thing to bear in mind is that a single urban complex accounts for 16 per cent of the national population in the case of Paris, 15 per cent in the case of London, and 7·5 per cent in the case of New York. The New York complex comprises some 11·5 million inhabitants (on a par with Tokyo), those of Paris and London some 9 million each, and those of Los Angeles and Chicago almost 7 million.

If 'Greater New York' accounts for only 7·5 per cent of the population of the United States this is precisely because the vast size of the country has led to the formation of other major complexes around Chicago and Los Angeles. The cities of America and Europe are thus swallowed up in a few megalopolises absorbing between 15 per cent and 16 per cent of the national population. But these megalopolises in turn proliferate to form what the Americans call 'strip cities'—ribbons of high-density population, long, continuous corridors of industrial and residential development from which nature has been banished almost without trace. In the United States three 'strip cities' (see the map on pp. 66-67) contain 45 per cent and will soon contain half of the total population. In Europe, where industrialization is less advanced, a similar phenomenon is already well under way (see the map on p. 68)

In Canada the Lithwick Report bases an optimistic view of the country's economic future on the fact that, as it estimates, by the year

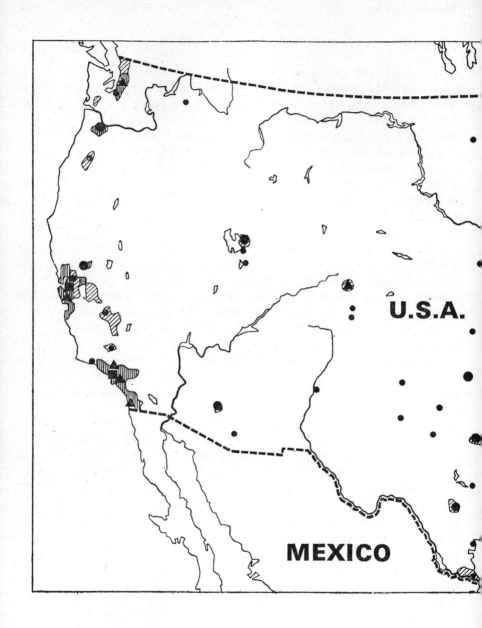

U.S.A.

MEXICO

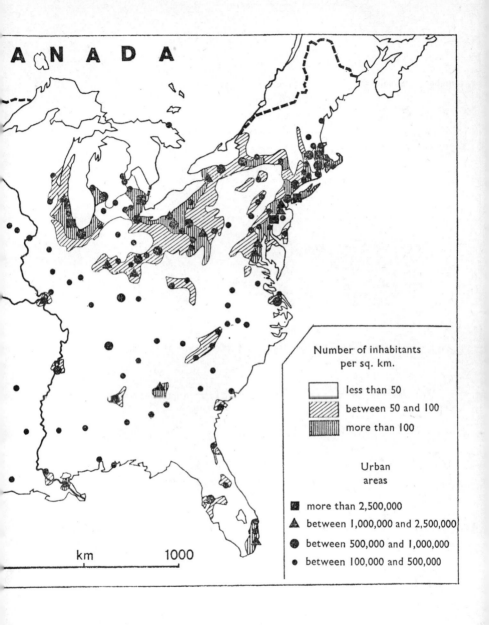

CANADA

Number of inhabitants
per sq. km.

less than 50
between 50 and 100
more than 100

Urban
areas

■ more than 2,500,000
▲ between 1,000,000 and 2,500,000
● between 500,000 and 1,000,000
• between 100,000 and 500,000

km   1000

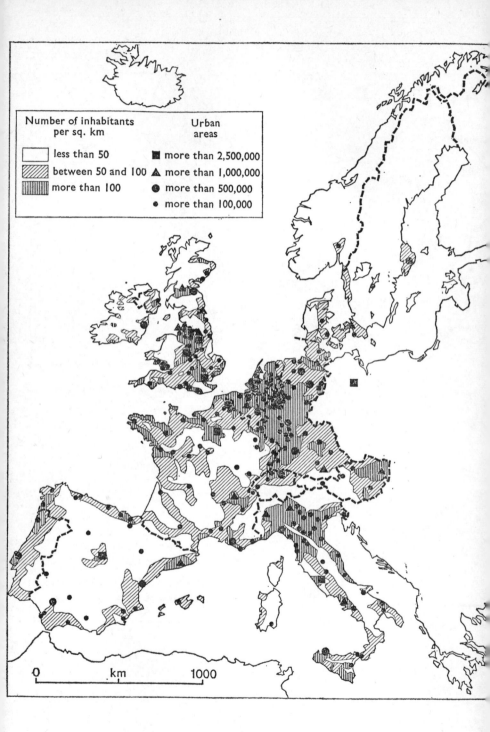

Number of inhabitants per sq. km	Urban areas
less than 50	more than 2,500,000
between 50 and 100	more than 1,000,000
more than 100	more than 500,000
	more than 100,000

0   km   1000

2000 Montreal and Toronto will each have more than 6 million inhabitants, Vancouver 2·5 million, Winnipeg and Ottawa more than 1·5 million, and four other cities approximately 1 million.

The connexion between economic expansion and the growth of towns is an incontrovertible fact of history. It was between 1831 and 1911 that the population of Paris rose from 780,000 to 2,900,000—a figure that still did not make it a monster city. But the modern world remains curiously attached to a conception dating from the last century, notwithstanding the technological developments, particularly in the fields of energy and transport, that have opened up the possibility of a better geographical distribution of industrial and residential centres.

While the United States is worrying about the exorbitant cost of salvaging its cities and searching—without success—for a better geo-economic equilibrium, Canada and Europe, with splendid insouciance, are pushing forward with the process of urban concentration. The 1960 plan for the reorganization of the Paris region still talked in terms of stabilizing an already disconcerting lack of balance by putting a brake on migration to Paris. Four years later a commission was anticipating that the proportion of city-dwellers in France would increase from 64 per cent in 1965 to 73 per cent in 1985, and that it would go on increasing until the end of the century. The master plan of 1965 was not content with noting its powerlessness to stem the flood; on the contrary, it suggested increasing the population of the Paris region from 8 million to 14 million by the year 2000. In this as in other respects the example of America makes no difference: Europeans refuse to take note of the lessons the Americans have learnt from experience. For Europe, America remains a fascinating 'model'—but a useless one. The Americans know the debit side of their urban balance-sheet: Europeans disregard it.

Suffocation

If the town was for a long time both a symbol and an instrument of progress, over and above a certain size it becomes subject to all the laws of regression. Buses in Paris travelled at 14 kph in 1952 and at 8 kph in 1970, i.e. the speed at which horses were pulling them at the end of the nineteenth century. A technical step forward—the internal combustion engine—has been cancelled out by increases in population and in the number of vehicles on the road. The rush-hour situation on the main arteries of the bigger provincial cities is even worse: 5 kph in Marseille, less still in Lyon and Strasbourg. The value of the time lost through travel is the sum of the consequent loss of earning power and the nervous strain involved in losing it.

Yet the facts show that this argument has no persuasive force whatever. In January 1972 the Rome city council, though already heavily in debt, offered free transport on the city's 1,600 buses for a period of nine days. Motorists were asked to leave their cars in the garage, the idea being that they could thus make a double saving—of time and of money. The experiment, which cost the city council some £30,000, was conclusive: the number of bus passengers increased—notably because quantities of children jumped at the chance of free rides—but the number of cars on the road remained the same, causing the usual number of jams. The vast majority of city-dwellers is quite obviously incapable of making a sensible choice. Society can only deplore the fact. But in this particular case it was a question of city-dwellers showing themselves to be not only blind to their own individual interest but also—which is more serious—insensitive to the general interest, and this fact society has every reason to find disturbing, for it strikes at the very principle of democracy.

That the public authorities have their share of responsibility in the matter needs no further demonstration: public transport remains grossly inadequate while the state, giving way to popular pressure, sinks vast budgets in public works that solve nothing at all. Traffic moves at a crawl not only in the narrow streets of Paris but also, at rush hours, on the *boulevard périphérique*, the ring road built at a cost of £150 million, i.e. £4·3 million per kilometre. The figure is double that for certain smaller axes such as the link-road from Maine-Montparnasse.

As a passenger the city-dweller accepts a greater and greater degree of inconvenience while as a taxpayer he puts up with higher and higher taxation. Experience shows that the public authorities have nothing to worry about here: contrary to what one might expect, deterioration in the field of transport carries no political risk. 'I'm surprised there has not yet been a revolt by public-transport passengers,' said a former *préfet* of the Paris region.[7] But the protests of passengers remain limited in extent and their demonstrations without consequence. Travel has become a chore that the modern city-dweller seems prepared to perform *ad infinitum*.

Has he in fact any possibility of controlling democratically the management of the urban community's interests? On the admission of a UDR deputy, urban development is at the mercy of pressure groups,

the 'dictatorship of speculators' money', and organizations such as the
'Caisse des dépôts et consignations' that are 'run in a non-democratic
fashion'.[8] In fact in very big cities of several million inhabitants as well
as in smaller towns embedded in urban regions municipal elections no
longer represent a means of solving city-dwellers' problems. Depending
on the degree of competence and the political affiliations of their
members, city councils can of course show a greater or lesser degree of
efficiency in erecting housing, schools, or kindergartens, providing
little parks, recreation centres, and so on—all of which things are by no
means negligible, but still only alleviate the problems without actually
solving them. The fact is that the solution is not to be found at the
municipal level: the national government alone is capable of decongesting the major urban areas.

In the megalopolises or 'strip cities' local councils have no alternative but to turn to the central government and ask it to finance
operations that are far too costly for the population directly concerned.
The State has financed two fifths of the major road works in Paris,
where only one sixth of the nation lives. The State also covers 70 per
cent of the Paris metro and bus deficit, and in 1970 that deficit was
twelve times what it had been in 1960. In 1949 passengers were bearing
84 per cent of public transport expenses in Paris; in 1970, only 50 per
cent. Urban concentration comes expensive for the nation as a
whole.

The areas of poverty we have been talking about coincide to some
extent with urban areas, but they are not of the same nature. A properly
conceived social policy should seek to draw into the circle of general
prosperity such social groups as have not succeeded in breaking into it
themselves because they start out with some professional, physical,
educational, or mental handicap. A social policy that thus goes beyond
merely handing out subsidies also pays economically. But in getting the
nation as a whole to cover their deficit the big urban regions are in fact
aggravating and perpetuating the very causes of that deficit. What the
state is doing is attacking the symptoms of the evil rather than
eradicating its causes. This kind of policy is economically disastrous. It
amounts to pumping fresh resources into urban areas not in order to
make them more habitable and more viable but in order to speed up the
growth that is the very source of their deficit. In the 'age of management'
and of the rationalization of budgetary decisions the state—the most
powerful firm of all—is pursuing an investment policy that leads to an
increased deficit. Over the last thirty years the burden of direct local

taxation—in constant francs—has increased four times more in the provinces than in Paris, so that the tax structure itself encourages urban concentration.

The introduction of 'revenue sharing' in the United States, whereby the federal government turns over a part of its resources to the states and municipalities, is not going to make it possible to avoid a degeneration of the urban environment. It will make the situation less intolerable in the bigger cities and favour an influx of population that will aggravate the problem. 'Subsidies' for urban areas become anti-economic in that they strengthen the very causes of the deficit they are intended to cover. The city is suffocating, and credit pumped in from outside is not going to help it breathe any better.

A mythical conception of progress

America's failure to tackle this enormous problem in a more timely and intelligent fashion has been due neither to ill-will nor to lack of dynamism. The causes of the blockage embrace all spheres of human activity and stem not only from the economic interests at stake but also from intellectual attitudes, political calculations, and a certain vision of society. By process of accumulation these various causes have brought urban civilization to a point of crisis.

An unfortunate confusion of ideas has led people to accept as evidence what are no more than assumptions and as ineluctable a process that no one has even attempted to control. The first towns were essentially places of meeting and exchange. Through commerce they developed into centres of economic, financial, and political power, and simultaneously into places of cultural importance through meetings and exchanges between writers, thinkers, artists, poets, and scholars. The industrial revolution, involving as it did a draining of manpower from the country towards the big centres, contributed further to the growth of towns. The history of major cities is further characterized by the property owner's fear of this massing of the industrial proletariat into overcrowded and insanitary districts that became so many potential centres of revolutionary agitation. But industrialization as the fruit of technological progress did not ineluctably give rise to the vast concentrations that the twentieth century continues to call 'cities' although they are no longer capable of performing the function of true cities. Technological development certainly led to the creation of cities of very considerable size. But it was the political authorities' capitulation to economic forces that was to give rise by a process of anarchical expansion to these monstrous agglomerations that a neologism has dubbed 'megalopolises'.

Lewis Mumford saw clearly that the human disaster and, as in the United States, economic insolvency of the big city threatened to usher in the end of an essentially urban civilization. For in the societies of the West the fate of the rural population is of course itself governed and dictated by the big urban complexes that constitute the seat of economic, financial, and political power as well as of every kind of blockage and paralysis. The crisis of the city is the crisis of an entire society.

In the United States the financing of towns and cities has become a major source of concern at the various levels of power. Most of the larger municipalities are insolvent. The federal power structure and the system of taxation that supplies the municipalities' budgets have the merit of not disguising this deficit, whereas in other countries the fact is camouflaged when the nation as a whole foots the bill for expenses that concern the urban population alone.

No one in America is in any doubt about the fact that this is a real crisis of civilization. No one, for example, has tried to reduce it to the more modest dimensions of a simple administrative breakdown.

The urban crisis is a prime example of the kind of problem that parties and politicians hesitate to tackle directly. The idea of the city is closely bound up with the concept of progress: the city is the engine of civilization where the country acts as a brake; innovations are born in the city, reaching the country only later; the tokens of comfort are apparent among city-dwellers well before they reach the rural population. History supports this analysis, but only in part, and the most recent trends in fact invalidate it.

There are 4,128,000 dwellings in the United States without running water, one million without heating, 6,900,000 without either bath or shower—and most of them in the urban areas. Furthermore they are overcrowded as a result of the migration of some 20 million country-dwellers in the space of a few years.

In the Paris region with its almost nine million inhabitants 64 per cent of dwellings have neither bath nor shower, and 43 per cent do not even have an inside lavatory. The situation is undoubtedly worse in *communes* of less than 5,000 inhabitants, where the corresponding figures are 87 per cent and 81 per cent, and where 32 per cent of dwellings are without running water, as against 12 per cent in the Paris region. But this situation is not surprising: it is due simply to the fact that rural *communes*, although numbering some 21 million inhabitants altogether, get a poor deal as far as the allocation of budgetary credits for housing is concerned. In the Paris region, nothing short of the rebuilding of entire quarters would, over a period of several decades, solve the housing problem. The present rate of housing construction, however, is barely sufficient to keep pace with the influx of population. Furthermore this kind of rebuilding is more expensive in Paris than in the provinces, and it is virtually impossible to provide temporary accommodation on a large scale for people living in dilapidated buildings in need of demolition before moving them into new accommodation. One or two exemplary rehousing schemes can blind no one to the fact that in Europe as in the United States the old urban fabric is decaying faster than it is being replaced.

A further myth contributes to the confusion of ideas although it is already belied by the facts: the megalopolis, so the myth runs, is a cultural capital, and new ideas and forms in literature and the arts find readier acceptance in an urban than in a rural environment. In reality, just as in the United States universities and towns of quite moderate size have their symphony orchestras, museums, and theatre groups, so throughout Europe it is the relatively small towns that attract theatre and music festivals. Theatre attendance in Paris has dropped by 25 per cent over the last ten years, while certain provincial towns are tending to play an avant-garde role. Similarly cinema attendance in France has dropped by half in ten years—and cinemas are of course an essentially urban phenomenon. Cultural life is tending towards decentralization, while the population of every country in the West is tending on the contrary to become more concentrated.

Writers, painters, and sculptors are increasingly deserting overpopulated areas and only using the big city for the purposes of publishing or exhibiting their works. Paris, London, and New York are shop-windows more than centres of creativity. The megalopolis attracts the careerist rather than the genius, which is no doubt why more than half France's architects—most of whom, to be fair, do not regard themselves as artists—have chosen to operate in the Paris region. The development of provincial universities too reveals a trend that is becoming more and more marked and that has been apparent in America for a long time: Harvard and Princeton have no cause to envy the University of Chicago, or Columbia University, situated in the very heart of New York.

'Places of pestilence'

There is a stubborn tradition that insists on the double equation: city = progressiveness, country = conservatism. Electoral sociology does not wholly substantiate this over-simplification, which would presuppose a clear-cut opposition between a truly conservative and a truly progressive party. In New York the city votes Democrat whereas the residential suburbs and the northern part of the state vote Republican, but the *arrondissements* of Paris, taken as a whole, show a majority of right and centre voters. In Italy the agricultural south is as loud in its claims as the workers of the north. In the United States the farmers' lobby that backed the New Deal was more concerned about subsidies for agriculture than about economic and social progress, and Roosevelt also received support from the agricultural south, a bastion of conservatism. In France the agricultural south-west has long voted left for reasons that have little to do with any modern conception of progress.

If it is true that towns and cities are on the whole more progressive than rural areas, the choice for the future does not lie between urban and rural populations. The real choice is between gigantic megalopolises becoming more and more congested and less and less solvent, and true cities of a size and economic dynamism that are compatible with a human style of life. It is no accident that, in France, towns like Saint-Nazaire and Le Mans have seen the emergence of strike movements that the Paris region was incapable of launching. Giantism is often synonymous with paralysis, even at the 'revolutionary' level.

It is not surprising, however, that all criticism of the phenomenon of the megalopolis is taken as criticism of the urban society of which it is a monstrous excrescence, and as a product of conservative attitudes. The right is often imbued with nostalgia for an agrarian existence powerless to resist the march of progress. Similarly bucolic dreams haunt city-dwellers as they spend eleven months of the year yearning for the return to nature represented by their holidays at the seaside or in the mountains.

In the United States this need is partly met by the national parks, an amenity that Europe too is belatedly beginning to introduce. But the Americans are under no illusions: their often magnificent national parks are none the less inadequate. They receive 164 million visitors annually—i.e. four-fifths of the total population—for visits of very short duration. They offer a practical holiday formula for a few days in the year and an effective way of preserving certain regions, but they in no way remove the necessity for reorganizing the megalopolises.

When Pétain preached from Vichy a return to the soil and in the same breath extolled the virtues of moral discipline, he rallied round him all the forces of conservatism. The Fifth Republic, however, is an example of the fact that regimes that base their support on the profiteers of chronic urbanization show themselves no less sensitive on the subject of the moral order.

In the United States Jefferson saw in cities the death of the democratic citizen and his institutions: 'I regard great cities as places of pestilence from the point of view of the morality, health, and liberty of mankind.'

The city is licence and vice; contact with nature is virtue: this moral over-simplification has never been the monopoly of Anglo-Saxon puritanism. Montesquieu was highly sceptical about the human equality of city-dwellers: 'The greater the number of men living together in one place, the greater their vanity and the more they experience a desire to distinguish themselves in little things. If their number is so great that the majority of them do not know one another, their desire to distinguish themselves is twice as strong for the fact that they have more hope of succeeding. It is luxury that lends this hope; each adopts the marks of the condition above his own.'[9]

Towns and cities are indeed the places where you find the luxury which is, as Montesquieu pointed out, based on an unequal distribution of wealth and on 'commodities that are obtained from the labour of others'—neither of which phenomena is of course particularly democratic. The notion of luxury evolves even faster than morality; the chief beneficiaries of the unequal distribution of wealth in France today are the 1·6 million city-dwellers who are able on occasion to flee the big city for the peace and quiet of their secondary residence or their yacht.

The choice between city and provinces has no ideological connotation whatever. The city offers both a comfortable anonymity and the 'desire to distinguish oneself' remarked on by Montesquieu. But anonymity also leads to the disturbed and traumatic states that David Riesman analysed in *The Lonely Crowd*. Nor is there any further doubt about the fact that big cities are, as Jefferson feared, 'places of pestilence' from the point of view of health.

Some 250,000 tons of sulphur dioxide fall on Paris annually, and in Marseille the air is even more polluted. 300,000 tons of soot fall on New York in a year, and the situation is even worse in Los Angeles; though the latter covers one and a half times the area of the former with only a third of the population, this only means that it can accommodate even more cars.

The dangers represented by these nuisances provoke highly contradictory reactions. Studies of air and water pollution and the effects of noise drive some people into a state of panic, whereas others greet them with a certain scepticism, pointing out in particular that environmental deterioration has not prevented a steady increase in the figures for life expectancy. It is true that the human organism has considerable powers of adaptation. The body learns to put up with the tensions of a hectic life and the strains to which a deteriorating environment gives rise. Moreover the progress of medical science makes it possible to alleviate the effects of these evils, however serious they may be. The city, it is claimed, is bringing about its own kind of natural selection: only the fittest survive the ordeal of urban civilization; the weaker always have the alternative of living in smaller developments.

Progress and capitalism

If urban concentration were a law of progress, no one would dare call it into question. What it is in fact is a law of industrialization under a liberal regime of which the chief driving force is the search for profit and in which the public authorities intervene as little as possible to place restraints on private interests. The industrial and technological revolution has indeed brought about progress in most spheres of social life, but the nature of that progress and the form it takes do not go unchallenged. A poll conducted in 1965 by the National Institute for Demographic Studies showed that, if 18 per cent of the population of France live in the Paris region, only 11 per cent would choose to do so if they could find work in less heavily populated areas. An adjustment of economic geography to meet the preferences thus expressed would reduce the population of the Paris region from 9 to 5·5 million. In the United States the way in which the better-off sections of the population are leaving the cities is evidence of the same disaffection. It is only the ups and downs of regional economics that force low-income workers to migrate towards the big industrial centres. The procedure of democratic consultation offers them no possibility of orienting the economic structure of the country to suit their own requirements.

The phenomenon of urban concentration is thus coming under increasingly heavy criticism. The trade unions, long accustomed to fighting for a higher *standard of living*, inevitably came to see that wage increases are not enough: they now also demand improvements in the *quality of life*, improvements that can only be realized in terms of slower production schedules, more humane working conditions, shorter hours, longer holidays, and more comfortable housing and transport facilities. What they are thus questioning is both the methods of production and the manner of life in megalopolises created by an anarchical process of industralization. In the United States this crusade is gaining daily in political weight, and it is within the bounds of possibility that it will become a frequently employed weapon against industries that make their profits by destroying the living environment and by polluting natural resources that do not belong to them.

In January 1971 President Nixon announced that the next ten years would be decisive in the battle against water pollution. In November the Senate voted 86 to nil for a bill requiring industries and municipalities to take all measures necessary to stop water pollution completely by 1985. The federal government immediately threw itself into energetic opposition to the project, which it estimated would cost the enormous sum of $94,500 million in a decade. White House economic and scientific advisers argued that such a law would drive American firms to emigrate to countries with less rigorous legislation. Once again the alliance between government and industry showed its cohesion.

The debate had the merit of throwing two points into clear relief. Firstly it showed that private firms find it entirely normal to make profits out of industrial processes that sacrifice the general interest by polluting rivers, lakes, and the sea; in one form or another they all devoted vast sums to publicity campaigns designed to portray them as servants of the public and of society. Secondly it showed that the government, in theory responsible for looking after the common good and acting as arbitrator in conflicts between opposing interests, was quite prepared to curry favour with voters by promising to combat pollution, but was not prepared to subject private industry to the necessary legislative controls. The Senate allowed for an expenditure of $3,500 million annually for four years. Mr Nixon wanted to cut them down to $2,000 million annually for three years. At the same time the Pentagon had no trouble in getting hold of the necessary funds for its B-1 bomber, which cost $11,000 million.

The citizen's powerlessness in the face of the coalition of 'public' authorities and 'private' industry is apparent in another example. 'America the beautiful. Today that beauty is in danger,' declared President Johnson. In 1965 Congress voted through the first law governing the billboards that cut off the view of the landscape along America's roads. But the removal of some 839,000 billboards would cost more than $300 million in public funds. The law also obliges the states to indemnify billboard owners. But the government hesitates to clash with the private firms involved, and the Transportation Department admits that at the present rate of billboard removal it will take a century to rid America's roads of this eyesore. Titillated and wooed as consumer, the citizen is virtually defenceless against industries that sacrifice to their own commercial interests a countryside that does not belong to them. The citizen, however, refusing to be reduced to the role of consumer, is becoming increasingly insistent on putting across his own point of view. The success of the campaign led by the young lawyer Ralph Nader against firms that supply the public with sub-standard cars, kitchen appliances, and food products is evidence of this discontent. Some groups go further: in Michigan, students equipped with power saws destroyed more billboards in one evening than the federal government has done in five years.

The economic aspect of these various nuisances reveals the incoherence governing the choice of priorities. American companies spend more than $20,000 million annually on publicity, yet the government does not feel it can make them set aside a sum only a third of that for the battle against pollution; on the contrary, it even toadies to them. When in 1967 the Department of the Interior set up a special group to combat pollution it entrusted the chair to Mr Charles Bueltman, head of the principal chemical industries lobby. In 1971 a Congressional committee estimated that it would cost $600 million to clean up lakes Erie and Ontario, but the federal budget for the same year allowed only $500 million for *all* lakes and rivers, i.e. the equivalent of the advertising budget of the three biggest detergent manufacturers. Billboard advertisements absorb $200 million annually, i.e. a bare 1 per cent of total advertising expenditure—but the removal of billboards would cost one and a half times that amount.

The industrialized societies of the West like to think they are scientifically and rationally organized. Spurred on by their conception of economic growth, however, they end up creating problems whose solution requires resources those societies are incapable of mustering. The law of profit acts as a stimulus to private interests but burdens the community with crushing financial responsibilities that ought to devolve on industry alone and be accounted for in its costing.

Urbanization, individualism, and anonymity

Yet these nuisances are not the chief danger facing the major urban concentrations. Even more serious is that other danger Jefferson feared —namely the big city as threat to the 'liberty of man'.

In the speech with which he promised the birth of a 'Great Society' President Johnson said: 'Expansion is eroding the precious and time-honoured values of community with neighbors and communion with nature. The loss of these values breeds loneliness and boredom and indifference.' Individuals may voluntarily reject 'contact with nature', or be without the necessary financial means that make it possible, or organize such contact in a variety of ways. But the 'sense of communal life' is at all events indispensable to every democratic society, especially in densely populated areas. In the last analysis this is a political problem involving a particular conception of man and of society.

Paul R. Ehrlich, Professor of Biology at Stanford University, claims that, certain appearances notwithstanding, and in contradiction of the ideal of the societies of the West, respect for human life decreases as demographic pressure increases: 'The increasing impersonality of big cities, where a citizen's appeals for help are often ignored by passers-by, tends to corroborate this point of view.' He adds that men are as a rule 'not aware of the influence that volume and density of population have on their mode of life and their way of looking at the world.'[10] This is due to the fact that significant changes in volume and density of population take place only slowly, rarely occurring within the space of a generation; man thus has time to get used to them gradually.

Large concentrations of population nevertheless entail anonymity, indifference with regard to the individual, rules and regulations that are blind to the particular case, and a general reduction of people to mere numbers. The teacher cannot take an interest in each pupil when the class is too large; the more accused he has to try, the less attention the judge pays to each one; in big blocks of flats people often do not know their neighbours; the motorist stuck in a traffic jam tends too easily to forget the respect he owes his fellows; over-large administrations have the effect of diluting responsibility and are very far from treating people as citizens with certain rights.

More than twenty years ago C. Wright Mills, who after his death was to become one of the intellectual father-figures of the more 'radical' section of American youth, noted that the city 'has become so impersonal at the top and bottom that a major problem is how to make it personal again, and still smooth-running and continuous.'[11] City administrators were not at that time asking themselves this kind of question. Two decades after Wright Mills's warning, however, the mayor of New York was defining 'the dominant malaise of the contemporary American' as follows: the citizen, John Lindsay wrote in an article entitled 'Can Cities Survive?', 'has the impression of having lost his individuality. The inhabitant of the City of New York, for instance, feels cut off from the city administration. He thinks the authorities do not understand his problems, that no one is interested in them or has any solution to offer him. This feeling of frustration gives rise to a deep and understandable bitterness.' The mayor of New York is mistaken: the people in his administrative charge do not just have the 'impression' of being anonymous—they really are.

A Gaullist idea has crossed the Atlantic, and John Lindsay considers that 'the best way to combat the deep malaise of our cities is to set up participation programmes'. But the mayor of New York has already discovered that the 'little city halls' created for this purpose and the improvements in citizen access to the various agencies and departments have done nothing to alter the problem. It is not enough to appoint 'receptionists', as France has begun to do. Citizens do not merely want to have the impression of controlling their own destiny: they want actually to do so. What they expect of a democratic administration is not just a more courteous reception but a real possibility of exerting some influence on decisions. Such a possibility simply does not—and cannot—exist in the megalopolis, for the megalopolis banishes democratic life.

In his inaugural lecture at New York University in 1970 Irving Kristol painted a sombre picture of the 'anonymous mass of individuals' living on top of one another in 'cosmopolitan, over-crowded cities', describing them as follows: 'Clawing one another in a sordid struggle for survival, for privileges, or for phoney honours, in their frantic existence showing reverence neither for God, nor for nature, nor for the political regime, such people are not of the stuff of which citizens of a free and autonomous republic are made.'

There are two problems here: on the one hand that of the behaviour of individuals who perhaps live and move in an administrative district of 80,000 to 100,000 inhabitants but have their being in an urban area of 10, 15, or even 20 million inhabitants; on the other hand that of the way democratic structures operate in areas of high population density.

For a long time liberal democracy entertained the hope that the emergence of a strong middle class would provide republican institutions with the stable base indispensable to their functioning smoothly. The very ideal of that liberal democracy was incarnate in a political leadership that was recruited essentially from among the liberal professions, leaders of the business world, landowners, and the universities.

4

These men possessed a certain culture, had experience of responsibility, and represented a way of life and a kind of moderation that constituted an example to the voters at large. Capitalism and the workings of democracy were to combine to develop numerically a middle class devoted to a body of values comprising wisdom, justice, order, and progress. This electoral base was credited with virtues rendering it immune to the two temptations capable of threatening democracy: authoritarianism and anarchy. The social class constituting the very foundation of the system would be a 'middle' class in every respect: *economically* it would be secure against poverty, enjoying a comfortable existence without having access to the privileges of the very rich; *culturally* it would have a sound classical or professional education while being hardly likely to share the dreams of poets and men of genius; *politically* it would be suspicious of the dangerous extremes of both disorder and totalitarianism.

This middle class has indeed emerged, and it is particularly well represented in urban areas, but it is far from resembling the model that was held up to it as an example. The values it was to imitate have become diluted and ultimately distorted in proportion as they have been adopted by a larger and larger number of people: a better standard of living has not automatically entailed a raising of the cultural level or a deepening of the social and political conscience. This middle class, the seat of power in every country in the West, is more afraid of disorder than of authoritarian measures, more concerned for its economic privileges than for social progress, and more attached to its material well-being than anxious for any broadening of its cultural mind. As Joseph Wood Krutch pointed out, 'middle' and 'mediocre' stem ultimately from the same Latin root.[12] Moreover this mediocrity permeates the whole of political life from election campaigns to government pronouncements, and from the contents of the mass media to the architecture of our suburbs. No democracy can be founded on such a basis.

On the other hand if the democratic form of society seeks in principle to cultivate the art of living together, in practice it cannot see itself existing without the kind of competition that fosters individualism. Whatever their ideological inspiration, the great figures who presided over the birth and development of the West's democratic regimes had a certain personal sense of mission. Electoral mechanics were such that a campaign was much more a duel between two individuals than a clash between two political platforms. Modern methods of publicity have reinforced this trend to the point of reducing the democratic debate to trivialities: charm, brilliance, and smoothness are more effective than the force of reason in moving the greatest number. It is generally agreed that John F. Kennedy beat Richard M. Nixon in 1960 by being more telegenic. The lesson was not lost on Nixon, who eight years later took more trouble over his television appearances. The problems at issue in the political arena—taxation, directions in scientific research, strategic concepts, investment programmes, budgetary priorities, foreign policy—are becoming increasingly complex and technical. In order to win votes the candidate chooses either to duck them completely or to over-simplify them, appealing to the middle-of-the-road concerns of a middle class that is satisfied with very middling ambitions for itself and for the society and world in which it lives. Its narrow individualism spares it the necessity of asking itself too many questions, and it does not expect the candidate to trouble its conscience by bringing them up.

Economic mechanisms foster even more effectively than political structures the individualist tendencies that are undermining the very foundations of democracy. They appeal directly to personal interest, which is held to be the driving force behind collective progress. Countless theorists have developed and continue to develop the thesis according to which the will and thirst for profit of the few is, by virtue of the laws of the market, automatically subordinate to the interest of the greatest number. If we are to believe what they say, the real dictators of the market are not the captains of the production industries in their search for bigger profits and faster growth but, democratically, the community of consumers, which has the final say. Vance Packard has shown just how far advertising is capable of deluding the vast majority of consumers. The intervention of governments obliged to keep a check on the quality of food and pharmaceutical products, the poison-content of cosmetics and various chemical compounds, the safety of cars, heating appliances, etc., shows that the citizen-consumer is at the mercy of grasping manufacturers. Since government intervention has proved inadequate, individuals have had to organize private associations for their own protection. John Kenneth Galbraith and others have shown that the laws of the market have never had the quasi-magical power that has been attributed to them. Speculators and pressure groups do not balance one another out. They are always prepared to sacrifice the general interest to private interests. Can one under such circumstances still talk of democracy?

In 1929–30 the individualism inherent in the capitalist system plunged the United States from euphoria into crisis. Forty years later, bowing to hard facts, the American government nevertheless waited until August 1971 before imposing wage and price controls. Commenting on these decisions later, John Kenneth Galbraith wrote in an article entitled 'Nixon Buries the Market': 'Once controls are in force—once it has been accepted that the market system has given way to another system involving a large measure of planning—questions of equity become crucial. Before, differences of income could be attributed to the blind decision of the market; superficially perhaps, here was a justification for inequality. Now that there are controls, income distribution depends clearly on human intervention, and towards human intervention people are going to be considerably less indulgent.'

The necessity for resorting to controls of a greater or lesser degree of severity confirms the vigour of a spirit of competition that has proved incapable of subordinating the individualist impulse to a respect for the general interest. That individualism can only be contained by means of personal decision—highly unlikely in a society that exalts it as a virtue—or by means of sociological pressure imposing the respect due to the body of citizens. Such pressure can be felt in societies on a human scale, but it grows indistinct or disappears in proportion as the individual loses his identity. The pilot of a B-52 is an anonymous person bombarding, from a great height, anonymous populations. Similarly the manufacturers who put harmful food products on the market are poisoning anonymous consumers.[13] The anonymity behind which the individual shelters in areas of high population density allows him to plague his equally anonymous neighbours with excessive noise, non-observance of the elementary rules of hygiene or courtesy, violence, and theft.

'We are far from inclined to reproach ourselves,' says Irving Kristol, 'with the fact that certain American milieux, which have their equivalent in the cities of other nations, are coming increasingly to behave like a mob having no respect for the law.'

This kind of behaviour becomes apparent as soon as the individual disappears behind a mob that grants him anonymity and with it impunity in the event of his infringing the laws of democracy. Large urban concentrations, the fruit of an anarchical process of industrialization, achieve the miracle of combining the opposites of individualism and anonymity, both of which are incompatible with the requirements of communal life within a democratic society.

The logical outcome of a process of industrialization that has run its course without the state, as guardian of the general interest, exercising adequate control over private interests, urban concentration has become the test of Western civilization. Irving Kristol does not hesitate to talk in terms of 'the evident incapacity of our democratic civilization' to solve the problems posed by this anarchical industrialization process.

Urbanization and speculation

Urban concentration is not the result of a choice of civilization. It is and has always been a minority's privileged means of enriching itself at the majority's expense.

In the United States the possibilities of making a fortune are becoming more and more restricted. A study of fortunes in excess of $75 million led to these simple conclusions: 53 per cent are inherited fortunes, left to their descendents by men who were able to amass their millions at a time when legislative controls were virtually non-existent and taxation extremely lenient; the rest (47 per cent) are the fortunes people have been able to put together themselves during their own lifetime. Of the latter, the first group are the independent oil magnates, living in Texas for the most part and reaping the benefits of fiscal legislation that grants them scandalous privileges, and the second those who have made their fortunes out of property deals on which legislative controls are notoriously inadequate.[14]

'Getting rich quick' through property deals is a phenomenon common to the entire West. The mechanics of it are more complex than they were in Baron Haussmann's time but the principles are still very much as Emile Zola described them in *La Curée* (1872). It began with the industrial revolution, which reduced the yield on agrarian incomes and opened up big opportunities for profit in the expanding fields of industry, banking, and commerce. While the rural patrimony dropped in value, industrialization pushed up land prices in the towns and their immediate vicinity. The new gold mine was laid.

This is the age of the 'developer'. One 'developer' bought a few years ago, at the price for agricultural land, some 250 acres about 15 miles outside Paris. Under subsequent plans for the extension of the Paris agglomeration, this plot was rezoned as 'building land': a simple administrative decision had netted the 'developer' a cool three-quarters of a million pounds. Philippe Saint Marc, former president of the Aquitaine Coast Planning Board, wrote in 1971: 'Buying cheaply land

that is zoned as not to be built on, getting a "waiver" from the administration entitling one to build on it, and then selling it for a vast sum is
common practice among countless builders. The waiver is the broad
highway to property speculation. A waiver can be the founding of a
fortune. Hence the tremendous pressure the administration is under to
grant them (. . .) There is no such thing as town-planning any more;
there is nothing but the tidal-wave of money. The property business
has become a state within the state.'[15]

Operations of this kind involve not only land that has been zoned
for non-development but also the density of building allowed on a
particular site (i.e. the height of the buildings). They are directed mainly
at the major urban areas and at tourist regions—seaside and ski resorts.
Philippe Saint Marc quoted the figure of 20,000 waivers granted in the
Paris region in the period 1960–64 and a further 80,000 since 1965. This
progression will continue and will accelerate until the target of 14
million inhabitants for the Paris region has been reached—at which
point there will be nothing to stop someone contemplating a further
extension.

Not all these tens of thousands of waivers are of course connected
with speculative deals. Some of them concern mere details of adaptation to make a new building fit better into the context of its neighbours.
But if Albin Chalandon, Minister of Housing and Public Works, is
right to point out that not all waivers are 'arbitrary' or the product of
'favouritism' or 'compromise'[16] he nevertheless admits that 'this kind
of increase in the number of dwellings built on a particular site to well
above the limit laid down by the town-planning authority involves a
genuinely unjustified gain for the developer if it is the community that
is financing the necessary public works.'

Various measures have been taken to limit this 'unjustified gain', but
real-estate operations are still among the most profitable as a result of
what the Minister calls the 'fantastic acceleration' of urbanization
following the Second World War. He talks about the 'intensive development of urban agglomerations' in terms of an unexpected 'tidal-
wave', a kind of natural cataclysm against which the public authorities
were powerless. This is to play down heavily the plan to increase the
population of the Paris region by two-thirds, a decision that is sufficient
in itself to send land prices soaring and thus make further huge profits
possible.

The system thus erected is rigorous in its logic. Building or renovation schemes are left in the hands of mixed or private firms. The

budgets involved in such operations are in any case very considerable. It is difficult to cut costs because, as the Minister says, 'the margin is a narrow one'. Feasibility then demands 'increasing returns by opting for the kind of building use that will offset the high cost of land— offices, for instance'. So more offices are built—in the Défense quarter of Paris, for example, but also all over Paris, as in the centres of American cities—which has the effect of encouraging new firms to move in, which in turn attract a workforce that has to be housed. The urban perimeter is pushed outwards, paving the way for lucrative deals in fresh land on the outskirts. The minister argues as if the public works paid for by the community as a whole were alone responsible for pushing up land prices. Yet a piece of agricultural land need only be rezoned as building land for its value to be many times increased. A regime that encourages urban concentration cannot overlook the fact that it is favouring certain private groups at the expense of the national community.

Profits and inefficiency

The public gets very excited about the various property scandals that periodically find their way into the newspapers of Europe and North America and sometimes even reach the political columns. But whatever the sums involved—and they are sometimes considerable—it is generally a question of the blunders and swindles of the small-fry of real-estate speculation. The real scandal, the one that is going on on the biggest scale, is the political decision to speed up urban concentration, thus paving the way for more and bigger speculative deals.

This decision is not dictated by any concern to ensure optimum economic development. On the contrary, it pushes up land prices and increases building, public-service, and transport costs. Moreover it reduces workers' productivity as a result of the constant fatigue which, thanks to the nuisances of the urban environment, cannot be eliminated even when job conditions are adequate. In addition to work fatigue there is the fatigue of travelling and that caused by the tensions of city life. It has been calculated in the United States that air pollution reduces workers' output by 15 per cent. Noise, in the working environment and during periods of recreation and sleep, is even more devastating in its effects. In France it is responsible for 11 per cent of accidents on the job and for the loss of 1,000 million working hours every year.[17] Noise can cut a manual worker's output by 30 per cent, an intellectual worker's by 60 per cent. Also to be taken into account is the proportion of the social-security budget represented by sickness and accidents arising out of these nuisances.

Neither does official encouragement of urban concentration stem from a concern to improve people's quality of life. One of the consequences of urban concentration is the disappearance of green spaces, despite the fact that every government proclaims its firm intention of preserving them. With $1·3$ m² per inhabitant Paris has more parks and public gardens than New York, but less than London or Rome (9 m²), and the bigger provincial cities are hardly better off than the capital: Lyon $3·5$ m², Bordeaux and Marseille, 2 m². Since 1900 the surface area of Paris parks has fallen from 2,250 acres to less than 1,500 acres, and they are still cutting down trees. 37,500 acres of forest have been cut in the Paris region; between 1965 and 1970, 4,750 acres of theoretically protected woodland were cleared. Wise administrative decisions protect green spaces that other administrative decisions—the famous 'waivers'—sacrifice to the developers' greed. Forests only bring in money when they are cleared to make way for buildings.

Lastly, if urban concentration does nothing for either economic progress or human progress, it is equally unproductive as far as political progress is concerned. The real power of elected assemblies decreases in the megalopolis, and by the same token the rights and powers of the citizen suffer a setback. The mayors of America's cities admit their powerlessness to balance their budgets, to provide decent public-health, educational, and road-upkeep services, and to protect citizens against a rising crime rate. So they turn to the federal government for fresh sources of finance. In Europe as in America the powers of the municipality in the more densely populated regions are subordinate to decisions taken at a higher level, for local authorities cannot finance by themselves the public works that become indispensable when the area in their charge grows in the space of a few years from a good-sized town to a city of several tens of thousands of inhabitants. They never cease to protest against extensions of the urban perimeter that drown them in a formless flood, but their protests are in vain. Elected assemblies continue to deliberate and pass motions and resolutions, but real power slips from their hands in proportion as they lose the right of control over their financial resources. That power passes more and more into the hands of planning organizations dominated ultimately by the will and the conceptions of technocrats. In the end the voter no longer knows his representatives—not that this matters much because his representatives have become mere supernumeraries who are required to pronounce on the consequences of decisions taken at a higher level.

Democracy is in a bad way in overpopulated regions where both voters and their representatives, depersonalized by anonymity, are at grips with blind administrative machines.

Corruption and the scandal of 'legal' speculation

If cities of vast size cannot be said to represent progress in economic, human, or political terms, what are they doing, dominating the industrialized West and growing bigger all the time? It was natural enough for the metallurgical industries to set up shop in the vicinity of iron-ore and coal deposits, but there was nothing to justify the enormous concentration of firms in areas that in many cases have no such deposits. Nothing, that is, except the possibility of exploiting a plentiful, underpaid, and ill-housed labour force. The first large-scale speculative real estate operations, which this concentration of humanity made possible, date from the last century when the workers had not yet managed to organize themselves. Once they had formed trade unions, however, they began to fight for their most pressing claims: decent wages, regulations governing child labour, and shorter hours. Meanwhile the law of profit-at-any-price pushed forward a process of anarchical industrialization and uncontrolled urbanization. It was the heyday of real-estate speculation, with fortunes being made overnight.

America and Europe may not be exactly in step but they are going the same way. In the United States corruption is more striking: there was a time when every American city had its 'boss' who ran the whole municipality, not just its prostitution and illegal gambling. 'The ties between vice and politics, and between "rackets" and the respectable business elements of the city, are too close to be easily broken,' writes Max Lerner. The crime syndicates have become slightly more civilized and introduced less obtrusive methods, but even today 'there is scarcely a big American city whose administration is not at least marginally involved in this trinity of crime, political corruption, and business favours.'[18]

The situation is no better in Europe, the sole difference being that the public is kept less well informed about it by its press and its elected representatives. Italian films such as *Heavy Hand in the Town* and *The Police Inspector's Confession to the Public Prosecutor*, however, have drawn attention to the kind of real-estate speculation that cannot succeed

4 *

without high-level protection and political complicity. Europe is well up with America as far as real-estate speculation is concerned; it is only behind in discovering and denouncing the scandalous profits some people make out of it.

So far in France the law has concerned itself exclusively with building societies that have artificially inflated the value of their assets, committed themselves to operations beyond their financial means, or misappropriated a part of depositors' funds, and then suddenly found themselves in difficulties. There are always savers who will let themselves be fleeced with promises of a higher rate of interest. But such scandals are marginal, the work of amateurs who want to have a piece of the cake but lack the backing of powerful consortiums or banks—and on top of that commit serious irregularities or imprudences. The real scandal, the 'legal' scandal is that of the promoters who practice real-estate speculation on a positively industrial scale, buying up hundreds of acres of cheap agricultural land around urban centres or seaside or ski resorts and, by securing all the necessary permits and authorizations, turning it into building land. In this they are aided and abetted by interested parties in the building trade.

Urban concentration can lead to big profits not only through extensions of the urban area but also through the renovation of city centres. 'Something has to be done about the defacement of our urban centres,' says Minister of Housing Chalandon.[19] Ten years of urban renovation in Paris have demolished 13,000 dwellings to erect 97,000 new ones on the same surface area. High-rise building makes possible a more unencumbered cityscape, but it also means, in this case, seven and a half times the density of population. Paris, like all modern cities, is spreading not only outwards but upwards, with tower-blocks shooting up at la Défense, at Maine-Montparnasse, along the Seine, at Porte Maillot, in the Italie quarter, and so on. Debate as to the aesthetic value of this kind of architecture is by no means negligible. But the essential problem is that of the steady growth of population in a city already twice as densely populated as New York. Paris is dreaming of building a new Manhattan at a time when the mayor of New York is at his wits' end and the better-off sections of the population are concerned only to get away from the great American metropolis.

In this respect what is happening in France is exceptional. The British government intends to cut the London population by one million over twenty years in order to fix it at a level—eight million—lower than that of the Paris complex. The new complexes designed to decongest

Greater London are being built between 30 and 80 miles from the capital.

Cities and the citizen

It it is absurd to increase the population density of the Paris region and if the policy of the British government appears much more satisfactory, the crises of urban civilization are not going to be solved merely by reducing the population of the London agglomeration to eight million inhabitants.

Even regarding towns less populous than London, a British study has led to some very pessimistic conclusions: 'The cost of implementing some of the large urban traffic plans is colossal,' writes R. E. Pahl, 'the figure of £250 million has been quoted for Liverpool, £200 million for Newcastle and £135 million for Leicester. It is doubtful whether we have the appropriate decision-making techniques for assessing the relative merits of different settlement forms and transportation systems, given the speed of technological innovation and change.'[20]

Indeed in terms of public works cities are already far behind not only what is required but what modern technology makes possible. Marseille and Lyon still have no Underground; both towns are about the size of Liverpool, where a modern transport system would cost £250 million to install. Such investments as well as the town-planning concepts that render them indispensable are doomed to the fate of those strategic weapons that are scientifically obsolete by the time they become operational.

Cities, like industrial enterprises, have an optimum size, though this is of course difficult to determine. But the congestion, paralysis, and asphyxia that characterize urban complexes such as Chicago and Los Angeles, with seven million inhabitants each, show clearly that they have overshot it.

It is hard to imagine two more different urban areas than Chicago and Los Angeles. Both megalopolises have about the same population, but as far as the city proper is concerned Los Angeles, though covering twice the area of Chicago, has half a million less inhabitants. Famous for its freeway system, the Los Angeles complex comprises literally dozens of independent municipalities, so that for example a 15-mile bus route has to be authorized by no less than six local governments. A few statistics will bring out the differences between the two cities (see table).

	Chicago	Los Angeles
Area in square miles	228	464
Population of the city in 1970	3,325,000	2,782,000
Change in population as against 1960	−6%	+12%
Number of inhabitants to the square mile	14,700	6,200
Population of the urban area......	6,894,000	6,960,000
Local taxation per capita (in dollars)	214	146
Outlay on education per pupil	659	758
Outlay on police per capita of population	56	33
Number of policemen per 1,000 inhabitants	3·2	4·3

Each of these physically very dissimilar cities illustrates in its own way the seriousness of the urban crisis. Car accidents cause 8·4 deaths per 100,000 inhabitants in Chicago, and in Los Angeles, despite its extensive freeway system, 7·2. But just because of its size Los Angeles has many more cars and its atmosphere is more heavily polluted with toxic gases. Richard Daley, mayor of Chicago, and Sam Yorty, mayor of Los Angeles, are both considered to be demagogues of dubious morality. Chicago is the only American city not to complain of financial insolvency, and this fortunate situation is attributed without any irony whatever to the fact that its municipal administration is reputed to be the most corrupt in the land. At any rate, the per capita burden of local taxation is one and a half times higher in Chicago than it is in Los Angeles, while per pupil outlay on education is 15 per cent lower. On the other hand Chicago's police are much better treated: the police-population ratio is only three-quarters what it is in Los Angeles, but Chicago's outlay on police, reckoned per capita of the population, is almost 50 per cent greater. In 1968, a particularly violent year, both cities were the scene of dramatic incidents: in Chicago, police brutality at the time of the Democratic Convention; in Los Angeles, Robert Kennedy's assassination. As regards theft, murder, and juvenile delinquency, the two cities make a comparable (i.e. equally disastrous) showing. Although the Watts race riots that caused thirty-four deaths in 1965 drew particular attention to Los Angeles, the situation in Chicago's black ghetto is just as explosive. But Mayor Daley's police keep a good eye on it.

Los Angeles shows that extension of the urbanized area involves vast expenditures on highway infrastructure without solving the problems of communication, pollution, public health, crime, education, and so on. Both cities show an equal abstention rate at elections, and the image they present of democracy is as unattractive in the one case as in the other. Both have elected mayors whom only a euphemism could describe as guardians of the public trust. Their administrations, as inefficient as they are corrupt, are sensitive to manipulation by powerful pressure groups while remaining indifferent to the claims of ordinary citizens.

Existing political structures hardly favour real democratic control: the sheer massiveness of such urban concentrations leaves power in the hands of technocratic administrations little suited to grasping the problem in its entirety. Each office handles with a greater or lesser degree of competence the sector for which it is responsible, but does so without any overall view. The overall view is equally lacking in the two cities' principal figures. Faced with a problem that is beyond them, whether in the form of grave social tensions or in the form of the rising crime rate, their first concern is to present themselves in the light of vigilant guardians of 'law and order': it is demagogic exploitation of this theme that wins them the votes of the socially and mentally middle class. Their election campaigns swallow vast budgets that every newspaper in America agrees cannot proceed entirely from natural sources. The real-estate speculation that out-sized urban areas encourage leads to surrenders of principle the voter is powerless to do anything about.

New York, Chicago, and Los Angeles—together with their urban areas comprising some 25 million inhabitants, i.e. one eighth of the total population—are not the only places where the quality of life is diminishing as public and private expenditure rise. This is also the fate of the 136 million Americans living in the big cities and their immense suburbs.

Because the public authorities have lacked imagination, breadth of vision, and a concept of the future and because they have also lacked courage and sometimes integrity in dealings with real-estate speculators, the megalopolises of the West have been delivered up to the greed of profiteers and unscrupulous local politicians who have left the citizen no more than a semblance of democratic control.

Originally a centre of progress, the city ceases to fulfil this role as soon as it becomes swallowed up in a megalopolis. Not only does it start to regress but it actually goes against the tide of progress. It is twenty years since Lewis Mumford called for an upheaval that the free-enterprise regime has failed to bring about. He foresaw that, as electrical energy came more and more to replace coal and as means of transport improved, industrial centres would be able to spread themselves more, thus decongesting the areas that had begun to develop in the nineteenth century. But the law of profit has decided otherwise, and the twentieth century has made worse what the nineteenth century began.

At about the same time Walter Reuther, president of the automobile workers' union, was saying something similar: 'The majority of our big industrial centres owe their geographical situation to the easy availability of coal or other sources of energy. As new sources of energy appear the advantages of such geographical situations may disappear and there could be big shifts of industries towards new areas.'[21]

Walter Reuther envisaged the possibility of using atomic energy to set up industries in less-developed regions. But despite the fact that the American metallurgical industry imports coal and iron ore, it remains based on the south shore of the Great Lakes near the (inadequate) Pennsylvania and Minnesota deposits. Economic liberalism is not up to exploiting all the possibilities of new techniques.

Modernization of plant and the progress of automation would have been further justification for moving. In the name of profit, however, managements have for the most part preferred to adapt their old plant.

Actually a number of textile firms did leave New England some thirty years ago to move to the South—not in order to modernize themselves but in order to employ cheaper (black) labour. The aeronautical industry grew up on the Pacific coast and the young electronics industry has made the South-West its home. But no significant moves on the part of industry have come to relieve the over-populated area that stretches almost without interruption from Philadelphia up to Boston and from Boston right across to Milwaukee. Thirty years of technological advance have revolutionized methods of production and distribution while leaving the geo-economic balance unchanged— indeed, even aggravating the phenomenon of urban concentration. Private interests have been unable or unwilling to place technological and scientific progress at the service of a new society. They have offered people more consumer goods that have won them profits and ensured their growth; what they have failed to offer is a living environment worthy of the promises of the technological age.

The responsibility does not in the first instance lie with them. By definition, private interests concern themselves with the general interest only to the narrow extent to which they think it worth their while to do so. A far greater weight of responsibility lies with the public authorities who have either felt it was none of their business to intervene in order to make private groups widen their field of concern or been too closely associated with those private groups to be in a position to intervene in any case.

To the degree that real-estate speculation, spurred on by developers and finance companies, has accentuated an already absurd degree of urban concentration, it was up to the public authorities to fight it with the only effective weapon: public appropriation of land, just as Lewis Mumford had advocated as early as 1938. The French Minister of Housing and Public Works, Albin Chalandon, himself declares: 'If we are not able to make the progress I hope for in this sphere today, I am afraid that later we shall be unable to avoid a possibly agonizing reappraisal of the right of ownership itself.'[22]

Does M. Chalandon intend to wait until a further three to five million inhabitants have come to clog the Paris region? One assumes so, since he holds his portfolio within a government that is encouraging this process of congestion.

The State has at its disposal the means of promoting a harmonious industrial development which would balance out over the country as a whole urban centres of a more efficient, more human, and less burdensome kind than the present megalopolitan monstrosities. Under the present system, when the State shoulders the greater part of the financial burden of major road works or of Paris' public-transport deficit it makes the provinces foot the bill for the consequences of concentration in the Paris region. Without any further infringement of the principle of free enterprise than is represented by credit measures and taxation, it could just as well promote the development of major industrial, commercial, and cultural centres on a human scale in the provinces.

If the urban crisis penalizes both the city-dweller, who has to suffer the resultant inconveniences, and the provinces, which have to meet the cities' deficits, it hits a third class of victims even harder than the others: the urban poor. It is they whose work and travel schedules are tightest. It is they who are the worst housed, and in the least attractive districts. It is they who, for financial reasons, hardly benefit at all from the few advantages the city still has to offer, and have least chance of affording a holiday in conditions of real relaxation. It takes a well-lined wallet to make city life bearable. For the families with the lowest incomes the megalopolis makes the proletarian condition even more inhuman. Excessive urban concentration increases the degree and aggravates the injustice of social inequalities.

Is there any hope of solving the crisis? Behind the United States in launching their motorway programmes, the countries of Europe will be behind the United States in calling a halt to them. Bankers and brokers are beginning to leave the city of New York to set up some distance away headquarters that are linked electronically with a small office on Wall Street. It is only a modest beginning, but it shows the way things are going. The State can fan this hope by devoting to decongestion and regional economic development the budgets with which it vainly seeks to plug the deficits run up by urban areas.

Reversing the trend toward excessive urban concentration means putting a brake on the greed of speculators, cleaning up their relations with the administration, and paving the way for a better geo-economic balance. It also means opening the door to a modern concept of the city in which cars designed for speed do not have the effect of slowing traffic down, in which pedestrians can walk around without having to breathe in exhaust, and in which there are plenty of green spaces everywhere. But above all it means protecting an increasingly numerous population from the arbitrary attentions—or inattentions—of a gigantic and consequently anonymous administration, and restoring in full its civil rights.

A process of industrial expansion leaving in its wake wide areas of poverty and leading to anarchical urbanization is after all evidence of a certain 'success' on the part of capitalism, for capitalism sees man merely as a producer and has never claimed to see him in his whole human potential as a citizen. But the intention of democratic regimes is precisely to correct by means of political intervention abuses of economic power. Harold Laski thought that in the United States capitalism and democracy had never achieved more than an uneasy marriage. The same goes for the West as a whole. In the last analysis the democratic 'credo' has been sacrificed to the 'imperatives' of production and the blindness of economic forces.

References

1 Lewis Mumford, *The Culture of Cities*, Harcourt, Brace, New York, 1938.
2 Population of the city proper: 7,781,984 inhabitants in 1960 and 7,867,780 in 1970. Population of 'Greater New York': 10,695,000 in 1960 and 11,410,000 in 1970.
3 Lewis Mumford, *From the Ground Up*, Harcourt, Brace, Jovanovich, New York, 1956.
4 Lewis Mumford, *op. cit.*
5 Statement to *Le Monde*, 11 February 1972.
6 Inhabitants per square kilometre: United States, 23; France, 91; Italy, 180; England, 224; West Germany, 230; Belgium, 330; Holland, 430.
7 Paul Delouvrier, statement to the 'Colloque du comité d'études pour un nouveau contrat social', *Le Monde*, 7 March 1972.
8 Paul Granet, UDR deputy for Aube *département*, *Le Monde*, 7 March 1972.
9 Montesquieu, *L'Esprit des lois*, Book VII.
10 Paul R. and Anne H. Ehrlich, *Population, Resources, Environment: Issues in Human Ecology*, Freeman, San Francisco, 1970.
11 C. Wright Mills, *White Collar*, Oxford University Press, New York, 1951, p. 172.
12 Joseph Wood Krutch, *Human Nature and the Human Condition*, Random House, New York, 1959.
13 The Food and Drug Administration estimates that between two and ten million Americans annually become ill as a result of eating 'contaminated foodstuffs'.
14 *Fortune*, November 1957.
15 Philippe Saint Marc, *Socialisation de la nature*, Stock, Paris, 1971, p. 53.
16 Albin Chalandon, statement to *Le Monde*, 11 February 1972.
17 Maurice Tamboise, *Le bruit, fléau social*, Hachette, Paris, 1965.
18 Max Lerner, *America as a Civilization*, Simon and Schuster, New York, 1957, p. 169.
19 *Le Monde*, 11 February 1972.
20 R. E. Pahl, *Patterns of Urban Life: The Social Structure of Modern Britain*, Longmans, Green, London, 1971, p. 130.
21 Cf. Claude Julien, *Le nouveau Nouveau Monde*, Julliard, 1960, vol. I, p. 207.
22 *Le Monde*, 11 February 1972.

CHAPTER THREE

The Citizen Scorned

- 'Law and order'
- A caricature of universal suffrage
- Broken promises, impossible choices
- Failings of the political class
- Democratic control
- Money and power
- From disappointment to rebellion

Does democracy need reinventing? The whole West is asking the same question. On coming to power President Nixon promised a reorganization of government institutions—nothing of which has been seen as yet—and Congress itself cannot throw off the traditional, inherited shackles that paralyse its activities, while the judges complain of delays and anachronisms in the machinery of justice. In France the regime introduced in 1958 faces the discordant criticisms of 'reformers', socialists, Communists, and all the nuances of the Left; but it is itself careful not to claim that all is for the best in this best of all possible worlds, continuing to promise that 'new society' whose outlines remain ill-defined. For all the respect with which it invests its institutions, Great Britain is no less dissatisfied: while the Conservative party, backed by a slender majority, is up against formidable difficulties at home and abroad, the Labour party is unable to agree as to the exact nature of the 'compassionate society' for which it longs. In Bonn the federal government, whose achievements on the home front are pretty slim, has seen the boldest aspects of its foreign policy exposed to the slightest accident of parliamentary procedure. Belgium and Italy lurch from ministerial crisis to ministerial crisis, heading for a crisis of regime that will in all probability solve nothing. And if American federalism has seen a strengthening of the authority of the central government over the last forty years, Canadian federalism is evolving in the opposite direction: the 'separatism' of French-speaking Quebec is not the only centrifugal force threatening to tear the country apart.

The malaise of the Western democracies has its origin in three different spheres:

Constitutional structures, which differ widely from one country to another, are tolerated without arousing any enthusiastic participation or even completely ignored by a large section of the electorate that neglects or refuses to exercise its right to vote. In the ranks of government and opposition alike they are criticized for their clumsiness and inefficiency by those who would like to see them improved, adapted, and brought up to date, and vigorously contested by those who would like to do away with them altogether. Their continued existence is essentially the outcome of a negative argument: the absence, inadequacy, or vagueness of a possible alternative.

Non-political structures are regarded as no more satisfactory than the organs of legislature, executive, and judiciary. Universal suffrage and the (more or less theoretical) separation of powers are not enough to guarantee the democratic character of a society. This is affected by many other forces that no one would venture to describe as being democratically organized: private or nationalized firms, news and information media, the educational system, voluntary groups and associations, public and para-public services, etc. All these factors together determine the physiognomy of a society just as much as do the legislative, executive, and judicial authorities with which they maintain a complex web of relationships.

Lastly, the *speed of operation* of these constitutional structures and different non-political mechanisms is becoming increasingly important in societies that the pressure of scientific and technological progress is continually confronting with fresh problems. Ernesto 'Che' Guevara said that the revolution is like a bicycle: if it is not going fast enough it will fall over—unless there is a circus acrobat in the saddle. But the same law applies to liberal, bourgeois regimes as well: they start to wobble and are threatened with collapse if they fail to move at the speed of modern techniques and fresh ideas and aspirations on the part of the people. In a society undergoing change new problems come up without warning, the public quickly becomes aware of them, but solutions are slow to emerge. Ten years after the assassination of John Kennedy arms are still freely on sale in the United States, anyone who wants to can go out and buy a bazooka—and the murders and assassinations go on. Throughout the West the 'pending' files pile up.

But the malaise does not stem exclusively from the inadequacy of existing structures and the speed at which they work. More obscurely it expresses an obsessive questioning: why democracy? To raise the level of consumption? To change man's way of life? The standard of living is indeed going up, though leaving wide areas of poverty and destitution in its wake, and the conditions of man's existence have changed overwhelmingly in the space of less than a generation. Yet man feels alienated, questions the sense of his work and of his life, pores over his anxieties or seeks desperately to escape them, and looks for fresh definitions of liberty, responsibility, community, progress, and justice. This search on the part of some and the refusal to question on the part of others sometimes assume violent forms and shake the very foundations of society.

The question 'Does democracy need reinventing?' naturally suggests a further question that the 'Club Jean Moulin' was asking more than ten years ago: 'Has it ever existed?'[1] The same report went on to answer, again in the form of a question: 'Was it not essentially the dream of a few eighteenth-century philosophers transcribed clumsily in the form of the political structures of the nineteenth-century West by a class that saw it as the synthesis between an idealism that was too vague and interests that were too specific?' But new social classes have appeared on the scene, their aspirations have become more concrete, and the interests with which they come into conflict have both increased their power and improved their techniques. The spread of education, the diffusion of news media (however imperfect), the growth of knowledge, and the transformation of custom have convulsed societies that are stuck not only with the institutions but also with the ideas of another age. Consequently the difficulties that democracy is up against in the West today are proof in a way of the success of the principles by which it is nourished. Democracy can thus be pleased with itself . . . But the pleasure promises only degeneration and death.

The conquest of rights

If the events of May 1968 shook society and the state in France and if similar upheavals have in varying degrees shaken West Germany, Italy, and Great Britain, the country most seriously affected has been the most powerful, the most prosperous, and the most modern of all. A distant, unpopular war, a large, repressed ethnic group, a highly dynamic student population, particularly brutal police forces, a clumsy and inefficient administrative structure, newspapers and television networks that pride themselves on their independence—the exact formula of this explosive mixture is not known, but it has brought to light all the weaknesses of the American system, forced President Johnson to retire from political life, obliged his successor to change the direction of his Vietnam policy, and made many individuals and social, economic, cultural, and religious groups re-examine their positions.

According to President Nixon:

We have been undergoing self-doubts and self-criticisms. But these are the other side of our growing sensitivity to the persistence of want in the midst of plenty, and of our impatience with the slowness with which age-old ills are being overcome. If we were indifferent to the shortcomings of our society, or complacent about our institutions, or blind to the lingering inequities, then we would have lost our way. The fact that we have these concerns is evidence that our ideals are still strong.[2]

Excellently put. But the 'doubts' had been sown by young people whom Nixon had no hesitation in describing as 'hooligans' and four of whom had been killed by the National Guard at Kent State University. The 'self-criticisms' were fed by a press with which Vice-president Agnew was then violently at war, by pacifists like the Berrigan brothers, who were imprisoned and ultimately acquitted, and by politicians who have virtually been accused of treason on account of their opposition to the Vietnam war. The 'want in the midst of plenty' was not discovered by the state, despite the powerful means of investigation at its disposal, but by men like Michael Harrington, who had the ear of John Kennedy, or like Cesar Chavez, who ended up in jail. The 'slowness' of remedies, the 'shortcomings' of society, the 'inequities' of which numerous citizens are the victims persist in the United States as they do in Europe. They may become less explosive once the government, jerked unwillingly out of its complacency, has taken 'official' cognizance of them, but it still cannot manage to eliminate them.

In a way this helplessness is good for democracy because it prevents people from falling into the kind of complacency for which they reproach the government. Such of course is the law and first requirement of democracy, under which the people gains nothing that it has not wrested by constant struggle: individual freedoms, trade-union rights, the rights of ethnic minorities—none of it has been volunteered by gracious governments; it has all been won from them as a result of campaigns and confrontations—sometimes violent, always stubborn, fraught with setbacks yet relentlessly renewed.

America and Western Europe are thus the scene of a confrontation between a majority of complacent or semi-complacent people who would be happy to see things evolve slowly and a restless, more demanding minority that questions the established order, the traditional truths, and the convictions that have become rooted in prejudice. But, as both America and Europe know, a minority can paralyse public transport, cut electricity supplies, disorganize the universities, force England to live by candlelight, and alter the course of a colonial war. As they also know, such a minority is capable of rousing larger masses, winning over numerous sympathizers, and exacerbating the contradictions between the complacent and the concerned.

The authorities' reaction is then in every case the same: first restore law and order. This was the slogan under which, in a dizzying piece of mutual out-bidding, Nixon, Humphrey, and Wallace contested the presidential election of 1968, and which was taken up again for the congressional elections of 1970. It was this theme that, in the wake of May 1968, returned to the French National Assembly an increased majority that had succeeded in playing on the electorate's fears. In the British general election of June 1970 the Conservative party gave the same subject more importance than education, pensions, agriculture, economic controls, or the health services; the Labour party, though more discreet about it, nevertheless gave it priority over unemployment, nationalization, economic democracy, or relations with Rhodesia.[3] In West Germany in 1972 the Christian Democrats raised the identical flag against Chancellor Brandt's coalition.

Law and order—the slogan draws all who have or fear they have something to lose by change. It expresses a natural reflex the force of which needs no demonstration. It is a useful slogan, bringing the party that knows how to exploit it a wide audience and often a majority. A blessed slogan, too, in that it does away with the woolliness in which too many debates get lost. For the banner of law and order spontaneously unites all the partisans of one of the two forces animating every democratic society: the 'resistance' party as opposed to the party of 'movement', the conservative as opposed to the progressive element, the Right against the Left.

Right and Left—difficult terms to define in a rapidly evolving world in which the Right, in order to preserve what it holds most dear, must make sacrifices to change and organize progress to its own advantage; in a world whose delicate and complex workings mean that the Left, if it is to promote movement and progress, must conduct itself with prudence and wisdom for fear of inflaming the Right and cracking the machine.

Rightist temperaments, wrote Emmanuel Mounier, 'take the side of continuity, fidelity, organization, hierarchy, and authority, of tested values and established situations', whereas Leftist temperaments 'are

more awake to the spiritual issues of progress and justice; they take the
side of human, scientific, and social adventurousness, of necessary
ruptures, of the governed and the oppressed, of liberty, the individual, and
democracy, and of the more mobile parts of the social organism: the
proletariat, city-dwellers, intellectuals.'[4]

But do the adherents of Left and Right today still recognize themselves in these definitions? There are clear-thinking men of the Right
who know that 'continuity' presupposes change, that 'hierarchy' and
'authority' cannot last without active freedom, and that many 'established situations' are threatened not so much by the will of men as by
the force of scientific, technological, and economic innovation. Similarly
the Left has its lucid spirits for whom 'necessary ruptures' are not synonymous with complete upheaval, who have seen the sense of authority
and discipline, who are aware of the difficulty of defining the 'proletariat' in modern societies, and who know how impossible it is to lump
all 'intellectuals' together and attribute to them an illusory monopoly
of culture and fresh ideas.

Mounier went on: 'Those whose lives are full of organized things and
who stand to lose by change will tend towards the values of the Right:
landed proprietors, owners of inherited wealth, the bourgeois, puncti-
lious officials, artisans, top civil servants, theologians, monastics.'

But those whose lives are solidly and securely organized sometimes
feel freer to throw them into upheaval, being aware of their emptiness:
there are 'landed proprietors' bolder than city-dwellers, 'bourgeois'
more revolutionary than tinkers, 'top civil servants' and 'monastics'
more controversial than certain professionals in the field of agitation or
revolutionary blather. Furthermore the Right is never on its own, and
the actors on the political stage have been known to switch roles: it was
under the 'Leftist' government of Pierre Mendès-France that the
Algerian war broke out, with a 'Leftist' minister, François Mitterand,
declaring that 'the only negotiation is war' and the Communist party
voting the government full powers—and it was to take a 'Rightist'
government to close the Algerian drama or withdraw France's forces
from NATO. Similarly in the United States the classic forces of the
Left backed Truman, who took the country into the Korean war, and
opposed Eisenhower, who took the country out of it; against a crusading
Barry Goldwater they backed Lyndon Johnson, who, while opposing
a crusade, escalated the Vietnam war, and then spurned Richard Nixon,
who was in a better position than any Democrat to bring about, if not
peace, at least a measure of de-escalation. There are myriad examples

of the Right accomplishing in the name of clearly understood interests gestures only dreamt of by a generous but ineffective Left.

The converse is no less true. Choosing his words with care, Emmanuel Mounier continued his parallel between the two opposing forces as follows: 'Those whose lives are full of hopes, dreams, and ideas and who stand rather to gain by what life has to offer will incline towards the values of the Left: all the small men aspiring to become less small, workers, intellectuals (*non rentas*), poets, city-dwellers, grant-holders, nostalgic officials, travellers, apostles', etc. But how many men of the Left put off indefinitely the fulfilment of their strongest 'hopes', turn their 'dreams' into empty reveries, and think they need only launch 'ideas' for life to have something to offer? How many 'small men' are content with their smallness, how many 'workers' have become middle-class and desire only to be more so, how many 'intellectuals' are primarily concerned with securing subsidies or hanging onto their privileges? Too many inhabitants of the big urban complexes find their time so taken up with work and the endless journeys there and back that they have no energy left for social life. Too many 'grant-holders' are concerned above all with not losing their means of support and with pursuing their personal careers.

Here too the roles can be reversed, and the Left sometimes agrees to do the Right's jobs as if anxious to show that it too has a feeling for the state, concern for the national interest, and respect for economic vitality. In the United States it was the Democratic Left that in 1950 voted article II of the McCarran Act authorizing preventive detention in 'concentration camps' for citizens suspected of subversive activities—a law that provided McCarthyism with one of its choicest weapons, and that was abolished under Nixon in 1971. In France men of the Left distinguished themselves in the colonial wars as they did in the Suez expedition. In Great Britain members of the Labour party restricted the immigration of Commonwealth citizens holding British passports.

Can one still talk in terms of 'Left' and 'Right'? Probably one can, but only with the greatest care, so fluid have these divisions become, though the Right recovers its cohesion as soon as it spots a threat to its most tangible interests, whereas the Left is quick to split up over vague projects or points of doctrine. The slogan 'Law and Order' is a prodigious catalyst of Rightist forces, while the terms justice and progress have become blunted by a divided Left. Yet both have in common their inability to conceive and put forward for people's approval a large-scale programme capable of attracting support and arousing enthusiasm:

'No aims rational enough and noble enough to appeal without deception to man's dynamism,' was the Club Jean Moulin's bitter comment.[5]

It is generally accepted that the technological society does not lend
itself to great visions and ambitious designs: the machinery is too
complex to be jostled. So it is all pragmatism and careful management.
But suddenly there rises from the depths to be shouted on the streets
and scrawled on the walls of the city the cry 'Let imagination rule!' For
men who feel perfectly at home in the technological society can no
longer stand the mediocrity of the pragmatists and the careful managers.
They charge them precisely with not knowing how to exploit the
possibilities the technological society has to offer in the way of creating
a new life that shall fulfil man's most ancient aspirations and put right,
to borrow Richard Nixon's phrase, 'age-old ills'.

Dazzled by the goods and commodities that the technological society
places at their disposal, perhaps people are no longer aware of ills so old
that in the end everyone gets used to them, aspirations so ancient that
they become eclipsed in the dark corners of memory. The forces of
'resistance' will have no trouble imposing law and order if the forces of
'movement' are no longer capable of seeing the ills afflicting society and
of reviving frustrated aspirations.

Yet this rediscovery is basic to the definition of new rights as yet
hardly glimpsed and still imperfectly formulated. And today as in the
past those rights are not going to be granted by a generous government
but wrested from it by constant struggle.

The right to democracy

Argue as they may about the structures and functioning of their
institutions, the majority of Westerners nevertheless appreciate living
under democratic regimes. They consider those structures ill-adapted
but have no doubt that they are more or less true to the principles they
claim to be based on. Winston Churchill would seem to have said the
last word on the subject with his humorous dictum, 'The democratic
system is the worst—with the exception of all the others.' In other
words the citizen has no choice: the democratic system must be kept,
for all its imperfections. The argument is doubtless a good one. But it
presupposes one thing: that the West is living under a democratic
regime. Is this so certain?

Despite their complaints and recriminations Westerners, or at least
the majority of them, do in fact enjoy freedoms that may be imperfect

but are more than merely 'formal': the freedom to form or join trade-unions (often excepting foreign workers and too often marred by cases of union officials being sacked), the right to strike (within limits), and freedom of the press and information (but with power and money having the advantage). These rights and freedoms represent so many conquests that are sometimes contested, sometimes thwarted, always precarious, and to be used with care. But real conquests none the less that need to be conserved and demand above all to be strengthened and extended. Their juridical definition has evolved hardly at all in a quarter of a century during which the objective conditions of their exercise have changed profoundly. In some instances these rights and freedoms have even lost ground; in any case they are none of them experienced in the fullness that a true democratic regime presupposes, and here lies the whole drama of Western civilization.

'Parliament has really no control over the executive. It is pure fiction,' said David Lloyd George.[6] Since then the pre-eminence of the executive has become steadily more pronounced and it has grown increasingly independent of parliamentary control. In Italy the fiction of parliamentary control finds striking expression in a never-ending series of crises: the only real freedom left to the legislative power is that of voting the government down in order to try out some other combination or go back to the country once more. But cabinet instability does not agree with the technological society. France tried it under the Fourth Republic, and in 1958 accepted a new regime in which parliament was reduced to a minor role.

A pretty good example of balance seemed to be the American system. But the role of the House of Representatives and the Senate has become progressively smaller while the federal government has increased its powers to the point where it pursues in its own way a policy over which the legislature has virtually no influence. Without the Senate's agreement the American government embarked on the Korean and Vietnam wars, mounted an operation against Cuba, and dispatched troops to the Dominican Republic. The size of its armaments orders allows the executive to wield a virtually discretionary influence over the economic life of the country. Whether in deciding to resume contact with Communist China or in announcing the non-convertibility of the dollar and a 10 per cent import surcharge, President Nixon has overthrown basic principles of American policy without first securing the agreement of the people's representatives.

Numerous examples show that in the United States the passing of laws, the voting of budgets, and the opening-up of credits are far from sufficient to ensure congressional control over government policy. Three main factors have brought about this shift of powers over the space of less than half a century. Firstly the economic crisis of 1929-30 called for increased federal intervention throughout the New Deal. Then the Second World War further increased the executive's role. Finally, right through the cold war and beyond, the confrontation between the two blocs has led the goverment to take initiatives on its own responsibility alone.

In all the countries of the West the state is intervening more and more in the economy and taking diplomatic initiatives on which parliament is invited to pronounce after the event. Whether it is a question of De Gaulle opening diplomatic relations with Peking or Willy Brandt carrying through his *Ostpolitik*, the secrecy of such negotiations is to a very large extent the condition of their success. Public debate on major decisions regarding money matters would likewise encourage massive speculation.

The fact remains that democratic control is shrinking dangerously, to the point where the British prime minister can be described as an 'elected monarch' in whose hands the reality of power is concentrated, no matter how slender his parliamentary majority. 'The main menace,' writes Andrew Roth, 'was put in a nutshell by Sir Winston Churchill when he said that he expected Parliament to endorse his policies after adequate debate.'[7] Elected assemblies are coming more and more to resemble mere recording bodies that, in order to preserve the façade of democracy, are allowed to debate freely and voice every kind of criticism provided that, in the end, faced with the *fait accompli*, they endorse the government's policy.

Of course governments are exposed to an *ex post facto* sanction. When the electorate goes to the polls there is nothing to stop it sending the prime minister or president packing and putting the opposition party in power. This form of democratic control cannot be under-estimated. It is constantly present in the minds of the head of state and the government, who have to think about their re-election, and consigning the members of the government to the minority gives them complete freedom of expression. Only the democratic procedure of changing the ruling team guarantees politicians and the current of popular opinion that they more or less faithfully represent from physical elimination or condemnation to silence. But this is clearly not enough to give 'decision-making' a democratic character.

The technical complexity of certain political options is sometimes invoked to justify the absence of debate. This argument amounts to saying that the electorate and its representatives, except those in power, are incapable of forming an opinion of the issues and of judging the national interest. The democratic system would thereby be reduced to an electoral technique giving citizens the illusion of deciding their own fate whereas in fact all major decisions are taken over their heads. Looked at in this way, the institutions of democracy are no more than a safety valve, the ritual of electoral consultation making it possible for people to believe they are in possession of a power that is not theirs at all. Liberal democracy would in this case be a sham to which adherents of the politics of the worst would be tempted to prefer an overtly authoritarian regime making no pretence and offering a wider flank to criticism. In refusing to live up to its principles and promises such a democracy would give away its counterfeit character and by the same token condemn itself.

Yet in every country large numbers of citizens tolerate a system that lends them the illusion of being partners in power. In placing their voting-papers in the ballot box, far from assuming any political responsibility they shift all such responsibility onto the shoulders of the candidate of their choice—and go back to their private affairs. Between elections they abdicate their citizenship and return to being mere workers, consumers, commuters, and telephone subscribers. This is particularly clear in the United States, where the national parties only really exist at the time of presidential elections, i.e. every four years. But no one would venture to claim that Europe's political parties, though they do not disappear between elections, have any profound effect on the life of society outside actual election campaigns.

This passivity on the part of citizens comes out even more clearly in the abstention figures. In 1968 the United States had more than 120 million citizens of voting age. A little over 73 million went to the polls. In other words 47 million Americans—39 per cent of the electorate— quietly abdicated their civil prerogatives. In the Western European countries the volume of abstentions stands at around 20 per cent, and that is already far too high.

On both sides of the Atlantic democracy is up against two main difficulties that in its long history it has still not succeeded in over-coming. Two types of decision are in fact crucial for the future of a country yet play only a minor part in election campaigns:

Long-term provisions and investments: Energy consumption doubles every twenty years or so and the choice of energy sources has to be made several years in advance (oil drills, electricity works, thermal or atomic power-stations). Similarly a country also has to decide how many doctors, physicists, or teachers it wants to have in ten, fifteen, or twenty years' time. Voters, however, are much more concerned with immediate problems and short-term projects than with the decade ahead. Election campaigns themselves centre around so-called current problems, absurdly excluding from this category decisions that have to be taken now if their effects are to become apparent in ten or fifteen years. Candidates and voters are thus borne along by events rather than determining their course. At best they will afterwards seek to steer that course in what seems to them to be the least undesirable direction. Meanwhile the decision has been taken by administrations or private groups without the majority of voters knowing anything about it. To quote only one example touching people's everyday lives, and one that called for no more than medium-term provisions, no Western government managed to take account early enough of the post-war population explosion in terms of providing against an increased need for school places five to six years later and for housing twenty to twenty-five years later. Nor have voters, though they are the first concerned, managed to use their votes in such a way as to make their elected representatives tackle these vital problems. The immediate present concerns them more than making provision for even the immediate future.

Decisions connected with foreign policy: The citizen's lot (employment, housing, schools, transport, leisure, health, etc.) is not determined exclusively in the place in which he happens to live. Decisions that passed unnoticed by the public at large involved the United States in the Korean and Vietnam wars and dragged France and England through the various bloody stages of decolonialization. The citizen's style of life depends to a great extent on his country's access to Middle-Eastern oil (as the Suez crisis brought home to Europeans), to copper from Chile (undergoing a democratic change of regime), to chromium from Rhodesia (which a United Nations resolution has decided to boycott), and on a humbler level to African, Brazilian, or Bolivian coffee, and imported bananas, cocoa, and so on. That style of life is also dependent on freedom of access to distant sales outlets; aeroplanes must be sold to Latin America, helicopters or lorries to China, and various other kinds of equipment to various other countries. A mass of decisions taken in or regarding far-off countries determine possibilities of buying and selling and directly influence employment and consumption. The voter, however, is primarily interested in his own neighbourhood or district and the candidates encourage this parochialism by aiming their speeches at local problems. It is taken for granted that the voter can see no further, and major problems of foreign policy play virtually no part in election campaigns. They figure by way of reminders in party manifestos and platforms—which few people read. But one day the storm breaks somewhere thousands of miles away and its repercussions make themselves felt in everyday life: a government sends troops to Vietnam, Cambodia, Chad, anywhere; contracts with remote countries no one knows anything about provide aircraft and motor factories with a few months' work; a revolution or some diplomatic snag results in the contract being annulled and the workers being laid off. Yet democratic debate rarely turns on major world problems. Politicians and voters alike proclaim their realism and pragmatism, their sense of the concrete, avoiding or dealing only superficially with questions from which hang such issues as war or peace, full employment or unemployment, even the very future of the planet.

Democratic debate is thus confined first of all to immediate problems, whereas it is the middle- and long-term issues that govern the quality of life, and secondly to local or regional problems, which always take precedence over major decisions of national (energy, scientific research, etc.) or international interest. If the latter do happen to be touched on, then any sense of reality is swamped under partisan pronouncements. The debate on education in France spent very much less time on requirements in terms of premises and staff than it did on considerations of an ideological nature, however important these might be. The entry of Soviet troops into Czechoslovakia stirred up public opinion in France although it did not appear directly to concern everyday life; actually it became one of the principal stumbling-blocks between socialists and Communists, thus weighing decisively on the political future of the country. John Kennedy's sending some twenty thousand 'military advisers' to Vietnam caused hardly a ripple of concern among the broad American public, yet it was the first step towards an unprecedented national crisis.

This inability on the part of most voters and the people they vote for to see any distance in time or space is no doubt the price we pay for our democratic regimes. The candidate in search of votes tries to find the highest common factor: he solicits electoral support, which is one of the laws of the system, but he forgets the other aspect of his role, which is to alert and inform opinion and suggest objectives. The art of

5

the election candidate consists in firing low, avoiding controversial subjects, pleasing the maximum number of people, simplifying every complex issue, and attacking the other fellow rather than putting across his own point of view. Hence the mediocrity of election campaigns; the quip that raises a laugh is more effective than an appeal to commitment; the opinion polls rather than any examination of the real issues dictate the subjects to be dealt with; the candidate's family and/or physical appearance are as important as his programme, and in the United States he hands out his wife's cooking recipes. It has been said that election campaigns in Europe are becoming more 'Americanized'. Too often this means that in our television age handshakes are as influential as speeches; in an age of mass education, mass media, and mass culture the trickery of advertising techniques counts for more than the rigour of reasoned debate.

If democratic life shows signs of anaemia it is primarily because its basic institution—electoral consultation—does not give citizens a chance of formulating clear choices and exercising their responsibility as trustees of the national sovereignty. Competition too often throws up candidates who deliberately keep their positions vague, or whose personality and past are ill-matched with the ideas they exploit. In France large numbers of voters who disagree entirely with Jacques Duclos' programme nevertheless agreed with him when he characterized the Poher-Pompidou duel with the phrase, 'Bonnet blanc, blanc bonnet' (or 'six of one and half a dozen of the other'). How many voters deeply hostile to everything Poher represented still give him their votes in the hope of defeating Pompidou? Democracy must wither and die in the minds of citizens when they see an electoral confrontation as a means not of paving the way for a world they believe would be better but of avoiding something they feel would be worse. Electoral consultation thus becomes the occasion for stopping a particular trend rather than starting society off in any clear direction. It ceases to be a positive act, a living, creative process. It is wrong what they say. Democracy can never be the art of the lesser evil: it can only be the art of the best possible.

In the same spirit Senator Eugene McCarthy expressed what millions of Americans felt when he said that there had not been a presidential election in the United States in 1968 but only a pretence of consultation. George Wald, Nobel Prize-winner and Harvard biology professor, expanded on this as follows: 'How could you choose between Humphrey and Nixon? Voting, after all, means choosing. We haven't had an election—just a ritual.'[8] Rituals can survive the loss of their meaning. But one day a generation comes along that is no longer content with empty gestures; it wants to rediscover their deep significance. It immediately comes into conflict with the defenders of a tradition from which all real life has fled, the 'doctors of the law' who are more concerned with the letter than with the spirit of their subject, the guardians of a sterile order.

And suddenly power ceases to reside in the elected assemblies and political parties that believed themselves to be the expression of the people's will. Power is no longer in the hands of governments, parliaments, and courts: it is in the street, where the barricades are up, in the paralysed universities, in the factories out on strike, in the black ghettos torn by riots. In the absence of adequate legal means, new forms of popular expression emerge: the street demonstration expresses for a moment what the electoral ritual is no longer able to express. But only for a moment. The guardians of tradition have at their disposal forces enabling them to stifle the explosion with the instruments of law and order. Fear makes the public an indispensable supporter of the process. The ritual gestures come back into their own in a creaky ceremonial that is remote from real life. The malaise has nevertheless been brought to light, and the authorities promptly begin treating the symptoms rather than the causes: reinforcement of the machinery for the maintenance of law and order, infiltration of subversive groups, legal sanctions, minor concessions to isolate malcontents. Then life resumes its normal course. If need be, some measure of liturgical reform will modernize the ritual. But the ritual belongs to the realm of magic. It has no effect on the concrete problems of a technological society in which increasing numbers of people are in the know or wish to be, wish to understand rather than drift along with the current, yearn to act instead of being acted on. Political parties, having felt the ground giving way under them, have begun to overhaul their platforms and think seriously about the current method of polling. The mechanics of elections are certainly important. They can falsify the outcome of the vote, allowing a minority of voters to send a majority of members to parliament, as has happened several times in the course of English history. Richard Nixon got to the White House with only 43·4 per cent of the votes cast, i.e. with the backing of 26 per cent of all citizens of voting age. In the French presidential elections of 1965 General de Gaulle was elected with 55·19 per cent of the votes cast, representing only 45·26 per cent of registered voters. In the French parliamentary elections of 1967 the UDR (Union pour la Défense de la République) received 8,448,982 votes, i.e. 37·73 per cent of votes cast or 29·85 per cent of registered voters (19·07 per cent abstaining). In June 1968, with 9,663,605 votes, the UDR received 43·65 per cent of votes cast, i.e. 34·3 per cent of the 28,171,635 registered voters (19·99 per cent abstaining). The referendum of April 1972 on Great Britain's entry into the Common Market resulted in 67·7 per cent of 'yesses', representing only 36·11 per cent of the registered electorate. Is it any wonder really that the people fails to recognize itself in a government with this electoral history? There is a growing gap between the real country and the legal country, but this is not, as Maurras said it was, democracy's doing: on the contrary, it is the direct consequence of a system that fails to respect fully the very principles of democracy.

The debate on methods of balloting ought not to obscure the basic problem, which is whether citizens are in possession of the elements of the real or formal choice being put to them. Are they able to give their verdict in full knowledge of what they are doing? Do election campaigns as held nowadays offer them the means of deciding the nation's future? The right to democracy is first and foremost the right to choose through the medium of an election that is something more than an empty ritual.

The right to choose

Governments and oppositions alike tend to rule out all possibility of a clear choice. Though often held up as an example, even British democracy is not exempt from this sleight-of-hand. Talking about Britain's entry into the Common Market, Hugh Gaitskell told the Labour Party Conference at Brighton on 3 October 1962: "We are now being told that the British people are not capable of judging this issue— the government knows best; the "top people" are the only people who can understand it; it is too difficult for the rest. This is the classic argument of every tyranny in history."

If allowance is made for a certain virulence of vocabulary—a badly functioning democracy is still a long way from a tyranny—the point is a valid one. Governments delight in calling in 'experts' to present problems in all their complexity and in language that is inaccessible to the majority of citizens and sometimes even to some members of parliament. These 'experts' too are supposed to be the best judges. The admission was made in its most grotesque form by an American Secretary of Defence who was, it is true, by common consent one of the most mediocre men ever to head the Pentagon. Asked about the criticisms that the leader of the opposition had just directed at his defence policy, Charles E. Wilson was pleased to reply: 'Do you think he is an expert in the matter?' When pressed furh,er by reporters he asserted that, 'the military chiefs think it is sountd and I think it is sound', and later, when asked about specific cases, added: 'In some cases, all you can do is ask the Lord.'[9] But the job of approving a particular policy is the responsibility of politicians, not of 'experts' nor of God. That responsiblity extends beyond the arguments of any experts, however qualified. By definition the experts' competence is limited to his sphere, whereas political choices take in the whole of life. The opinion of experts is irreplaceable as a guide, but it is by its very nature too specialized to make the final decision, and it can always be countered by the opinion of other experts.

Eight years after Hugh Gaitskell's pronouncement, when the 'experts' had already put forward the British government's main arguments in favour of entry into the Common Market, public opinion was still not convinced. In December 1970 a poll showed that 16 per cent of Britons were in favour of and 66 per cent opposed to joining. But a further inquiry revealed that two-thirds of the population were certain that the government would take Britain into the Common Market in spite of this large measure of hostility.

The very principle of democracy is affected when the majority is convinced that it cannot change the government's policy. Then the democratic system is no longer even a safety-valve giving people the illusion of deciding their own fate. That the minority should bow to the majority is the law of democracy. But that the majority should feel coerced by the will of the government means that democracy is in danger, even if there are grounds for thinking that the governments' policy makes sense.

A year after the election of the Heath government, which has since taken Great Britain into the Common Market, a poll conducted in June-July 1971 on the eve of publication of the White Paper showed that 70 per cent of Britons still did not feel well enough informed to make a choice. This is not surprising: in the 1970 election campaign the problem of Europe was touched on by only a very small number of candidates (38 per cent of Conservative and 23 per cent of Labour candidates). Yet Great Britain's entry was to be the principal outcome of replacing Harold Wilson by Edward Heath as head of government.

Here, taken from the best study on the subject, are the chief problems dealt with by candidates during the course of the campaign:[10]

% of candidates mentioning the problem	Conservative	% of candidates mentioning the problem	Labour
92	inflation	84	education
76	unemployment	82	the economy
72	trade-union reform	77	balance of payments
66	housing	73	health services
63	abolition of selective employment tax	70	housing
		67	pensions
60	'law and order'	63	examination
58	tax cuts		reform
58	social services	50	social services
57	help for home-owners	47	transport improvements
38	COMMON MARKET	23	COMMON MARKET

In other words 62 per cent of Conservative and 77 per cent of Labour candidates chose to avoid the subject of the Common Market in the presence of the voters whose support they were after, which was enough to rob the process of consultation of any real significance. But even among those who had the courage not to ignore a problem of such importance more than half took refuge in an ambiguous position, leaving their hearers utterly confused as to their real intentions. The authors of the analysis just quoted then point out in disillusioned tones that Wilson and Heath had refused to promise a free vote when the project should come up before the House of Commons, but that Great Britain's joining the Common Market 'was plainly one on which some MPs would feel obliged to take an individual stand. However, less than one major party candidate in sixteen committed himself to flat opposition to British entry, while two out of three made no mention of the subject at all.'[11]

Another problem, important both as regards the principles at issue and as regards the feelings it aroused in the public, ought to have had a special place in this election campaign: that of the entry of Commonwealth citizens into Great Britain. The official policy of the Conservative party, which favoured a stengthening of immigration controls, was clearly very popular in the wake of the various racial incidents that had been hitting the headlines. Yet only 26 per cent of Conservative candidates dealt with the subject in their election speeches. As for the Labour candidates, who would have had here a theme—anti-racialism —that theoretically no 'left-wing' party can do without, a bare 2 per cent thought fit to mention it.

The problems to which the two parties gave their whole attention were not by any means negligible: unemployment, housing, education, social security, taxation, transport, etc. These constitute the *pièce de résistance* of electoral speeches in every country. As abiding problems they ought to have been dealt with but not to have eclipsed the two burning topics of the Common Market and immigration. But above all they ought to have furnished the occasion for a genuine debate in which the two parties presented their respective platforms to the public at large.

In fact in Britain as elsewhere election campaigns are rather negative confrontations: each party, instead of putting forward plans to which it is committed and by which it will be judged by the voters, prefers to embark on criticism of its opponent, if need be attributing to it intentions it does not have. Harold Wilson, for example, devoted 75 per cent of his speeches to criticizing the Conservative party, 20 per cent to cracking up Labour's achievements, and only 5 per cent to the future plans for which he ought in principle to have been canvassing support. Edward Heath's attitude was not much different: he devoted 70 per cent of his speeches to criticism of the Labour party, 19 per cent to generalizations about freedom and the need to pave the way for a better life, and only 11 per cent to his party's plans for the future of the country.

Thus the subjects most frequently touched on were not treated in any depth, the two parties being moved by a common concern to duck the two most urgent issues and discuss in vague terms why each thought itself the most fit to sit in the seats of power. Such an attitude amply deserves the following severe but carefully phrased verdict:

There was no great correspondence between the subjects that, according to the polls, were of most concern to the public, and those

that the politicians concentrated on. Mr Wilson and his colleagues
had little to say to those whose main anxieties were about taxation,
strikes, housing or the cost of living. The Conservatives, as the opposition, could and did attack on all of these themes, but remarkably
few of their speeches were devoted to the remedies which, for good
or ill, they had offered in their manifesto. Certainly it cannot be said
that these handouts of campaign speeches offer the raw material for
what the rational elector envisaged in democratic theory could
regard as well-reasoned argument over the real choices to be faced
in the next five years.[12]

Yet who would venture to claim that Britain has the sad privilege of
a monopoly over this kind of election campaign? We find the same
situation throughout the West. Furthermore the principles of democracy are respected with varying degrees of fidelity and occasionally
violated outright by the governments thus elected. They are violated
when the president of the United States talks about an accused man's
guilt before the courts have passed their verdict, when in the United
States or elsewhere the party in power hands out favours on the side
and fills its election funds by dubious methods, when it tries to intimi-
date the press by confiscations (in France under the Fourth Republic) or
prosecutions (of the *New York Times*, for example, after its publication of the Pentagon Papers on Vietnam), or more simply when the
government fails to keep parliament informed or deliberately misleads
it. But the democratic system is failing to operate from the outset, or is
operating very badly, every time an election campaign does not give
citizens the chance to look at the various opposing parties' plans,
compare them, and choose between them.

It is further necessary that a government keep the promises by which
it has secured election. In France the 'Front républicain' set up by Guy
Mollet and Pierre Mendès-France in 1956 owed its success at the polls
to its promise to put an end to the Algerian war—which it in fact
intensified by sending more troops. Lyndon Johnson did the same
thing in the United States in 1964 with regard to the Vietnam war, and
in 1968 Nixon managed to persuade people that he had a 'plan' that
would lead to an 'honourable solution', though he was careful not to let
slip a single detail and in effect asked voters to sign him a blank cheque.
A similar procedure had been used in 1952 when Eisenhower promised
to go to Korea, but he kept his promise and put a stop to the war. On
the other hand his speeches on internal problems were disturbingly

platitudinous, and his two consecutive terms at the White House were to be marked by the rise of black militancy, by serious economic difficulties, and by significant favours granted to big private firms (notably as regards offshore oil and the exploitation of atomic energy in processes perfected by scientific research that had been paid for out of government funds). John Kennedy promised a big effort on behalf of Latin America in his election campaign, as yet ignorant of the fact that very soon after coming to power he would be letting loose on Cuba the military operation set up by his predecessor, and would have to take the responsibility for its failure. In West Germany Willy Brandt was certainly not elected exclusively for the sake of his *Ostpolitik*, which in fact became rapidly less popular with the public. He had also promised to 'undertake sweeping reforms' in the fields of education, taxation, and penal law, none of which has yet seen the light of day. All Germany has seen so far have been a few measures regarding housing, workers' rights within firms, and worker capitalization—but these sops to the working class have been powerfully offset by increased unemployment and rising prices. The German Social-Democrat/Liberal coalition is not the only one whose internal contradictions make it virtually impossible for it to keep its election promises. In Italy the election of President Leone at the twenty-third ballot—breaking the record set in France with the election of René Coty, last president of the Fourth Republic, which had become incapable of dealing with a serious crisis—illustrated the artificial character of fragile coalitions that are kept in power only by the absence of an alternative solution. The election promises of the parties forming the coalition do not coincide—so how could they find expression in deeds once the coalition is in power? Both in Italy, with a government that cannot govern, and in France, with a government enjoying a docile majority, the two Communist parties offer themselves as government parties. Yet neither in Italy nor in France can Communism secure a majority without the help of allies with whom, assuming they managed to hammer out a common election platform, it would merely reproduce on the Left the powerlessness of the majorities it seeks to replace—unless, that is, it were to violate the basic principles of democracy.

The familiar inability of coalition governments to keep their election promises has led to the imagining of all kinds of solutions: systems of alliances and rewards to the majority in order to broaden the government's parliamentary base, legislative agreements, threats of dissolution and a fresh general election. Elsewhere, in countries like Great Britain

5*

and the United States where the theoretically simple, clear, and efficient two-party system operates, the actual link between election promises and the achievements of the elected is a slender one. Britain puts in power the leader of the majority party; America has frequently experienced the difficult situation of a Republican president cohabiting with a Democratic congressional majority, or *vice versa*. But whatever the differences in constitutional structure the two-party system in Britain and the United States leaves large numbers of voters dissatisfied. Election campaigns only give the illusion of a genuine choice since the government that emerges is not absolutely bound by the promises that won its votes. The forms of democracy have been respected but the ritual has nothing very much to do with life.

In the two-party as in the multi-party system, with one or two ballots, with a majority ballot or with all the various systems of proportional representation, the principle of democracy has ceased to work—if it ever really did—right at the initial stage of the whole ritual, namely when voters are summoned to the polls. Universal suffrage, as wrested by democracy from autocratic regimes, is something sacred. It offers guarantees that citizens are not prepared to relinquish. But as practised it does not allow citizens to choose their own destiny, it does not oblige parties to commit themselves to precise programmes, it makes it possible for candidates to avoid the burning issues, even encouraging them to take refuge in generalizations, it fails to make them the authentic mandatories of a popular sovereignty unambiguously expressed, nor does it even expose them to a rigorous *ex post facto* democratic sanction, for the following election will be conducted according to the same abstract ritual.

Democracy is sick because citizens do not give their votes to politicians of whom they expect concrete achievements along the lines laid down by precise commitments. Electoral consultation is not a positive act by which citizens make their will known and give their representatives an imperative mandate to carry it out. It is essentially a negative act by which citizens, instead of backing a constructive programme, choose the lesser evil: it becomes a question of 'stopping' the forces of conservatism, or of progress, or of Communism. Every institution dies once it becomes purely defensive in a world where the conditions of existence, production techniques, received ideas, and popular aspirations are changing rapidly at the rhythm of life itself, which refuses to be reduced to a mere ritual.

This divorce between the people and its political institutions comes out in the indifference or discontent of those sectors of society that know they have no purchase on the machinery of power. It is also apparent in the resurgence of extremes: almost ten million votes for the racist candidate Wallace in the United States in 1968, right-wing activism in Italy, France, and England, left-wing activism and its proliferation of groups of varying allegiance, and recourse to violence on both sides of the Atlantic—kidnappings (James Cross in Montreal, Robert Nogrette in Paris), assassinations (John and Robert Kennedy, Martin Luther King, and union leaders in the United States, Pierre Laporte in Canada, René Pierre Overney in Paris), and bomb attacks in Italy, Britain, the United States, Ireland, France, West Germany, Quebec.

Violence is theoretically the last resort, after all legal procedures have been exhausted. One is forced to the conclusion that democratic procedures leave large numbers discontented and even desperate. Yet how could it be otherwise, when the ritual is becoming increasingly meaningless?

> Right now, about 75 per cent of a presidential campaign is hoopla, manufactured movement and entertainment designed to bedazzle. Substance, and there is some, is largely buried and ignored in the rush of the jets, the bands, rallies and booze. Ensnared in all this tinsel, the candidates come up with ridiculous pledges, like the one about setting foot in all 50 states (Nixon in 1960). That is an exercise in locomotion, not intelligence. Rushing madly along the trail, looking over their shoulders at the pursuers and scared to death of making misstatements in the blur, the men have tended in recent years to grow more and more reluctant to commit themselves on vital issues.[13]

After the Congressional elections of 1970, in which President Nixon intervened personally in support of the candidates of his choice, public opinion polls expert John F. Kraft wrote:

> We asked: How do you feel about Senator Goodell's proposal to pull everyone out of Vietnam right away, by the end of 1970? That got 3-to-1 approval. Then we'd ask them how they thought the President was doing about pulling people out of Vietnam. And again, we found 3-to-1 approval. Theoretically, there's a distinct difference between what Goodell was proposing and what Nixon was doing, but in the public mind they were doing the same thing.[14]

Can one still talk in terms of democracy when a majority of citizens can no longer distinguish the opposition's from the government's proposals? Or can one speak of democracy when the majority of citizens is subject to a tax system it does not understand? One hears repeated throughout the West what has been said in France, namely that 'the notion of taxation is synonymous with obscurity, endless complications, and incomprehensibe regulations'.[15] Can one speak of democracy when election campaigns pass over the technical complexities of problems—whether economic, financial, military, diplomatic, or scientific—and throw up a smoke-screen of generalizations, abstract affirmations of principle, and vague declarations of intent?

Democracy can live and become dynamic only when the opposing candidates and parties at general elections offer voters the means of choosing between programmes that have been clearly worked out by competent experts, and when those programmes form the object of popular debate during the campaign. Democracy can only be based on universal suffrage. It is fashionable to be ironical at the expense of countries where 'universal suffrage' gives the government majorities in excess of 99 per cent. It is too easily inferred that democracy is respected in countries where universal suffrage only just manages to arrive at a slender majority more or less capable of governing. But such countries discovered long ago how to practise universal suffrage without giving voters the chance to make a clear choice. De Gaulle's referendums carried the phoney choice to an extraordinary degree of perfection, but the result is much the same when both Labour and Conservative parties avoid mentioning the Common Market, when Democrats and Republicans vie with one another in making promises they will never keep, when Richard Nixon solemnly commits himself to presenting a balanced budget and ends up with a $25,000 million deficit for 1971–2, and when election campaigns in every Western country rule out the possibility of rational choice.

This malaise of democracy is common to all the countries of the West, notwithstanding their very different constitutional structures. It is not going to be remedied by constitutional reform or changes in polling methods. It calls into question first of all the very course of election campaigns with their pseudo-dialogue between voters and candidates and then between voters and those they have voted in. It also very directly calls into question a 'political class' that cannot consider itself and is coming to be less and less considered as the mandatory of the sovereign people.

The right of those elected

Elected (though hardly 'chosen') at the close of a pseudo-competition that has left the main problems unmentioned, hardly representative of a people that has been deprived of all opportunity of making a reasoned choice, the faithful servants of a government from whom they expect favours and assistance in securing re-election or its scattered adversaries within a heterogeneous opposition, the members of the parliamentary body are as it were the flies in the ointment: they prevent the government from governing. The executive keeps them as far as possible in the dark about its plans except for the purposes of soliciting their unconditional support, preferring to present them with a *fait accompli*.

'The best of the *députés* on the majority side are losing faith in their mission,' writes Georges Vedel, former dean of the Paris law faculty. 'Neither on the benches of the *Chambre* nor in the proceedings of their party do they have any hand in the mechanics of decision. The institution of parliament is sinking in a mire of indifference.'[16]

The lot of opposition members, however, is no more enviable. In France they have virtually given up tabling motions of censure, which they know will inevitably be crushed by the size of the government's majority. The rules of the *Assemblée* have deprived them of their former recourse to interpellation. Debate no longer takes place in parliament but has assumed other forms: accusations in the press, like those directed against Chaban-Delmas in connexion with his tax return, ripostes on television, demonstrations and violence in the streets. A parliament that is bound hand and foot and prevented from carrying out its task of supervision, control, and criticism does not make the government's job any easier. No society is prepared merely to lie back and accept its fate: 'the more controversy is banned from institutions, the more it breaks out vigorously elsewhere' in the phenomenon that has been dubbed 'suppletory democracy'.[17]

But this curious form of democracy, which tends to make up for the institutional kind that no longer works, is of limited effectiveness. In Italy and France trade unions have sometimes seemed to be in possession of a power that political parties lack or that has been denied them, but workers know they must be careful not to blunt the strike weapon, so they reserve it to back up their claims for better wages or working conditions and hesitate to use it in support of general political objectives.

In the United States, where the powers of Congress have become more and more limited while the executive's power has grown enormous, 'suppletory democracy' appeared earlier than in Europe, though without producing better results. The agitation on the Berkeley campus was three years prior to May 1968; it very quickly petered out. Before that students committed to the civil rights movement had tried to force the hands of overtly racialist local authorities; but school integration, legally compulsory since 1954, is far from being a reality, and there are still 7·5 million Negroes out of a total of 10·9 million who are prevented from voting. The campaign against the Vietnam war was at its peak in 1968, then enjoyed a resurgence in 1970 with the entry of American troops into Cambodia; but it was virtually moribund when bombing was stepped up again in the spring of 1972. Admittedly the opponents of the war scored a point with the public outcry caused by the 'Pentagon Papers', but these documents concerned the Johnson administration, and in any case their publication proved incapable of relaunching the campaign in the universities and the streets. The war continues, however, with other methods. 'Suppletory democracy' has changed its style and sent Lyndon Johnson back to his Texas ranch, but it did not put an end to hostilities. It did reduce the number of American victims; it did not reduce the amount of destruction in Vietnam one whit.

A further phenomenon shows how the democracies are in poor working order. Like the United States recently in connexion with Vietnam and Pakistan, and like France not long ago at the time of its colonial wars, West Germany too has had its political 'leaks'. As early as the summer of 1970 the Springer press published the dossier of Egon Bahr, who was negotiating the Treaty of Moscow. Since then fresh indiscretions have marked each stage of negotiations with the Kremlin. In December 1971 one of the papers in the Springer group published extensive extracts from the inter-German agreement on transit between Berlin and the Federal Republic. That such 'leaks' raise delicate problems of principle is hardly in doubt. What they also show is that the yearning for the sensational and the interest in the secret and confidential are sometimes not unconnected with a legitimate desire on the part of the public to be informed about major decisions concerning it. The fact that civil servants and members of parliamentary committees who have access to documents of a confidential nature sometimes see fit to communicate these to the press merely proves what must in any case be clear to everybody: democracy does not like a secret, even if it is a question of diplomatic problems that cannot at a certain stage be debated in the public arena without imperilling negotiations in progress.

But there is something worse than this. Not only do governments fail to inform but on occasion they actually deceive citizens, the press, and the nation's representatives. A press conference of Richard Nixon in December 1970 prompted so respected a commentator as Richard H. Rovere to remark: 'It is not unusual for a President to say one thing and do another—or to say today precisely the opposite of what he said yesterday.'[18] It was under Lyndon Johnson that the expression 'credibility gap' was coined to refer to the public's mistrust of words belied by deeds.

At one time or another all the governments of the West have had to suffer the effects of this 'credibility gap' they have themselves created. For if candidates for election to parliament avoid committing themselves clearly before voters, governments are equally disinclined to present parliament with a clear choice based on solid arguments and full information. At the beginning of the Indochina war, the truth about the bombing of Haiphong was carefully concealed. No government can resist the temptation to act behind a smoke-screen. The argument is always the same: efficiency in secrecy is better than the paralysis resulting from authentic democratic debate. But when governments shroud their preparations in secrecy it does not make them any more efficient. In connexion with Great Britain's joining the Common Market, Andrew Roth writes:

> Mr Heath is not the first Prime Minister to expect Parliament to take vital decisions without having the necessary facts. His sponsor, Harold Macmillan, was never more than half-truthful about his 1956–8 effort to break up the E.E.C. or about his 1961–3 effort to break into it . . . This pattern of misleading Parliament, the Press and the people by half-truths reflects the near contempt for the very Parliamentary democracy that Prime Ministers and their lieutenants proclaim to be protecting.[19]

'What is scandalous,' write Georges Bernanos, 'isn't telling the truth but not telling the whole truth, introducing by omission a lie that leaves it intact externally but eats away like a cancer at its heart and entrails.'

The machinery of democracy thus gets jammed at two levels. Democracy presupposes that members of parliament should secure not only a majority of votes but also a clear mandate from their electors to carry out precise projects or at least work along definite prescribed lines. Democracy further presupposes that the government should not merely content itself with governing but should actively seek—instead of avoiding—parliamentary debate that will permit it to put across its arguments and the opposition to expound its criticisms; but real debate is as rare between government and parliament as it is between parliamentary candidates and voters.

If it is hard to achieve 'permanent revolution', it is impossible to imagine democracy as only intermittent: by definition it is and has to be permanent, otherwise it withers away, leaving free rein to a government that escapes all democratic control, to an all-powerful administration, to despotism, and to unconstitutional forms of criticism and protest. Democracy is in decay if the only power it grants the citizen is that of slipping a voting-paper into a ballot box every four or five years. When members of parliament complain of the smallness of their audiences at election and constituency meetings, they are faced with evidence of a crisis to which their conception of political debate with the public has itself contributed. When the same members complain of the pointlessness of certain parliamentary debates, they are putting their finger on another aspect of the same crisis, responsibility for which lies first and foremost with the government itself. At every level, fear of debate stifles democracy. Permanent, sustained debate is not the prerequisite of some 'ideal' democracy impossible of achievement. It is the prerequisite of any kind of democracy at all.

Political parties can and very rarely fail to criticize the institutional framework—and it really is ill-adapted—within which they have to operate. But do they themselves pursue, within the structures they have voluntarily imposed upon themselves, a democracy that tallies with the ideal they profess and with the demands of modern society?

> There is unquestionably a form of political action that does not meet the aspirations of citizens who are daily up against the difficulties of industrial society, its nuisances, its rhythms, its swindles, and its deep injustices (. . .) There is a modern form for parties that has yet to be discovered. That is why we are getting so many new institutions in the form of clubs and study centres (. . .) Political parties must be given a new kind of tone and a new popular impact.

These remarks were made not by some embittered denigrator of the pseudo-democracy obtaining in the West but by a member of the French government, Mlle M.-M. Dienesch, Secretary of State for Social Action and Readjustment.[20]

But what parties can boast of respecting in their own organization the democratic principles of which they claim to be the guardians? In the days when Guy Mollet was general secretary of the socialist SFIO ('Section française de l'Internationale ouvrière'), two federations alone determined the majority at party congresses. But even when democracy prevails in their congresses, it does not automatically follow that parties are democratic in their relations with their electoral base. Party politics is too often the politics of party bosses, even if these no longer fit the definitions of forty years ago. It is still a question of 'controlling the machine'.

In the United States the national conventions that select presidential candidates are a kind of circus designed to camouflage the power struggles and the often scandalous behind-the-scenes negotiations and deals that nevertheless sooner or later come to light.[21] Moreover these conventions are themselves undemocratic in composition, if only for the reason that they include very few women and very few blacks.

In Great Britain the fact that the trade unions belong to the Labour party can be misleading, for here too it is the high-ups that count politically—in this case the union leaders. 'The weaknesses,' writes Andrew Roth, 'are by no means new. They are rooted in Britain's uneven evolution over the last century from a tightly controlled oligarchy into a more broadly based democracy.'[22]

Oligarchical customs predominate, in England as elsewhere. Almost as soon as he is elected the politician becomes a personality, a dignitary, already concerned to preserve his position and secure re-election. To this end he cultivates the 'big voters' rather than the rank and file electorate. He goes after potential contributors to his next campaign fund. He tries to get a few local projects financed to increase his popularity in the constituency.

But national politics is never the sum of local projects. The elected representatives of a particular district may get an existing school modernized or new technical college built and yet take no interest whatever in curriculum reform, modernization of teaching methods, or teacher training (of 23,000 mathematics teachers in French secondary schools only 8,000 have a degree in mathematics, and it will not be one of them that is appointed to the brand-new tech.). Whether left-wing or right-wing, of middle-class or working-class origin, these new 'notables' may in their desire to secure re-election obtain far from negligible benefits for their constituencies without democracy being any the healthier for it.

And yet such as they are, with their good qualities and their limitations, their public spirit and their more personal preoccupations, their courage and their fears, these men and women are the representatives of the nation and are on rare occasions even considered as such by the government. Lyndon Johnson bartered support for a senator against construction of a hydro-electric dam in his state. Raymond Barrillon has remarked that 'priority in the granting of investments is often given to regions that vote well'.[23] Granted that throughout the West 'the nature of the decisions required of a modern state is such that they in fact usually lie with the executive surrounded by its various bodies of experts'.[24] But this strengthening of the executive's role in no way exempts it from accounting to parliament, nor does it authorize it to purchase agreement or dispense rewards for loyalty.

France's *députés* are not the only members of parliament to be 'humiliated and insulted by the regime', nor the only ones whose powers 'are *de facto* or *de jure* curtailed'.[25] Their British, German, and Italian colleagues complain likewise of not having access to the information they need if they are to do their job. The 'restricted area' that the executive shields from parliamentary control is spreading in every country in the West. The tradition is an old one, although the expression was first used in connexion with Gaullisme. To take only one example, the Suez expedition of 1956 was preceded by no parliamentary discussion whatever, either in Paris or in London. In France parliament was kept in the dark about the negotiations that ended the Algerian war, and was consulted neither about the withdrawal from NATO nor about recognition of Peking. The United States Senate was deceived when, after the alleged Gulf of Tonkin incident, it was stampeded into a vote that was to plunge the country into a major crisis by authorizing the bombardment of North Vietnam.

It is not of course easy to bring democracy to bear when it is a question of delicate diplomatic negotiations or risky military operations. But how often is it because the initiative towards debate is taken too late, or because the projected decision goes against the principles of democracy? Democracy is the loser every time the executive curtails parliament's role. Accepting that in certain cases the government's concern to be effective prompts it to act without prior agreement from parliament, it ought at least to submit itself to parliament's judgement after the event; moreover this procedure could never be anything but the exception, whereas now it is becoming the rule. If effectiveness sometimes demands secrecy and the surprise element, who is to be the judge of that effectiveness? And would not the greatest effectiveness lie in the establishment of a genuinely democratic regime?

Kept on a short leash, too often deprived of any real chance of doing their job, how many members of parliament fail to attend decisive debates? Throughout the West too many debates are held before empty benches. In 1960 John Kennedy took part in only 35 per cent of the Senate's votes; in 1968 Eugene McCarthy's record was only 5 per cent. A constitutional amendment put forward by Mrs Margaret Chase Smith—it has little chance of being adopted—proposes the automatic exclusion of any member who is absent from 40 per cent of the votes taken in his branch of Congress. But would not the best way of combating absenteeism be to give parliament back its full dignity and members their proper responsibility?

The first condition of responsibility on the part of a member of parliament has to do with the availability of his voting record. In this respect the accounts of debates in the *Journal officiel*, the *Congressional Record*, *Hansard*, etc., clearly do not reach a wide enough public. The analyses published in the press have the disadvantage of ephemerality. In the United States the AFL-CIO distributes before every election the voting records of all members of Congress on questions concerning the working class. It is an effective method but somewhat limited in its scope. It could well be extended so that all voters, while listening to their candidates' declarations of faith, could at the same time be in possession of outgoing members' voting records. Every citizen could thus see what had been his member's attitude to the principal questions placed before the *Assemblée*, Congress, the House of Commons, or whatever. The debate between voters and members, instead of wandering off into generalizations, would thus become concrete. A direct link would be established between election campaigns and parliamentary debates.

But parliament must also be able to do its job. In the United States Congress keeps trying to abolish the seniority rule that gives the chairs of committees to the venerable aged rather than to the people most competent to occupy them. Three Congressional committees have chairmen of 80-plus, three of 75-plus, eight of 70-plus, and nine of 65-plus, Congress is also trying to reduce the possibility of systematic obstruction by making it possible to stop a filibuster with a three-fifths majority instead of the present requirement of two-thirds.

Members of parliament must also have the financial means of doing their job, and in this respect the United States undoubtedly offers an example. A Representative or Senator cannot possibly meet all his innumerable obligations on his own—attending sessions, preparing himself beforehand, attending committee meetings, examining the 30,000 or so bills (many of them superfluous) tabled every year, keeping in touch with his constituency, answering voters' letters, meeting the press, writing speeches and lectures, etc.

In the United States a member of Congress earns $42,500 (£16,000) a year. If he sits in the House of Representatives for a constituency numbering more than 500,000 inhabitants he can recruit sixteen assistants, paid by the state, at a maximum salary of $29,000 a year. If he sits in the Senate he gets a staff budget fixed according to the population of the state he represents, the ceiling being $478,000; the maximum salary for a senatorial aide is $35,000, and certain senators, who admittedly pay some of their aides out of their own pockets, can recruit a staff of up to sixty. On top of this there are expenses for travelling, telephone bills, mail, telegrams, etc.[26]

Parliaments have become so discredited that even in the United States these figures are regarded as excessive by certain sectors of the public. Yet the running costs of Congress, including upkeep of buildings, printing costs, and the Library of Congress, are $396 million annually, that is to say 3·6 per cent of the cost of the B-1 bomber. Gambling, drugs, police, military equipment, cosmetics, advertising—each of these costs immeasurably more than the nation's representative body.

But what of those European countries where several members of parliament sometimes share the services of a single secretary? Europe prides itself on having entered upon the technological age, yet its elected representatives work in positively primitive conditions. Europe fails to offer its MPs, *députés*, *membri*, etc., salaries that might attract the best minds—unless they have a private income—nor does it make it possible for them to employ the staff they simply cannot do without if they are to study the problems that the technological society dumps on their desks every day.

To increase parliament's slice of public funds would doubtless be an unpopular move. Yet can one, without paying the price, expect democracy to work as it should? A section of motorway, a speculative real-estate operation, or a military aircraft all cost more than a parliament. A people stands accused when it allows its democratic institutions to be run on the cheap while allowing at the same time, even if unwillingly, vast sums to be sunk into less essential and sometimes quite useless activities. So an effective parliament would be an expensive item? But money is a long way from having nothing to do with the debate on the future of democracy.

The rights of money

The election of Richard Nixon in 1968 officially cost the Republican party $29 million. Some say it cost a lot more. Walter Pincus, for example, wrote:

> The Nixon campaign organization reported raising some $25 million at the national headquarters level. That figure does not include expenses of Nixon-Agnew committees in every one of the 50 states. Since the total for one statewide Florida committee ran to $380,000 one could guess that at least another $10 million nationally was involved for such 'citizen' committees at the state level.[27]

At the beginning of 1972, even before he had officially announced his candidature, Senator Muskie had already spent $1 million, and the 'primaries' were soon to run the bill up a lot further. In 1970, of fifteen candidates standing for important senatorial seats eleven were millionaires—and were elected.

Nelson Rockefeller spent between $7 and $10 million in 1970 on securing his fourth mandate as Governor of the state of New York; his Democratic opponent, Arthur Goldberg, spent only $2 million. The senatorial campaign in the same state cost $6 million. In California Governor Ronald Reagan spent $2·4 million on getting himself re-elected, his defeated Democratic opponent $1·1 million; John Tunney was elected senator after having spent $1·7 million, as against $1·5 million spent by his opponent, outgoing senator George Murphy; and candidates for the thirty-four seats in the California House of Representatives spent $5·4 million. Altogether these elections in California officially cost $12 million, though the real figure was no doubt higher. Is it absolutely necessary that such vast sums be spent on such disappointing campaigns?

Election campaigns in both America and Europe are fraught with scandals that throw serious doubt on the functioning of democracy. The American press shows more enthusiasm in exposing them than does its European counterpart. In February 1972, for example, it revealed that the International Telephone and Telegraph Company (ITT) had apparently promised to contribute $400,000 to the Republican party on condition that the Department of Justice drop the suit it had filed against the company under the anti-trust laws. The Attorney-General, as it happens, was John Mitchell, who headed Nixon's election campaign in 1968 and left the Department early in 1972 to run the new campaign. His place at the Department had been taken by his closest associate, Richard Kleindienst, who personally took part in the negotiations with ITT and whose appointment was nevertheless ratified by the Senate.

The affair is in no way exceptional. In March 1971 the Department of Agriculture announced that the government would not be increasing the subsidies for milk production. Thirteen days later, after a conference of milk-industry chiefs at the White House, the same Department announced that federal subsidization would be increased by 6 per cent. 'Contributions to the GOP and to President Nixon's re-election campaign totaling some $300,000 poured in from the dairy industry,' wrote *Newsweek*.[28] *Time* quoted the figure of $322,500.[29] A complaint has been lodged by the young lawyer Ralph Nader and various consumer-protection organizations. The complaint gives details of the arrangement arrived at between the milk industry and some hundred Republican pseudo-committees, enabling the party to get round the law limiting individual contributions for electioneering purposes to $5,000. Such practices come under the provisions of the law against corruption that has been in force for almost half a century but has never been applied. Furthermore in the last three years thirteen senators and forty-seven Representatives have tabled draft bills providing for increased federal subsidization of the milk industry, which has rewarded them with election-fund contributions to the tune of $187,000. Among the recipients: Senators Muskie ($3,936), Humphrey ($15,625), and Vance Hartke ($4,100).

The identical procedure is of course current in Western Europe as well. The danger is less in West Germany, for example, where the state subsidizes the parties' election campaigns. 'The facts have shown,' writes Alain Clément, 'that this arrangement has not undermined the two-party system (balanced by the liberal FDP) that emerges from every German election. In the United States, on the other hand, one of the main objections to subsidies for political parties is that they might lead to the emergence of third parties disturbing the Republican/Democrat alternation. Would this be a bad thing? Or would the scourge of venality and the courting of private means reappear in another form?'[30]

In any case the 'third party' is already a fact in the United States (though perhaps only a transitory one) with the candidacy of George Wallace, who collected 13·5 per cent of the votes in 1968, and in West Germany and Great Britain with the presence of Liberal parties. Elsewhere the multiplicity of parties removes the problem. But is it a real problem? For it amounts to saying that only money makes it possible to win votes, and that the way to avoid dissipating votes is to confine the possibility of financing an election campaign to the traditional political formations.

A funny kind of democracy, though, where money opens the door to power and at the same time to the chance of making more money. Yet money—and lots of it—is indispensable to the staging of an election campaign. Either the candidate gets hold of the necessary resources himself, in which case the theoretical equality of citizens is violated because wealthy candidates or candidates with wealthy relations are at an advantage: this was the case with John Kennedy in the United States or—implying no comparison—with Jean-Jacques Servan-Schreiber in Nancy. Or the money is put up by the party, which involves just as much compromise and guarantees the candidate's 'unconditional support' not of a particular political doctrine but of the party's sources of funds. The whole debate about 'unconditional support' would be considerably clarified if, instead of this being treated as some quasi-mystical loyalty to an ideal, it was looked at in its true and more prosaic light: the backing of the party financing the election campaign is the key to power—even when the real powers of members of parliament are reduced to their simplest expression.

The fact is election campaigns are costly—and are becoming steadily more so. In the United States the presidential campaign of 1968 is said to have cost twice as much as that of 1956. A campaign for a Representative's seat costs between $40,000 and $70,000, for a senator's seat $1·5 million, and for a governorship $1 million. These sums amount to a kind of 'property qualification' not for voters but for candidates. Is such a 'property qualification' in line with the requirements of modern democracy?

> These huge sums, despite the traditional claim of politicians that every dollar came in crumpled bills from the man on the street, are raised from the wealthy few: it is estimated that 90% of political funds are donated by 1% of the population.[31]

Can universal suffrage be anything other than a ritual as long as election campaigns are not democratically financed and those finances democratically controlled?

Of very modest origins himself, Senator Muskie remarked humorously, in connexion with the vast resources and backing that Edward Kennedy had at his disposal: 'I am glad to discover that a poor boy can become President of this country if he can pick up twenty million dollars for expenses on the way.'[32]

The problem is not one of knowing whether, as American mythology would have us believe, a 'nobody' can, in a democratic, free-enterprise society, rise to the presidency: we have Richard Nixon to prove that this *tour de force* does in fact lie within the reach of an enterprising, stubborn, and intelligent man—provided that he gets Alger Hiss condemned on a wave of anti-Communist hysteria, that he stirs up prevailing passions rather than enlightening opinion, that he manages to latch onto the coat-tails of a prestigious personality like Eisenhower, that he succeeds in clearing himself of a charge of embezzlement, and that he subsequently gives himself a political face-lift and runs as a respectable man.

The problem is rather one of knowing whether money alone makes it possible to offer public opinion the plans and criticisms that are the *raison d'être* of an election campaign. Victory is not necessarily assured to the candidate who invests a bigger sum in it than his opponent. But a democracy denies its nature when it allows money—for posters, hand-outs, bookings, travel, television appearances, telephone bills, etc.—to become the unequal condition of debate.

Citizens regard with suspicion the enormous financial resources mobilized into canvassing the popular vote. Are their votes then worth so much? And is all that money put up by philanthropists? President Pompidou had to defend himself on this count at his press conference of 23 September 1971, but even those who do not feel the need to justify themselves must be aware that they are not above suspicion.

The United States is putting through a law to place a ceiling on the amount that can be spent on an election campaign. But there will still be ways of getting round such a limitation. There is a law of 1925 that forbids a candidate to accept more than $5,000 from any one contributor, but American trade-unionists have long been telling the following story, which is still topical today:

The ancestral head gathers together all the members of the DuPont de Nemours family and tells them: 'In a few months' time we are going to have to win an election. The law forbids any citizen to give more than $5,000 in support of the candidate of his choice. *Ergo*, each of us will contribute $5,000.' And every member of the clan, in obedience to the ancestor's wishes, gives $5,000. Eventually it is little Peter's turn. Peter is five years old, and they tell him: 'Peter, your party needs you.' Whereupon little Peter replies: 'I shall uphold the DuPont tradition.' Forcing back his tears, he generously smashes his piggy-bank, from which fall $5,000 in brand-new bills. Grandfather DuPont then resumes: 'We have now fulfilled our obligations towards this committee. But the same party has formed another election committee that is also asking for our help. The law forbids any citizen . . . *Ergo* . . .' And each member of the clan coughs up again. Little Peter spontaneously goes off in search of another piggy-bank, from which he takes $5,000 without shedding a tear. For the clan has meanwhile taught him the supreme wisdom: it is a good idea to have a number of piggy-banks . . . Each member of the family thus contributes $5,000 to each of the committees set up by the Republican party at each level. And so does each member of the Rockefeller family, Pew family, Mellon family, and so on. For all are equal before the law: workers too are allowed to contribute $5,000 per head to each of the election committees of their choice. A working-class family of four persons can legally contribute $20,000 to the national committee of the Democratic party, and the same amount to the state committee, the local committee, and so on. All citizens have the same rights—just not the same incomes.

'The resources of political parties,' said President Pompidou on 23 September 1971, 'are not all people think. They are usually somewhat obscure, for reasons that vary widely and are not necessarily immoral. I am all for keeping a check on them, but it won't make much difference.'

If keeping a check does not make much difference it means that the mechanics of supervision are inadequate—not that the principle must be abandoned. A democracy presupposes that documents and records—all of them—should be available to the people as the final judge. Politicians and parties continually underestimate the mistrust with which they are surrounded on account of their 'slightly obscure' resources. Too many mysteries shroud the financing of political organizations—mysteries on which the occasional scandal throws some light. If the reasons for this secrecy 'vary widely and are not necessarily immoral', no party can refuse to open its account-books for inspection.

The democratic regimes of the West are sick because behind a façade of more or less faithfully observed ritual they violate the very principles of democracy. Through either indifference or complacency large numbers of citizens are accessories to this violation. More consumers than citizens, they are content to see their standard of living go up, and above all they feel helpless in the face of a cumbersome machine over which they have no control.

Not only are voters accessories—they are also victims. Election campaigns, as C. Wright Mills has put it, are pitched more 'to the belly or to the groin than to the head or to the heart'.[33] They rarely offer them the chance of choosing between candidates committed to concrete projects. The art of the 'good' candidate consists in promising all things to all social and professional groups and to every age group, well knowing that not all those promises can be kept—or else in shutting away the more complex problems behind vague declarations of a kind that will subsequently leave room for every justification. Citizens are further victimized by the fact that political parties, which are rarely democratic in terms of internal structure, are vote-catching machines rather than the instruments of a continuing dialogue with the public. The citizen, said Jefferson, ought to 'take part in the government of affairs not only at election time (. . .) but every day.' Furthermore, as John Quincy Adams remarked, a man wants 'to be seen, listened to, discussed, approved of, and respected by those around him'—a privilege that is denied not only to inhabitants of the megalopolis, lost in the anonymity of dense masses of population, but also to the 'ordinary' citizen who feels himself disregarded by the administration, parliament, the political parties, and all the wheels of a power that is often blind except to the mighty.

On their own or as members of political parties, members of parliament are themselves for the most part accessories to this weakening and undermining of the democratic spirit. How often are personal convictions and the requirements of a democratic society sacrificed to the pursuit of a political career? How many pronouncements and how many silences are dictated by opportunistic calculations, by personal considerations, and by fear masquerading as caution or wisdom? If ability is indispensable, courage is no less so. The public understands a mistake but will rarely countenance cowardice. Of the elected representatives who, while criticizing him on occasion, recognized the pluck shown by John F. Kennedy, how many either in Europe or America would figure in that portrait gallery he entitled *Profiles in Courage*? An entire parliament, with the exception of a tiny minority, collapsed in June 1940, burying the French Republic. In 1958, at the time of the Algiers *putsch*, were the outgoing President of the Council and his successor-designate, who each tried to shuffle responsibility off onto the other, so much less courageous than other parliamentary leaders in search of a saviour? Where were the *députés*—majority and opposition —in May 1968? In the United States what did congressmen—with the exception of one senator, McGovern—say in February 1965 to the first bombardments of North Vietnam? If there was a revolt of Labour members at the time of Suez, how did France's parliament react to the same crisis? But then where was the courage of British MPs in 1970 when the majority of them quite simply avoided all mention of the subject of their country's entry into the Common Market?

In a society devoted to its rituals all criticism of members of parliament is looked at askance, for it immediately seems like a crime of 'lèse-democracy'. But an institution can never lose its credit without the active collaboration of the men who are its life-blood.

Besides being accomplices, a nation's elected representatives also become the appointed victims of this decay of parliamentary institutions. A bodily function that operates inadequately or incorrectly ends up by atrophying the organ concerned. The executive for its part tries to encourage and speed up the process, gnawing away at the real powers of the legislature, assuming every right, bending the constitution, creating a new *de facto* situation, and too often finding a majority of members of parliament to sanction, if only implicitly, their own decline or suicide.

Too many organs of state are beyond any real control by the people's representatives. In the United States there are more than 3,200 committees, commissions, and agencies holding advisory powers within the federal government and Congress. They employ more than 20,000 people, including 4,400 salaried experts. The executive has set up 140 'presidential commissions', 31 'inter-governmental committees', and 190 'federal inter-agency committees'. They meet in secret and their transactions are confidential. One of these advisory committees managed to hold up an important anti-pollution programme for seven years. Senator Lee Metcalf has shown for example how 'within a year, the Budget Bureau began to develop advisory committees, although the act provided no statutory basis for them. These committees deal with banking, chemicals, communications, equal employment, fats and oils, meat packing, natural gas, oil, railroads, trade and utilities. These committees are housed within the Advisory Council on Federal Reports, which terms itself the official business consultant to the Budget Bureau. Yet it states it is responsible only to the business community. In fact it is funded by private groups, not by the government.'[34] Most of the members of these committees belong to the industries concerned and operate like pressure groups in their favour.

One advisory committee has met four times in ten years; another has not even produced a report for the last twenty-three years. The president can disregard the conclusions of these committees, whether for political reasons—as Nixon did in rejecting the report on pornography and censorship, which had cost $1·8 million—or to please industry—as Johnson did with the report on technology and automation and Nixon with the report on urban problems (cost: $1·5 million). But in general these committees, whose existence is unknown to the general public and which are thoroughly infiltrated by private industry, meet and deliberate behind closed doors, forming as it were a secret government, and get the executive to adopt their conclusions without their being subject to any democratic control whatever.

In France what real democratic control is there over such organizations as the 'District de Paris', the 'Caisse des dépôts et consignations', the nationalized banks and industries, etc.? What parliamentary control is there over the sale of military aircraft or the refusal to deliver them? An investment boom can be encouraged by tax reductions, which require a division in parliament, or by lowering the bank rate—a generous present to the business community that depends on a simple ministerial decision. In France a law passed by parliament does not come into force until publication of the relevant *décrets d'application*; the government was thus able to hold up for four years the law on contraception passed in 1967. The Prime Minister deplores this delay and promises to 'speed up the process' of publication of *décrets d'application*.[35] But it is not just a question of speed and efficiency. The 1967 law laid down a six-month limit for publication of the *décrets d'application*. In the name of what principle of democracy can the government break the law with impunity?

Though a victim of this kind of violation of the democratic spirit, parliament is nevertheless still the place where major problems must be debated and brought to the attention of the public. This presupposes that parliament shall not forget that it is nothing without the citizens who elected it and that it be willing to engage them in a dialogue of longer duration than the few weeks of an election campaign.

Three conditions are essential if relations between members of parliament and their constituents are to be clarified:

Firstly there must be some democratic control over the funds spent on election campaigns and over the financial resources of political parties. Universal suffrage postulates equality of citizens at the polls. If in reality the vote cast by a big contributor of funds has more weight than that cast by the ordinary wage-earner, then at least let the fact be recognized and admitted.

Secondly all members of parliament know by experience that only a small number of voters are aware of exactly how their representatives vote on the occasion of the principal roll-calls of the period covered by a particular legislature. Electoral campaigns only become fully meaningful when an independent organ issues voters with the candidate's voting record. If members of parliament want to avoid being 'unrepresentative' and therefore vulnerable, it is up to them to restore election campaigns to their true importance as an occasion for the electorate to pass judgement on them for their own voting record on the one hand and for their plans for the new legislature on the other.

Thirdly, when none of the candidates for a seat comes up to the public's requirements, the 'blank paper' should be officially allowed in order to give voters the chance of keeping them out by refusing them a majority of votes cast. The risks inherent in such a system are by no means negligible. It can lead to an impasse, with no one name emerging from the ballot. But it is the only way in which citizens could reconsign to private life those politicians who, lacking any real support in the electorate, contribute to a different kind of paralysis and a very much more serious impasse. Members of parliament cannot duck their own share of responsibility for the poor functioning of democracy, which is connected not only with democratic institutions themselves but also, too frequently, with the mediocrity of a certain political class. It is normal, if deplorable, that voters should abstain. It is abnormal, and even more deplorable, that the 'blank paper' should not give the public the opportunity of rejecting the false choices it is too often presented with.

Such reforms will not be enough in themselves, but they could help make it easier to achieve what one statesman has called 'a coherent policy, based on a conscientious study of the facts, clearly put before the country and accepted by it'. The same statesman has also deplored certain politicians' lack of courage and character, adding that such weaknesses 'are not unique to governments and parliaments. They are extremely widespread throughout the country, in individuals as much as in groups of all kinds (. . .). What counts more than improving the laws are those much more sweeping and admittedly much more difficult changes that concern men and their actions. The men in power first of all, and also all those throughout the country who constitute the administrative, political, professional, social, and military leadership of a great nation that is today a prey to a kind of generalized disorganization and discouragement the effects of which could be disastrous in the near future.'

Indeed it is too easy to heap criticism on the institutions of the West, as if the better to excuse the men behind them. These severe remarks are, alas, already twenty years old. They were made by a man who has got himself widely hated in political circles—Pierre Mendès-France.[36]

Members of parliament may denounce the restrictions placed on their authority and competence, criticize the extension of the prerogatives of the executive, and deplore the fact that, as a result of this twofold trend, the forum of debate is moving to the street and sometimes assumes violent forms; but they will be voices crying in the wilderness as long as they have failed to make political parties like 'glass houses' and until they have changed both the style of their election campaigns and their standards of action.

The future of democracy lies in the hands of citizens and those who have of their own free will chosen to solicit their votes. The spirit of democracy has become as anaemic as its institutions are paralytic. Can these be restored to life?

Yet the sphere of democratic life is not confined exclusively to political institutions. It embraces all sectors of social, economic, and cultural activity. If all the countries of the West are experiencing in varying degrees this same crisis of adaptation in their political institutions, do they show signs of greater vitality in other fields of activity?

References

1 Club Jean Moulin, *L'Etat et le citoyen*, Editions du Seuil, Paris, 1961, p. 11.
2 State of the Union Message; see *The Times*, 22 January 1972.
3 David Butler and Michael Pinto-Duschinsky, *The British General Election of 1970*, Macmillan, London, 1971, pp. 437–8.
4 Emmanuel Mounier, in *Esprit*, March 1938.
5 *L'Etat et le citoyen*, op. cit., p. 14.
6 Quoted by Ian Gilmour, *The Body Politic*, Hutchinson, London, 1969.

7 Andrew Roth, *Can Parliament Decide?*, Macmillan, London, 1971, p. 202.
8 Cf. Claude Julien, *Inquiète Amérique*, article II, 'La renaissance du rêve', *Le Monde*, 29 January 1970.
9 Quoted by C. Wright Mills, *The Power Elite*, Oxford University Press, New York, 1956.
10 From David Butler and Michael Pinto-Duschinsky, *The British General Election of 1970*, Macmillan, London, 1971.
11 *Idem.*, pp. 439–40.
12 *Idem.*, p. 445.
13 *Time*, 31 January 1972.
14 *US News and World Report*, 23 November 1970.
15 *Le Monde*, 16 February 1972.
16 Georges Vedel, 'Le régime parlementaire a-t-il un avenir?', *Le Monde*, 1 December 1971.
17 Roger-Gérard Schwartzenberg, *Le Monde*, 24 February 1972.
18 Richard H. Rovere, in *The New Yorker*, 19 December 1970.
19 Andrew Roth, *Can Parliament Decide?*, op. cit., pp. 2–3.
20 Mlle Marie-Madeleine Dienesch, in *Le Monde*, 8 February 1972.
21 There are many studies on this theme. For concrete illustration see among others Theodore H. White, *The Making of a President*.
22 Andrew Roth, *Can Parliament Decide?*, op. cit., p. 12.
23 Raymond Barrillon, 'Démocratie et oppression', in *Le Monde*, 10 March 1972.
24 Georges Vedel, op. cit.
25 Raymond Barrillon, op. cit.
26 *US News and World Report*, 22 March 1971.
27 Walter Pincus, editor of the *Morning News*, in *The New Republic*, 11 December 1971.
28 *Newsweek*, 7 February 1972.
29 *Time*, 2 February 1972.
30 Alain Clément, 'Le pouvoir de l'argent et l'argent du pouvoir', in *Le Monde*, 19 January 1972.
31 *Time*, 23 November 1970.
32 The *New York Times Magazine*, 22 November 1970.
33 C. Wright Mills, *The Power Elite*, Oxford University Press, 1956, p. 356.
34 See *The New Republic*, 20 February 1971.
35 See *Le Monde*, 13 January 1972.
36 Pierre Mendès-France, 'La réforme constitutionelle suffira-t-elle?', in *Le Monde*, 10 April 1953.

CHAPTER FOUR

Man and Capital

- Power and inefficiency
- The limits to growth
- The price of economic expansion
- How labour is sacrificed
- Useful and non-useful products
- The privileges of money
- The injustices of taxation

Prosperity gives rise to areas of poverty, and technological progress fails to do away with the jobs at the bottom end of the qualification and wage scale. Social policies relieve, with a greater or lesser degree of effectiveness, the victims of that poverty, but without eliminating its causes: in the United States it has even been established that welfare has often had the effect of keeping its recipients—particularly blacks—beyond the pale of prosperity.

On the other hand, notwithstanding the incoherencies of its urbanization policy, the West has never had a real revolt (with something to show for it afterwards) on the part of public-transport passengers or the homeless, or against inadequate school or recreational facilities. Citizens simply put up with it all, and when some of them do succeed in launching a protest movement, their campaign is too easily diverted from its aims: 'The membership of air and water pollution boards in thirty-five states is dotted with industrial, agricultural, municipal, and county representatives whose own organizations or spheres of activity are in many cases in the forefront of pollution,' wrote the *New York Times*.[1]

Instead of being nurtured, all desire to participate and accept responsibility is systematically discouraged. Citizens are helpless not so much against the problems, though these are extremely complex, as against the unwieldiness of institutions or the blindness of the authorities. The loser thereby is the democratic spirit, which in fact ought to be gaining ground with the spread of education and information media. Does the state by the same token get more freedom to govern? 'Never has the state had more power to impose respect for the common interest,' one jurist has observed, 'and never has it seemed so impotent. The weakening of parliament together with the links between government, the administration, and the business world have given money free rein:

controls, far from restraining money, provide a maze within which it moves with ease.'[2]

The power of the economy and the power of the state are inadequate to solve the biggest and most urgent problems. In the United States the *New Yorker* is by no means the only publication to have observed that 'many nations with economies feebler than this country's have much better records in health and education'.[3] Another journal has pointed out that the United States, with its 'unparalleled resources', has a 'social instability' problem that is perhaps also unequalled among the industrialized nations.[4]

The two kinds of growth

Yet it is in the United States that the economy has achieved the most influence and the state possesses, whether *de jure* or *de facto*, the most extensive powers—by virtue of the structure of the constitution and by virtue of the budget, which it controls. Is all this power a mere illusion? Its bankruptcy is evident in the very streets of the federal capital. When Richard Nixon came to power in January 1969 he was appalled by a spectacle that shocks every visitor to the White House: 14th Street is littered with piles of rubble, the all-too-visible traces of the race riots that followed the assassination of Martin Luther King in 1968 and caused \$24 million worth of damage. To give the city back some of its dignity the President gave orders that the ruins should be speedily cleared away, entrusting the job to one of his associates. But, as this associate said, presidential decision or no presidential decision, the most minor town-planning project took twelve years. It is the same in Los Angeles: Watts is still littered with the ruins left by the 1965 riots that caused 35 deaths and \$220 million worth of damage. The wealth of the nation and the powers of the president are here up against a brick wall.

Yet it is easier to rebuild a street or city district than it is to alter ingrained attitudes. And here all the powers of the economy and the government show themselves to be dangerously ineffective. Daniel Bell, professor at Columbia University and author of *The End of Ideology*,[5] has said: 'We see here all the symptoms of a blocked society. The administrative structure is all awry. We have to invent new mechanisms, redefine the echelons of power, reform the political system, make it possible for the public to assume its responsibilities, facilitate citizen participation in the life of local communities.'[6] He goes on to sketch a picture of the urban crisis and list the technical solutions that are theoretically applicable in the light of the most recent developments, adding, however, that these techniques, though available, cannot in fact be applied because the crisis is *politically* insoluble.

When a powerful economy and a powerful state cannot manage to solve problems within an acceptable period, is reforming the political system, the echelons of power, and the structure of the administration going to be enough? Doubtless it will also—and primarily—be necessary to redefine real power both in economic terms and in political terms.

The problem is not exclusive to America. It occurs everywhere in Europe where the economy has achieved a high growth rate and where there has been a strengthening of the powers of the executive. In West Germany 'the malaise stems from the feeling of impotence that the government gives', despite the fact that it 'sought to be particularly active', according to Alfred Grosser.[7]

In its directives to the 'Commissaire général au Plan' in June 1960 the French government wrote:

Whatever may be its positive aspects, there is no doubt that industrial civilization gives rise, when its effects are not balanced and humanized, to many dissatisfactions that are coming to be more and more deeply felt: noise, air pollution, lack of green spaces, barely adequate water supplies, long daily journeys between home and place of work, difficulties regarding the employment of leisure time.

Clearly perceived here were some of the problems that lie at the heart of the current 'crisis of civilization'. But what is the situation thirteen years later? Noise and air pollution have got worse, the equivalent of the Bois de Boulogne and the Bois de Vincennes put together were wiped off the map in the Paris region alone between 1965 and 1970, efforts made since the 1964 law have not reduced the risk of water shortage, new means of transport have not cut travelling times, and leisure facilities have still to catch up with demography. Yet throughout those thirteen years the economy has been in a state of expansion and the government has enjoyed a stable majority, enabling it to pass all the credits it has thought necessary. The power of the economy and the power of the state have done less than nothing to solve the problems to which the government drew the attention of the 'Commissariat au Plan' thirteen years ago.

Economic growth and the strengthening of the powers of the state have failed to overcome a deep-rooted powerlessness: society remains 'jammed'. The state has become a giant caught in the toils of the immense apparatus it has itself created. As for the economy, it is not necessarily more powerful for simply producing more: its efficiency is also dependent on what it produces and how.

Yet it is more than a decade since Galbraith pointed out the divorce that exists between what man produces and the usefulness of that product. In *Economie et Société*, François Perroux too showed the consequences of putting quantity before quality.[8] The entire West has nevertheless chosen to develop its economic power by increasing production quantitatively without asking too many questions, despite the warnings it has received, about the usefulness and quality of its products or about its methods of producing them. Increase in gross national product has become both the goal and the yardstick; growth has become an end in itself. Yet, as Pierre Drouin writes, 'it cannot be too strongly stressed that, beyond a certain rhythm, expansion tends to give rise to more problems than it solves; its *external costs*—too often left out of official accounts—tend to increase.'[9] But opinion is so conditioned that the letter Sicco Mansholt sent Malfatti on 9 February 1972 caused all the consternation one could imagine, notably on account of the sentence: 'The society of tomorrow cannot revolve around growth, at least not in the material sphere.' His argument is essentially an ecological one: to establish a balance between population and natural resources, to keep sufficient sources of energy for the future, and to set up a 'non-pollutive system of production'—all of which would amount to a 'marked reduction in consumption of material commodities per inhabitant' and consequently a 'lowering of the standard of material well-being', which are to be 'compensated for by an increase in non-material benefits: social insurance, a blossoming of intellect, leisure and recreational provisions, etc.'

As conceived in the West economic growth carries with it a real risk of disturbing and one day no doubt destroying the natural balance essential to life. Ecologists have long been proclaiming the danger, and certain economists are now becoming aware of it as well. Paul Fabra has written:

> The expansion we have so prided ourselves on is being shown up for what it is: man has as it were usurped his present well-being by using up the natural resources that he has inherited and that he will no longer be able to hand down in the same state (. . .). Even the least complacent appraisal of the effort needed to repair the damage

inflicted on this earth over the last twenty-five years—the time it has taken to bring Lake Geneva to the brink of disaster, for example, whereas the previous six thousand years of human history had left it intact—takes absolutely no account of the permanent risks to which the natural environment is exposed as a result of a conception of economic growth that revolves around short-term objectives.[10]

But the West's conception of growth does more than inflict damage on nature. The goals it has set itself have undoubtedly involved a heavy drain on natural resources, but the means it has chosen to reach those goals have had two disastrous consequences: they have led to increased wastefulness, and above all they have devalued the nature of human labour.

In order to increase production the West has applied itself to producing on the one hand useless commodities that require the consumer to be conditioned by skilful and expensive advertising to persuade him to buy them at all and on the other hand commodities whose useful life is artificially limited so that the consumer shall be obliged to replace them more frequently. In order to sell all it produces the West has had to increase purchasing power faster than productivity has increased, thus institutionalizing inflation. It has also—and this is the most serious part—had to keep prices as low as possible not only by exploiting all the resources of technology, but above all by importing at the most favourable terms raw materials that are the principal resource of the 'proletarian nations' and by inflicting on its own proletariat inhuman quotas and working conditions. So to the 'damage inflicted on this earth over the last twenty-five years' we must add the injury and insult to the labour of certain categories of wage-earner, whose toilsome and ill-remunerated efforts have, by an unconscious perversity of the system, been deliberately directed towards producing unnecessary or unnecessarily ephemeral goods.

In this form, are not economic growth and power simply delusions? In comparing gross national product and growth rate from country to country, the West has neglected to ask itself the most important question: since economic power and the power of the state cannot be ends in themselves, towards what conception of man and society shall they be the means? Despite some sharp ideological confrontations, the problem has rarely been discussed in concrete terms. Not the least virtue of the protest movement has been to give new impetus to a debate that was becoming increasingly academic. Expanding societies with democratic

regimes of a more or less stable nature have discovered in themselves defects forcing them to re-examine firstly their objectives and
secondly their structures and institutions. For economic progress and
democracy only make sense if they lead to an increase in justice, equality, liberty and knowledge, and a general blossoming of human qualities in societies of a more fraternal nature. The West knows—but may
have found out too late—that economic expansion may very well be
accompanied by pronounced injustices and inequalities and in fact
sacrifice the very spirit of democracy.

If it is to survive in a form compatible with its declared ideals, must
the West put a brake on its economic growth? This growth is leading
to the waste of non-replaceable natural resources, the diminution or
exhaustion of which would condemn the West to investing vast sums
in research into new raw materials; meanwhile investment in the tools
of production would be cut, leading to the obsolescence of industrial
plant; without agricultural implements, fertilizer, medicaments, etc.,
the population would swiftly decrease: it would be the end of a civilization based on a high level of consumption. Such, briefly summarized,
is the analysis that a research team from the Massachusetts Institute of
Technology drew up at the request of the Club of Rome and on which
Sicco Mansholt based his case. The authors drafted several 'scripts' for the
future, all culminating in the same catastrophe around the year 2100.[11]

If the forecasts analysed in *The Limits to Growth* are realistic, is Sicco
Mansholt justified in concluding that it is necessary to reduce per capita
consumption of material commodities? The MIT team foresees catastrophe at the end of the next century providing that consumption continues to increase at the same rate as at present. Is it actually necessary
to reduce consumption, or would it be enough to stop stimulating it
artificially? If an apocalyptic vision of the future prompts industry to
cut down waste it will have benefited not only the West but also the
under-developed world, which sells the West its raw materials.

The MIT team's methods and conclusions have of course been dis-
puted. Faith in progress as being able to solve all problems is as firmly
rooted in some people's minds as it was at the end of the nineteenth
century: science offers unlimited perspectives, so economic growth,
with synthetic products and new sources of energy, will also continue
ad infinitum.

But is perpetual growth indispensable to the proper functioning of
the system? Or more exactly: does perpetual growth have to be prim-
marily material growth, with 'fringe benefits' in the fields of public

health, culture, and the amenities of existence? Is it not possible—without artificially stimulating production, without squandering natural resources, without polluting the environment, and without destroying the biological balance—to conceive of other forms of development that would meet man's needs in a different way? Ought the economy to meet man's needs, or must those 'needs' be stretched at enormous expense in order to enable the economy to grow and develop? Does rejecting perpetual growth mean cutting right back to 'zero growth' or even a reduction of consumption?

An attitude is emerging in the United States that questions not technological and scientific progress but the way it is used by a profit-hungry industry. Lewis Mumford denied that there was any 'irresistible impulse' driving man to achieve everything that is technologically possible rather than confining himself to those technological possibilities that are of use to the race. The lively public-opinion campaign that got the project for the SST supersonic aircraft shelved illustrates a state of mind that comes down to this: we don't need to halve flying time between Paris and New York; what interests us is getting to work quicker and in more comfortable conditions without aggravating noise and pollution problems. If most Europeans were impressed by the conquest of the moon, many Americans condemn the space programme and complain that it has diverted funds that would have been more usefully employed in improving urban transport or education. America knows it is technically and (for the time being) economically possible to give each family two or three cars, but it is worried about this kind of proliferation. A Harvard scientist sees heart transplantation as a wonderful technical achievement but one that does not really benefit mankind, particularly not in a country that, like the United States, is short of doctors.[12]

The Americans said that Mikoyan 'could have sold ice-boxes to Eskimos', but they themselves stimulate their own growth by selling air-conditioners in temperate zones where they are totally unnecessary. In the interests of growth the West can further put on the market such 'useful' appliances as the electric tooth-brush, the electric carving-knife, and the electric corkscrew. And why should not every high school have one microscope per pupil, as those of Chicago do? Some 29 per cent of families have at least two cars: so the market is unlimited . . . Not many families have a refrigerator and a television set on every floor of the house yet: but fear not, if there is room for progress, the advertising industry will take care of it.

6*

The first step toward a solution is to know how far to push material growth. Valéry Giscard d'Estaing suggests an ambiguous answer when he writes: 'Is economic growth still the central, determining goal, the raw material of other forms of progress? (. . .) It all depends on the level already reached (. . .). This will continue to be France's case for a relatively limited period of probably between ten and twenty years. Until then we shall have to live with economic growth. And since this has its debit side, we must allow for and correct it.'[13]

But on the basis of what criteria does one decide that 'the level already reached' is still insufficient? By reference to other countries, such as the United States? In a competitive world, comparison is hardly to be avoided. But if it is allowed to come to that, international rivalry will result in a 'growth race' as entirely comprehensible and quite as absurd as the 'arms race': the fear of being left behind by the others will keep everyone pushing ahead.

If in the United States, with a per capita income three times that of Europe, growth and affluence had eliminated poverty, social injustice, and the exploitation of certain categories of worker, the temptation would be strong to follow its example. But the experience of that country, which entered the age of technology and consumption earlier than Europe, destroys any illusion: expansion has not got rid of poverty, it has raised the standard of living more than improved the quality of life, it has multiplied the number of jobs in which work loses all human interest whatever, it has created a virtually uninhabitable urban environment, and it has broken all the records for pollution and other nuisances—and to achieve all this the United States has had to mobilize all the resources of its 'frontier-less empire'[14] in order to channel essential resources towards itself. And Europe is in the process of doing likewise.

If America is to be their exemplar, it is not for a 'relatively limited period', as Giscard d'Estaing puts it, that the countries of Europe will have to devote their whole energy to material growth. In fact they would be putting off indefinitely the moment when, in the French Minister of Finance's words, 'the cultural ascent of our society shall take the place of economic growth'. For will the point of 'saturation of material aspirations' ever be reached? America itself has not reached it: a well-to-do class seeks only to consume more and more, trading in its cars, refrigerators, television sets, etc. more and more often, while several tens of millions of citizens are still living in poverty.

Like the 'threshold of poverty', the 'material saturation point' tends to rise in proportion as industry floods the market with new products or old products that have been slightly modified or improved or merely better presented. The American government, at any rate, sees no other solution to the difficulties it faces than headlong advance.

Announcing his 'new economic policy' (non-convertibility of the dollar, 10 per cent import surcharge, wage and price freeze) on 15 August 1971, President Nixon declared: 'The time has come for American industry, which has produced more jobs at higher real wages than any other industrial system in history, to embark on a bold programme of new investment of production for peace.' This plan goes against every analysis showing that commercial production is overvalued in relation to other human requirements.

Galbraith, for example, writes in *The Affluent Society*:

> The scientist or engineer or advertising man who devotes himself to developing a new carburetor, cleanser or depilatory for which the public recognizes no need and will feel none until an advertising campaign arouses it, is one of the valued members of our society. A politician or a public servant who dreams up a new public service is a wastrel.[15]

And he adds the following example, which well illustrates the situation obtaining not only in the United States but to an increasing extent throughout the industrialized West:

> Automobile demand which is expensively synthesized will inevitably have a much larger claim on income than parks or public health or even roads where no such influence operates. The engines of mass communication ... assail the eyes and ears of the community on behalf of more beer but not of more schools.

The production-advertising-consumption mechanism, which continually increases the volume of more or less useful commodities launched on the market, creates distortions that Giscard d'Estaing admits must be 'corrected' when a certain 'level' has been reached. It is this mechanism that exploits an unqualified and ill-remunerated labour force at the same time as squandering vast resources. It is not really balanced out by a compensatory system that parallels commercial advertising's stimulus of material consumption by encouraging consumption of those non-marketable commodities that are no less necessary to man's well-being: health, education, culture, leisure, sport, parks, etc. 'Advertising' of these non-commercial commodities can only come from citizens who organize themselves in private associations, trade-unions, and political parties. The means at their disposal for revealing or awakening these needs have up to now been very limited—and have moreover very often been used to back demands that only facilitate the increased consumption of products launched by private industry.

The example of the 'expensively fabricated' demand for cars that Galbraith quotes is in no way hypothetical: it forms part of Richard Nixon's 'new economic policy'. Following his appeal for 'new productive investments', the President expounded the second point of his booster programme: abolition of the 7 per cent tax on cars. He commented as follows:

> This will mean a reduction in price of about $200 per car. I shall insist that the American auto industry pass this tax reduction on to the nearly 8 million customers who are buying automobiles this year. Lower prices will mean that more people will be able to afford new cars, and every additional 100,000 cars sold means 25,000 new jobs.

Looked at in this light, the West has got its values backwards: it is no longer working to produce what it needs to consume but is, absurdly, invited to consume more in order to be able to produce greater quantities. Furthermore President Nixon's decision deprives the state of tax resources that would mean it could increase community investments, which at the moment are sorely inadequate. Granted that numerous sectors of industry are over-equipped and consequently not operating at full capacity. Does that mean the state has to encourage society by means of tax reductions to consume more so that private industry, in whose investments citizens have no say, can work at full swing? A 7 per cent tax cut clearly benefits the automobile industry, but it means that the state loses part of its income and is prevented from increasing the 'non-productive' investments of which society nevertheless stands in greater need.

But are such investments in fact 'non-productive'? Quite apart from the fact that health, education, green spaces, music, painting, literature, travel, etc. are useful to man and society, they also provide work for doctors and nurses, teachers and lecturers, gardeners, musicians, painters, writers, publishers, printers, and librarians, hoteliers and restaurateurs, etc. who are equally capable of buying those 100,000 new cars and providing those 25,000 new jobs.

Economic growth is doubtless both necessary and inevitable. It does not automatically make it possible either to reduce social injustice or to satisfy those of man's aspirations that no management enters in its books or that, if it does take account of them, it rates second to his purely material aspirations, even when these have been artificially created by advertising.

Appearances notwithstanding, economic power and political power too often attract the weak: once they have acquired it, they rarely know what to do with it. This is why affluent societies are powerless to alleviate the deep social tensions that stem from economic and racial inequalities, anarchical urbanization, and all the vital needs that remain unfulfilled. It is also why powerful states are powerless to sustain a dialogue with their peoples, to give an authentic kind of democracy free rein, to promote a flowering of ancient or newly glimpsed freedoms, and to meet men's yearning for more justice, greater truthfulness in the state's dealings with voters, and increased fraternity among citizens.

The curse of work

Economic growth is based undoubtedly on technological progress but also, as the West has tended to forget, on human labour. The hopes aroused by automation continue to occupy men's minds and encourage them to dream of better things. Machines do do some of the dirty work but plenty of men and women still have to do jobs that are boring, exhausting, and often unpleasant and unhealthy as well.

In France in 1968 'semi-skilled' workers, who numbered 2,650,380, constituted 13·4 per cent of the voting and tax-paying population and 39·5 per cent of the worker population. These figures are very much higher, however, in certain sectors of industry whose products daily reach consumers who could not conceive of doing without them: 50 per cent in textiles, leather goods, and electrical construction.

At the same period manual workers, who numbered 1,489,140, represented 22·4 per cent of the worker population. But this figure can run as high as 33 per cent in the glass industry.

Altogether, unskilled workers doing the least interesting and worst-paid jobs made up 61·9 per cent of the worker population. Technological progress, far from reducing this category of worker, has augmented it: four years earlier it constituted only 51·1 per cent of the worker population. Many of these workers are women.

The inhuman character of high-speed production-line work is widely recognized; the nervous fatigue and boredom induced by endlessly repeated movements have been denounced as well as all the nuisances of noise, smell, heat, and dust that are present in some factories. Unions secure improvements of detail from time to time; managements are aware of the problems and do something about them, if only in the interests of productivity. But tens of millions of workers throughout the West are still doing jobs in which it is generally accepted that they can hardly blossom as human beings. Industrial societies appear to think that they are subject in this respect to the law of the machine and of industrial civilization, whereas what they are in fact subject to is primarily the double constraint of competition and the 'growth race' that dictates an inhuman pace of work and all the drawbacks of assembly-line production in order to keep prices competitive and hang on to or increase a given share of the market. The competition between capitalist and socialist countries means that no regime is exempt from this kind of slavery. In fact what is at issue here is not industrial civilization as such but one particular form of industrial civilization, based on the quest for maximum profits, on frantic competition or agreements to maintain the status quo, on the growth race, and on the practice of encouraging customers to replace everyday appliances at frequent intervals.

To take only one example, given the number of cars on the road, is it really necessary for the West to turn out some 18 million more annually? Slightly modified lines, the inclusion of some new 'extra', a fresh range of colours—this is all the advertising industry (employing vast budgets that would be better spent elsewhere) needs to persuade customers to trade in their cars every year or so. Has the system led to any significant progress? Over the last quarter of a century the motor industry has introduced fewer innovations than the aircraft industry.

Assembly-line labour with all its attendant degradations has developed solely as a result of the fact that cars are not designed to last and that the advertising industry has conditioned the public always to want the 'latest' model. The first Fords and 11CV Citroëns were as indestructible as the first nylon stockings. The system got off the rails when, to ensure its own survival, it started not only producing ephemeral goods but even encouraging people to replace them *before* they wear out. Certainly no law of 'progress' is at work here. This false logic has won acceptance only through the West's failure to work out and put into practice a different conception of production and growth.

If man wants the machine to serve him and not the other way round, the things he produces with it must recover 'the durability he took so much trouble to deprive them of, which will make it possible to combat pollution more effectively and steer more and more capital into community investments and into everything that will tend to right the ecological balance.'[16] If this happened customers would be prepared to pay more for something that would last longer, production could be cut down, assembly-line rhythms slowed, and wages kept at least constant.

A proposal to this effect was launched with a certain amount of ceremony in Britain in January 1972 with the backing of thirty-three internationally famous British scientists. They asserted that unchecked industrial and demographic expansion could only lead 'to the breakdown of society and of the life support systems on this planet—possibly by the end of this century and certainly within the lifetime of our children.'[17] They put forward concrete solutions in terms of penalizing firms that consumed large quantities of non-renewable raw materials and encouraging firms that spent more on labour. According to their plan, an industrial product designed for limited durability would be heavily taxed (up to 100 per cent of its value), whereas a product designed for prolonged use would be free of tax.

Certain firms using assembly-line labour have tried various experiments to make jobs more human, less stupefying, and better adapted to man's natural rhythms instead of subjecting him to the rhythm of the machine. All such experiments are doomed to only limited effectiveness as long as they take place within the context of the particular form of industrial civilization that has developed in the West.

What are the forces that might lead the West to conceive of more human forms? Various ideas are emerging in the United States and in Europe: 'advertising' for so-called 'non-productive' investments would counter-balance that put out by the firms binding society to the law of consumer production; research to establish—even if only approximately —the real value in monetary terms of such commodities as air, nature, calm, silence, culture, etc. would one day make it possible to balance the quantitative by the qualitative; taxation and eventually legal sanctions would place heavier penalties on firms that pollute nature and organize the squandering of raw materials by producing commodities of limited durability; trade-union and consumer action could secure a slowing-down of production, a humanization of assembly-line labour, better working conditions, and could force firms to change their concept of production, management, and advertising.

Such currents can only prevail in the context of an authentic democracy in which men conduct themselves first and foremost as citizens rather than as consumers and in which political power harnesses economic forces in the service of the general interest.

The success of such currents of opinion also presupposes a reversal of ideas that tradition has solidly established. The West accepts that, in order to stimulate human endeavour, the highest salaries must be paid to the men with the highest degree of skill and the best professional qualifications. Since, however, the least qualified jobs are showing a tendency to increase while the number of candidates for those jobs is decreasing, the law of supply and demand ought to operate in favour of an increase in the wages paid for them. Substantial wage-increases for manual and specialized workers would not of course make their work any more agreeable, but volume of production would diminish if commodities were designed to last and could consequently be sold at higher prices, and the working hours of unskilled labour could be reduced.

In fact the gap between supply and demand for unskilled jobs is plugged by immigrant labour in Europe and by black, Puerto Rican, and Mexican labour in the United States. A developed society supports at home or recruits from abroad a pool of workers that are referred to as 'fringe labour' not because they are not essential to the process of production—far from it—but because production as that society conceives of it keeps them 'on the fringe' of prosperity.

The form of industrial civilization that has developed in the West favours qualified personnel, managerial staff, university graduates, etc.: the time spent on their education and training is regarded as an investment from which they will eventually draw some profit. But in countries where education is free and where certain students (hospital interns, students at France's 'grandes écoles') receive a salary, it is not the student himself making the investment but society. Consequently it is not the resultant graduate but society that is entitled to the profit from that investment. The situation is quite different in the United States where a course of study at one of the major universities costs the student or his family a great deal of money: there it really is a private investment. Yet precisely in the United States the difference in income between an unskilled worker and a university graduate is very much less than it is in Europe. In 1969 average annual incomes stood at $25,000 for a surgeon or doctor (only $12,000 for staff doctors), $13,000 for an engineer, $9,415 for a teacher (primary and secondary),

$9,522 for a foreman, $7,693 for a skilled worker, and $6,248 for an unskilled worker.[18] By and large, European and American professional and managerial personnel enjoy a roughly comparable standard of living, whereas the European worker is very much less well paid than his American counterpart.

In Europe, the income spread is very much wider. The skills of managerial and professional personnel are rewarded primarily with more interesting jobs than manual or semi-skilled workers get to do. The universal aspiration of industrialized societies leads the former to look for jobs that draw upon their skills and allow these to blossom: the remuneration they expect is obviously a factor, but it is not the only one, and at certain levels it is even beginning to count for less and less. Boring, tiring, dirty, and unpleasant jobs on the other hand call for a twofold compensation: more money and shorter working hours.

An optimistic vision of the future made possible by technological innovations has prompted research into better 'timetables': a redistribution of working and leisure hours in the day, week, and year.[19] This would be a big step forward. But it would not touch the heart of the problem, which is to change the very nature of certain jobs in order to bring production techniques more into line with the desire for dignity of labour. The West has transformed a work mystique into a mystique of production and consequently of consumption. From working in order to live, live better, and let others live it has gone over to producing furiously in order to consume more and more of what is not even necessary to life, building wastage into the production process to enable it to produce in greater volume.

Not only raw materials, then, but also a great deal of human labour is squandered in the process of producing commodities whose durability is artificially limited so that they have to be replaced more often and the need for which is artificially engendered in order to stimulate growth. It is not only manual labour that is affected: America has made the discovery that the activities of numbers of bureaucrats are also completely unnecessary.

Department heads in the large companies ask for and are assigned additional assistants, coordinators, planners, and programmers who fill up new acres of office space every year. And everyone appears to keep busy: attending meetings and conferences, flying around the country, and writing and reading and amending memoranda. That a large proportion of these employees are not necessary was illustrated when, due to a long labour dispute, one large corporation took the unprecedented step of firing one-third of its white-collar force. The wholesale departure of these clerks and executives had no effect on the company's production and sales.[20]

The development of the white-collar class is regarded as the natural consequence of technological progress, which reduces the proportion of blue-collar workers to the total active population. But this shrinking of the manual-labour bracket in no way implies that the activities of all those bureaucrats are necessary: 'Parkinson's Law' and the 'Peter Principle' have poured scorn on this inflation of bureaucratic hierarchies that began in America and is now over-running Europe as well.

The emergence of the white-collar worker in the United States has followed a classic pattern. During the Second World War, writes Andrew Hacker:

> The American economy had learned some significant lessons in efficiency. The improvements in productivity that were achieved did not, as classical economic theory might have dictated, bring about a reduction in the prices of commodities and services. Even if it took fewer man-hours to manufacture a car or a bar of soap, the cost to the consumer remained the same. Thus postwar business found itself taking in a good deal of unanticipated money—far more than was needed for paying dividends to stockholders and too large an amount to be consumed even by replacing old machinery or building new facilities. To be sure, no business organization regarded this windfall income as superfluous cash. It was seen rather as money that could be liberally expended on hiring new employees.[21]

These new employees arrived on the labour market *en masse*. Most of them were demobilized soldiers to whom the government, anxious to avoid large-scale unemployment, offered the chance of completing a course of higher education. Thanks to the GI Bill university matriculations went up drastically and, Hacker adds, 'these Americans, upon graduation four years later, looked forward to entering a new stratum of society: they took for granted that positions befitting their status and education would be waiting for them. In this they were not disappointed. (. . .) Were all these new job-holders really needed? This is a question best not asked, for an objective answer is impossible.'

In fact these new jobs had a decisive effect on the economy by stimulating consumption. America did not worry too much about the productivity of certain categories of white-collar worker. The graduates all found jobs, started drawing high salaries, and stimulated the demand for commodities and services. But the bigger firms took a more pragmatic view of the situation when recession or rather 'stagflation' set in: many white-collar workers in some of the higher income brackets found themselves out of work.

Wearisome for a manual worker, less objectionable for a bureaucrat not burdened by any real responsibility, non-creative work is always a form of slavery that man accepts only insofar as he grasps its real usefulness. Various techniques have been attempted to *give the impression* that a particular job is useful. But this so-called 'job enrichment' is to the wage-earner what conditioning by advertising is to the consumer. Is he working to some purpose, in order to improve the world and the quality of human life, or merely in order to stimulate consumption as a means of accelerating growth for its own sake? This form of economic expansion has undoubtedly led to considerable progress in fields regarded as non-productive (and which are still very under-equipped in relation to the productive sector), but such progress had been achieved at the cost of a colossal waste of resources and of human energy expended in dehumanizing and sometimes perfectly useless jobs.

A society is certainly characterized by its productive capacity, but more so by the forms of labour that it offers its population. It stands condemned when, aside from professional activities that constitute creative work in the context of what must be called a 'vocation', it condemns large numbers of individuals to jobs whose superfluity makes them degrading. In return it offers them a rising level of consumption (but one which will never reach saturation point), the escape of leisure facilities made mediocre by the fact that cultural investments are way behind productive investments, holidays that represent their only chance (often spoilt by the inadequacy of tourist facilities) of living at a human pace, and, since all this is clearly not enough, the 'synthetic paradise' of drugs. But work itself, which takes up most of their time, remains for too many people a curse: so society has to invent constraints to make man accept it as such.

The people responsible for the apparatus of production, especially if they work very hard and like their work, will always find it hard to understand the occasional person who rejects the servitude they offer. Fifteen years ago a novel called *The Man in the Grey Flannel Suit* met with enormous success in the United States. It told the story of a man— with whom many executives identified—who refused promotion in a big company. The promotion was accompanied by a substantial increase in salary, but it also involved some serious drawbacks: reports to be read at home in the evenings, to the detriment of family life, week-ends spent in study sessions or meeting clients, etc. The hero of the novel did not want to *have* more money: he wanted to *be* more himself.

The chance of turning down promotion is of course only available in an affluent society, to the sensible individual who considers his material needs covered. The last decade and a half of expansion in the United States has multiplied the number of people who can identify with the hero of Sloan Wilson's novel. In fact their number has given rise to a kind of intellectual subversion rejecting traditional values, particularly those connected with work. 'For the people of my generation,' says Harvard professor Roger Revelle, 'work is an essential part of life. Young people today are wondering whether there is not something more important in life than work and material success.'[22] What would that something be? Revelle replies:

> Many young people have discovered the notion of disinterested service and are not so much concerned with earning money, which shocks both the older generation and the millions of Americans who lack the bare necessities and are consequently obsessed by material preoccupations. In their concern to be of service many young people want to become doctors, lawyers, engineers—but they embark on these careers out of a desire to be useful members of society rather than to make a pile.[23]

Professor George Wald, Nobel Prize-winning biologist, makes the same diagnosis:

> Among young people the happiest are the medical students. They do not want to be like the doctors of previous generations: they are conscious of preparing themselves to serve others. I would say the same of the students who want to become lawyers or engineers—or even of military-school cadets: they are giving new meaning to the words *career* and *profession*.[24]

Work in the service of the GNP, unlimited growth, ever bigger markets, and ever fatter profits for industry and commerce? Or work in the service of human society and of the satisfaction of needs that are not all material? Lewis Mumford: 'The older generation got its objectives wrong. Every professional group has now got to re-examine its objectives, its values, its concepts, and its methods.'[25]

But the men and women at the lowest levels of the apparatus of production have little chance of seeing their work as being a useful service to society. Theirs is the harsh law of quotas, costing, and competition. Businessmen and technocrats with eyes glued to their production charts and balance-sheets are blind to the fact that their concepts and their methods have robbed certain jobs of the only meaning that might have justified them. It is of this kind of job that the novelist and poet Claude Roy has written:

One day people will no doubt be amazed that man should have had to experience that lesser death: *work*. As we are amazed that even today seven out of ten babies die in early infancy. It will be beyond them perhaps to understand how the pleasure of doing and the need of surviving could have become so dissociated. Or that human beings should have been obliged to divide their lives into two unequal parts: servile activity, in which one died that one might live, and free activity, in which one spent in living the little time that was left over from the dreary time of work, which one spent dying. Work without either joy or sense will seem like a childhood ailment of mankind (. . .). I pretend to no superior wisdom in the field of economics in saying this. What bewilders me is that this commonsense truth still counts for so little in modern societies.[26]

The divorce between so many partial, meaningless, stupefying, and degrading jobs and the will to live is not the inevitable outcome of mechanization and technology but of the use these have been put to. The high priority given to the quest for economic power is the cause of injustices, inequalities, a de-humanization of labour, and growing social tensions. That priority has shaped societies in which dissatisfaction is on the increase, protest is tending to become more and more violent, and civilization is showing signs of disorder and crisis. Yet that priority was not decided as a result of any democratic process of consultation. It was imposed by the mechanisms that guide investment, and the political authority, the theoretical guardian of the general interest, was inadequate, unable, or unwilling to play its role. In Europe as in America 'the power to make investment decisions is concentrated in a few hands',[27] and it is this power that defines the balance or lack of it between the activities of production and commerce and activities of a non-commercial nature. It is this power that fashions society.

Now this power is autocratic or oligarchical in character: it belongs to the owners of capital alone. In the United States, for example, approximately one-third of the shares quoted on the stock exchange change hands every six months, and half are the property not of individuals but of companies. These giants dictate the course of investment, production, advertising campaigns, and consumption—an important aspect of everyday life. And as Andrew Hacker wrote: 'A corporated institution may profess to speak for its stockholders. But many of these are not human beings; and of those who are, a vote is cast for each share owned and not by the conventional democratic standard of one ballot per individual. Neither our constitutional law nor our political theory is able to account for the corporate presence in the arena of social power.'[28] Here too, in economic life, whose impact on people's everyday existence is even more considerable than that of an apparently powerful state, democratic society has accepted a kind of 'property qualification'. But it is an uneasy acceptance, and it will continue to be so as long as the basic democratic principle of one vote per citizen, whatever his wealth and education, is not applied to economic decisions as well.

One of the biggest factors of the 'crisis of civilization' that the West is passing through lies in this contradiction between the hopes of large numbers of educated and well-informed people who legitimately aspire after a democratic society, and the constraints to which they are subject as a result of the paralysis of democratic life in political institutions combined with the absence of democratic life in economic structures.

Aneurin Bevan summed up as follows a situation justifying criticism of the democratic West in the name of the very principles of democracy:

> Those who have been most successful for the time being, the money owners, will in the sum of their individual decisions determine the character of the economy of the future. (But) the kind of society which emerges from the sum of individual choices is not one which commends itself to the generality of men and women. It must be borne in mind that the successful were not choosing a type of society. They were only deciding what they thought could be bought and sold profitably.[29]

This observation, already more than a decade old, is what underlies every present-day form of protest: not only the radical and occasionally violent action of 'leftist' groups but also the criticisms, however timid, raised by trade unions and political parties, the representatives of the oppressed, be they nations or aliens, the victims of growth, those who have been sacrificed to urbanization pursued for profit alone, the homeless, public-transport passengers, families that have no green spaces for their children to play in, students and teachers, and all the citizens whom the paralysis of political institutions and the weight of economic structures prevent from fulfilling their role.

Certain societies declared themselves to be 'democratic' and democratic they were in relation to the systems they had overthrown, but they had only taken and are still only taking the first steps on the road to democracy. They declared and kept on declaring that the people was sovereign, with the result that the people eventually came to believe it. But the people is gradually discovering all the inroads that have been made into its sovereignty and all the restrictions that have been placed upon it: the people is in revolt. Without that revolt democracy would die of self-satisfaction. A civilization cannot afford not to live up to its declared principles—under pain of appearing 'repressive'. The citizens of democracy demand not only that it shall be more liberal than the feudal or dictatorial systems that it has replaced or that still exist in other parts of the world; they also expect it to live up to its ideals and fulfil the high hopes to which it has given birth. Otherwise it stands condemned, even if its fall involves society in a return to archaic forms of authoritarianism. 'Democratic growth' is even more vital than 'economic growth': any lack of balance between them can only result in dragging both to ruin.

One of the prime movers of the protest movement in America, Paul Goodman, compares major waves of protest to attempts on the part of prisoners to escape:

> To be free of the constraints of modern society, even without knowing where one is going, for too many people feel themselves totally useless. Not only the 420,000 inmates of our prisons but also 78 million under-20s, some 20 million over-65s, 30 million Negroes, Puerto Ricans, Indians, and Mexicans, to say nothing of the 1,874,000 hospitalized mental patients and the 1,500,000 others in psychiatric treatment. And of course the majority of women, even if they do not belong to the Women's Liberation Movement. Of course these figures overlap, and they cannot be added up. But altogether the majority of Americans feel themselves useless—useless and impotent, in the face of the complex machinery of society.[30]

'This society,' writes Erich Fromm in *The Revolution of Hope*, 'produces many useless things and, for the same reason, many useless people.'

Useless—even in the society that holds all the records for production. A quarter of a century ago every American, whatever his sphere of activity, was proud of his country's economic power, seeing in it a means of alleviating the difficulties or solving the problems of humanity. Since then that power has increased, and the problems, both internal and external, have become increasingly urgent: power is no panacea. Every American used to think that his work, by contributing to his own personal prosperity and that of his country, would lead to greater happiness, greater justice, and greater freedom. But the shadowy side of his own society disturbs the happiness he thought to find in the affluence he has worked so hard for. Either he retreats into a defensive attitude and tries desperately to ignore violence, riots, assassinations, racialism, corruption, drugs, and poverty. Or he faces up to them, still hopeful of achieving the promise of the 'American dream'. But the tasks before him are enormous: racial integration, social justice, urban reorganization, political renewal, keeping the peace, combating pollution, etc.

The very vastness of these tasks leads him to doubt a fundamental dogma. The Puritan ethic, which conquered Roman Catholic and Jewish circles as well, glorified work and saw material success as a sign of God's blessing. The material success is there, ubiquitous, dazzling, triumphant—with all it has left in its wake of dissatisfaction, frustration, injustice, and exploitation of the weak. So is it perhaps not a token of divine pleasure after all? The Puritan work ethic is undermined; the powerful myth it supported has shattered into a thousand pieces. Modern forms of labour have doubtless brought broad sectors of society to a level of material success that would have been unthinkable one or two generations ago, but they have not ushered in the joyful and harmonious society man continues to dream of.

This quest for happiness on earth questions not work itself but its methods and its purpose.

The methods: just as students are coming to demand courses more relevant to life, man is less and less prepared to accept work that in his eyes has no meaning. The harsh law of highly specialized labour is coming more and more under fire because it cramps the personality and prevents it from blossoming, even granted a high standard of living.

The purpose: modern forms of labour have brought society to an unprecedented level of economic power and many individuals to a degree of affluence they never dreamt possible. But this is not enough.

Human labour cannot be reduced to a mere means to power and affluence. Happiness has larger requirements: the quality of life is not measured in material possessions.

The 'leisure civilization' that has been made so much of is beginning to become a reality. It only makes more urgently apparent the need to bring about a genuine 'work civilization' at last, one in which human endeavour shall cease to be an absurd constraint and become once more something to free man from his real needs rather than enslave him to the artificial needs no consumer society can do without. Economically less powerful and less affluent than the United States, Western Europe has to realize that growth and expansion, far from being a satisfactory solution, can only serve to further dissociate what Claude Roy calls 'the pleasure of doing and the need of surviving'.

Robbery and the law

Human labour has been perverted through being harnessed to the service of objects not its own. A source of creativity and an instrument of survival, it has been sacrificed not to the demands of technology and the machine but to the thirst for profit and the will to power.

Taking a purely materialist view of society, does work at least represent a means of getting richer? *US News and World Report* asked a team of economists 'how to become a millionaire'.[31] Their analysis established first of all a number of facts: over the past twenty years the common stock listed by Standard and Poor had earned an average of 14·3 per cent per annum (in dividends and capital appreciation); but the figures were as high as 16·7 per for the shares of radio and television manufacturers, 18·4 per cent for electronics, and 22·7 per cent for office equipment. Furthermore twenty-five top-performing shares showed earnings at a rate of 15–36 per cent per year. These are not of course averages but the results obtained by the most successful companies.

According to the magazine, a young man of thirty who judiciously invests $10,000 at 15 per cent compound interest (and he could do even better with electronics or office-equipment shares) will find himself at the age of sixty-five in possession of $1,331,800 earned not by his own labour but by the efforts of those employed by the companies in which he is a small shareholder. This will admittedly not put him in the category of 'major fortunes' (in excess of $50 million), but nevertheless his (inherited) starting capital will have brought him in $550,000 in the space of thirty-five years. Between the ages of thirty and sixty-five he will also have worked for his living. At a salary of $20,000, which will put him in the privileged minority (8·3 per cent in 1969) earning more than $15,000 a year, his work will bring him in over the same period $700,000—i.e. slightly over half the amount he will have acquired without lifting a finger except to invest the initial $10,000.

The lesson is obvious: assuming that the acquisition of wealth is the aim and object of life, an American, even in a well-paid job, cannot get as rich by his own efforts as he can by the efforts of others, thanks to the shares he owns. It is a fundamental fact of capitalism.

But this example is exceptional. What usually happens is not that a person invests a lump sum at the outset and leaves it to accumulate: the 30,850,000 Americans who own shares are for the most part wage-earners who set aside a part of their savings each year to buy shares. So the *US News and World Report* economists took another hypothesis that was closer to reality: a thirty-year-old American begins investing $1,000 a year; at sixty-five he has $1,013,346, i.e. $200,000 less than the man who invested $10,000 at the outset, but still $300,000 more than he has been able to earn in thirty-five years' employment at the unusually high salary of $20,000 a year.

In both cases the mechanics are the same: even a modest capital investment, if wisely placed, will bring in very much more than even a well-paid job. There is nothing mysterious about this profit: it derives from the labour of the personnel of the companies in which the investor is a shareholder and from the customers of those companies who help contribute the profit a part of which is paid out to share-holders in the form of dividends.

Capitalism would not merit the name if it did not remunerate capital more than labour. But if the societies of the West are based on money, they are also based on the political equality of citizens, which ought in theory, in a democracy, to make up for and counter-balance economic inequalities. How does practice compare with the theory?

In the United States the poorest 20 per cent of families shared 5 per cent of the national income in 1947 and 5·6 per cent in 1969. At the top of the pyramid the richest 20 per cent of families shared 43 per cent of the national income in 1947 and 41 per cent in 1969. According to these figures there was in fact some evolution—slight, no doubt, but never-theless in the right direction—towards greater equality: at first glance the democratic principle appears to have been at work.

But the national income stood at $199,000 million in 1947 and at $769,500 million in 1969. Expressed in absolute figures rather than in percentages, what the poorer families actually received was $9,950 million in 1947 and $43,080 million in 1969, while the richer families received $85,570 million in 1947 and $314,490 million in 1969. In other words the sum total of the poorer families' incomes increased by $33,130 million while that of the richer families' incomes increased by $228,920 million—that is to say, seven times as much.[32] Far from narrowing, the gap between rich and poor had been growing wider all the time, thus violating the principle of democracy.

How inequality increased

	1947		1969		Change	
	$ thousand millions	%	$ thousand millions	%	$ thousand millions	%
National income	199		769·5		+570·5	
Rich....	85·57	43	314·49	41	+228·92	−2
Poor....	9·95	5	43·08	5·6	+33·13	+0·6
Gap	75·62	38	271·41	35·4	195·79	−1·4

The 20 per cent of families at the top of the income scale enjoy two advantages: they have the best-paid jobs, and they have the possibility of investing part of their savings in shares that will bring them in dividends far in excess of their salaries. In spite of all the welfare programmes and in spite of the 'war on poverty' the gap is widening—and is doing so by virtue of the system itself. This system, together with the anti-democratic inequalities it accentuates, can be corrected by means of a variety of measures that fall into two main categories:

External measures, tending to mitigate distortions without removing their cause: graduated income tax, social subsidies, medical aid for the needy, family allowances, scholarships, etc. As applied in varying degrees in the various countries of the West, these methods have prevented worse distortions but have failed to prevent the gap between rich and poor from widening.

Internal measures, attacking the root cause of the distortions: such measures must inevitably be directed at the degrees of remuneration accorded to capital and labour respectively.

The West remunerates capital at a higher rate than labour on the grounds that it is necessary to promote investment in order to stimulate growth. However, the democratic societies have got to decide whether they are going to continue to give priority to capital, thus aggravating the inequalities they claim to want to correct, or whether they are going to opt at last for putting the emphasis on human labour. Only this second aim (which presupposes if not a change of regime at least a switch of values) can possibly justify on the economic level democratic systems that will otherwise go on sinking further into lethargy for having given up their goals.

The chief cause of poverty throughout the West is connected neither with unemployment nor with illness but quite simply with low wages (see Chapter One), corresponding to jobs that require no qualifications and for which applicants are beoming fewer and fewer. The French employers' association 'Entreprise et Progrès' was careful to point out that in France between September 1967 and April 1971 manual labour had risen in the wage scale as compared with administrative work, while the situation of foremen had got relatively worse. It quoted the following figures. Incomes of manual and semi-skilled workers had progressed by 49 per cent, while those of lower- and middle-grade office workers had increased by 39 per cent and those of foremen by only 36 per cent.[33] Here again the percentage figures look all right but absolute figures belie this superficial impression. Let us take three cases, using round numbers for the purposes of demonstration:

A *worker* was earning Fr. 1,000 (per month) in 1967; by 1971 his income had risen by 49 per cent, i.e. an increase of Fr. 490; new income Fr. 1,490.

An *office-worker* was earning Fr. 1,500 in 1967; by 1971 his income had risen by 39 per cent, i.e. an increase of Fr. 585; new income Fr. 2,085.

A *foreman* was earning Fr. 2,000 in 1967; by 1971 his income had risen by 36 per cent, i.e. an increase of Fr. 720; new income Fr. 2,720.

Despite a higher percentage increase (on a lower initial figure) in the first case, the gap between the incomes of shop-floor worker and office-worker had increased from Fr. 500 to Fr. 595, that between the incomes of worker and foreman from Fr. 1,000 to Fr. 1,230.

	Monthly income Sept. 1967	Gap 1967	Increase over 4 years	Monthly income April 1971	Gap 1971
Manual worker	Fr. 1,000		49%= Fr. 490	Fr. 1,490	
Office-worker ..	Fr. 1,500	Fr. 500	39%= Fr. 585	Fr. 2,085	Fr. 595
Foreman	Fr. 2,000	Fr. 1,000	36%= Fr. 720	Fr. 2,720	Fr. 1,230

The 'Enterprise et Progrès' group not surprisingly concludes that it would be a good thing to continue this 'revaluation' of manual labour. As long as the percentage differences do not get too great the process will only serve to widen the income spread rather than tighten it up. The worker's and the foreman's wives do not do their shopping with percentages but, like everyone else, with francs. The technocrats of the private sector know as well as those of the public sector how misleading percentages can be. The real situation only emerges from absolute figures.

By the same token, the percentage gap between the average incomes of a white family and a black family in the United States is diminishing, whereas the real gap, in dollars and cents, is widening.[34]

The racial aspect of the problem is important, but from the strictly

Average income	1950	1969
White family.................	$5,290	$9,794
Black family	$2,848	$6,191
Difference in $	$2,442	$3,603
Black in relation to white	54%	63%

economic point of view it does not count: given the same degree of professional qualification, a white and a black worker have the same productivity. What counts is the type of job—and hence the salary level—to which the black has access: in this sphere anti-democratic inequalities are flagrant.

The social aspect is important too because of the living conditions his income imposes on the black worker's family. But the essential thing is still his job, to which the black man gives eight hours of his day: a more useful job than that done by some of the white-collar workers whose productivity is virtually nil; a job he has to hold onto, because if the firm is prepared to reward a graduate handsomely for performing ill-defined bureaucratic functions, it is not inclined to give anything away to blacks, who are the last to be hired and the first to be fired; a job that is often boring, mechanical, repetitive, tiring, and dirty, and that offers little scope for initiative; a job, above all, that is scorned by a society that reserves this kind of work for its sub-proletariat, and paid at a rate that is insulting in relation to the general prosperity.

Following the big explosion of May 1968 in France, workers got wage-increases of 14 per cent and managerial personnel of 11 per cent. A worker on Fr. 1,500 a month and a middle-management employee on Fr. 4,500 thus saw the gap between their incomes increase from Fr. 3,000 to Fr. 3,285 a month. The gap between the same worker and an upper-management employee getting Fr. 8,000 a month increased from Fr. 6,500 to Fr. 7,170.

In 1970 a United Nations study showed that inequality of remuneration between management and shop-floor personnel was greater in France than in the other industrialized countries of the West. Two years later the *Centre d'études des revenus et des coûts*, headed by Paul Bacon, former Minister of Labour, confirmed these findings in more detail, with a few nuances regarding factory managers and managing directors, whom Great Britain and Italy pay better than France, although France shows a bigger gap between these jobs and those of foreman or engineer than either the United States, West Germany, or Holland.[35]

It would be a good thing if all the countries of the West closed up their salary ranges in order substantially to revalue the jobs that figure at the bottom of all job rankings. The case of the United States is often cited as an example. But it is itself far from satisfactory, maintaining and even increasing too many inequalities to the detriment of the least attractive jobs.

This penalization by income of human labour and particularly of manual labour is further reinforced by taxation. According to Pierre Uri, labour, which receives only 60 per cent of total income, accounts for 75 per cent of taxable income.[36] Maurice Duverger rightly speaks of the 'structural injustice of the French (tax) system',[37] but despite the diversity of their systems the same stricture could be applied to the majority of the Western countries, with the exception of Sweden.

The principal injustice in France stems from sales tax, which accounts for 61 per cent of the state's fiscal revenue, whereas graduated income tax accounts for only 17·7 per cent. Sales tax is the most unjust because it hits the lowest-paid worker almost as hard as it hits the top income brackets. The last Ministry of Finance inquiry in France, writes Gilbert Mathieu, 'shows that the proportion of indirect taxation to expenditure varies very little from bottom to top of the income scale: 12·7 per cent for an annual income of approximately Fr. 2,500 per unit of consumption, 13·5 per cent for an income of double that, and 14·4 per cent for an income of four times that. In the meantime studies carried out by the *Commissariat général au Plan* had reached exactly the same conclusions: indirect taxation absorbed between 12·6 per cent and 15·1 per cent of expenditure on consumption according to socio-professional grouping and between 14 per cent and 17·5 per cent of the expenditure of wage-earners according as their incomes vary from x to $5x$.'[38]

Here by way of comparison is a table showing the origin of fiscal revenue in the United States, where sales tax is a very much smaller factor and where taxation consequently corresponds more closely to real income:

	1967		1970	
	$ million	%	$ million	%
Company income tax	34,918	23·5	35,037	17·9
Personal income tax	96,329	64·9	141,101	72·1
Property tax	3,014	2	3,680	1·9
Purchase tax	14,114	9·6	15,904	8·1
		100		100

As for income tax, though theoretically 'graduated', it too penalizes those wage-earners who have already been heavily hit by sales tax. In 1966 the National Assembly's finance committee estimated the tax-evasion possibilities of wage-earners at 8 per cent, those of tradesmen, artisans, and members of the professions at 147 per cent, and those of companies at 160 per cent. 'A more recent estimate puts tax evasion at 3 per cent for workers, 10 per cent for middle- and upper-management employees, and 47 per cent for the independent professions.'[39] The fact that out of 10·5 million taxpayers only 53,276, i.e. 0·3 per cent of the voting and taxpaying population, declared a taxable income of or above Fr. 100,000 in 1969 is clear indication of the extent of tax evasion in France. It is impossible, on this figure, to account for the number of secondary residences, yachts, and sports cars and the prosperity of the luxury trade.

In February 1972 the parliamentary Communist party in the French National Assembly tabled a proposed resolution on taxation that was worded as follows:

> The big fraud is at the level of the big companies, and it is perpetrated by a minority of powerful opportunists, by the parasites with which the capitalist system teems, by firms and categories of taxpayer that command the means of concealing a part of their resources and exploiting the impenetrable jungle of bourgeois taxation to the full (. . .). It is inadmissible that the mass of the people, who bear 80 per cent of the tax burden, should also, by virtue of an aberration of accounting, have to support the myriad privileges granted the holders of capital.

Is this virulent accusation justified by the facts? A famous book has exposed the methods by which, in France, the rich can shield a large part of their incomes from taxation.[40] If techniques vary from country to country, the result is the same everywhere. 'Taxation certainly does not make much difference to social inequalities' in France, writes Gilbert Mathieu.[41] And it is the same in the United States, despite what many Europeans think: 'The distribution of income after taxes is not very different from what it was before taxes', an American study shows.[42]

The volume of tax revenue in relation to GNP is smaller in the United States than it is in certain European countries. In France, Sweden, West Germany, Austria, Norway, Holland, and Great Britain tax revenue amounts to between 33 and 41 per cent of GNP;

in the United States, Canada, Belgium, Italy, and Denmark it only represents between 26 and 30 per cent. Then come countries such as Algeria, Uruguay, Brazil, and Iraq with figures lower than 24 per cent.

Furthermore the share of tax revenue accounted for by corporate income tax went down from 23·5 to 17·9 per cent in the United States between 1967 and 1970, whereas the share accounted for by personal income tax went up from 64·9 to 72·1 per cent. A government expert has shown that incomes other than salaries are 'under-assessed' for taxation by 33 per cent[43]—so the situation in the United States is about the same as it is in France. An Internal Revenue Service investigation carried out at the request of the Senate Finance Committee showed for example that half of the 3,000 doctors investigated had been concealing 'a substantial amount of their income' and that in some cases 'the omission exceeded $100,000'.[44]

The volume of tax revenue could thus be bigger in relation to the GNP, which would make possible an indispensable increase in community investments, benefiting the community as a whole and the lower income brackets in particular. The weight of taxation could also be more equitably distributed in order to relieve those with smaller incomes: their labour would thus be the better rewarded and inequalities reduced. Reform of this kind would presuppose more stringent restrictions on tax-evasion and fraud; it would also presuppose a fresh distribution of taxation between corporate and personal incomes.

Not only is the proportion of tax on corporate incomes to total tax revenue tending to diminish: such incomes also enjoy exorbitant privileges by virtue of which capital is better remunerated than human labour.

Senator William Proxmire had the *Congressional Record* publish a list of the major oil companies with their profits and taxes.[45] The picture that emerged, drawn from the journal *Oil Week*, constituted what the Senator called 'a disgrace'. For example a modest Standard Oil of New Jersey employee with an annual income of $6,000 paid 16 per cent tax while the company itself, with an income of $2,400 million in 1970, paid only 10·8 per cent. Standard Oil of Ohio, with an income of only $66 million, paid no tax at all; it even got a 'tax credit' of 10·4 per cent which it could deduct from subsequent income. Texaco paid 6·4 per cent tax on an income of $1,100 million, Standard Oil of California 5 per cent, Atlantic 4·1 per cent, and Gulf 1·2 per cent. These figures must be compared with the normal rate for companies in other sectors

7

of industry—46 per cent. Altogether the American oil companies paid
7·3 per cent tax on $8,000 million income in 1969, and 8·7 per cent on
$8,800 million income in 1970.

In 1970 the lowest wage-earner, with a taxable income of under
$2,000, paid between 14 and 18 per cent tax, i.e. a rate twice that of the
oil industry. The middle bracket, with taxable incomes of between
$18,000 and $20,000, was as hard hit (46 per cent) as the rest of industry,
where gross profits reached the figure of $82,100 million in 1970. Of
this sum the companies concerned paid $37,800 million in taxes and
$25,200 million in dividends, leaving them an undistributed profit of
$19,100 million. With $53,500 million free of tax, they thus had a cool
$72,600 million at their disposal.[46] Nearly seven million private
persons are more heavily taxed than they are.

Tax evasion on the part of oil companies is made perfectly legal by
virtue of the 'depletion allowance' on deposits inside the United States.
Democrats have been denouncing this scandal for forty years; the
Republicans, who support it, were unable to prevent a reduction of the
rate of allowance from 27·5 to 22 per cent in 1969. President Truman
denounced the 'inequitable' character of the allowance in his 1950 fiscal
message. John Kennedy too wanted to abolish it: it was in the oilmen's
fief that he was assassinated. Richard Nixon, however, travelled Texas
in his 1968 election campaign saying: 'I continue to believe that
America's security requires the maintenance of the current oil depletion
allowance.' In Dallas itself, speaking to the Texas Mid-Continent Oil &
Gas Association on 12 October 1971, John Connally, former Democratic governor of Texas and, at that time, Richard Nixon's Secretary
of the Treasury, declared:

> Before the Congressional committees of the Congress, without fear
> whatsoever or without embarrassment or without shame, I say that
> I think profits are too low in this country. This is why I can sit there
> and say to a Congressman or a Senator that 'No, I don't think we
> ought to impose any more taxes on the oil and gas industry' . . . I
> thought the Congress had gone too far in reducing individual income
> taxes $36·4 billion over the last five years while raising corporate
> taxes $3·2 billion. I thought it was basically unfair.

Connally's figures are somewhat inaccurate. Between 1965 and 1970
income tax on private individuals did not go down by $36,400 million:
it went up by $51,620 million (from $48,792 million to $90,412
million). Nor did corporate taxes go up by $3,200 million but by

$7,368 million (from $25,461 million to $32,869 million). In other words individual income tax went up from 41·8 per cent of total tax revenue to 46·7 per cent while tax on companies went down from 21·8 per cent of total tax revenue to 16·9 per cent.[47]

So the Texan oilmen knew which party's money box to put their contributions in—as do other companies. Human labour is taxed more and more heavily, while the yield on corporate tax goes down, though company profits increase. Former Treasury Secretary Joe Barr, quitting his job in 1969, foresaw a 'revolt' of taxpayers indignant at 'the high-income recipients who pay little or no federal income tax'. This anti-democratic privilege is the preserve of the big companies, the individuals to whom those companies pay high salaries, and those who draw a large part of their income not from their own labour but from dividends.

Companies have the legal possibility of setting up 'domestic international sales corporations' (DISC), through the medium of which they can do their purchasing in one of the states of the union that has no sales taxes or sell abroad without paying tax as long as the profits are not written up to the mother company. The system of subsidiaries, intermediary companies, etc. makes it possible for companies through out the West to shield a part of their profits from taxation. The non-salaried professions can also conceal part of their income, as can certain upper-management personnel whose real income includes, apart from their salary, certain fringe benefits entered under the company's general expenses. Only the lower income brackets are taxed on the whole of their income—the people who live by nothing but their own labour. And labour in what kind of jobs? Society as a whole tends to forget just how boring, unattractive, and unhealthy such people's jobs can be. The cult of money has stifled respect for human labour.

The labour of the lower income brackets is the most heavily taxed by virtue particularly of the 'family quota', which favours the higher incomes. There is nothing more anti-democratic than a system that amounts to considering that a child of poor parents costs less than a child of comfortably off or wealthy parents. If a 'democratic' society finds it normal to put a ceiling on the portion of income subject to social deductions, it ought at least to put a ceiling on the portion on which the family quota is allowed. If it is not to amount to an anti-birth policy, this will presuppose a scale of salaries with a coefficient of tax-relief for each level, varying with the number of children in the family and decreasing as incomes increase. Every fiscal structure that does not tend to iron out inequalities in real income after tax goes against the principles of democracy.

At the end of an analysis of taxation in the United States one American observer arrived at this conclusion:

> The unpalatable fact is that the gap between rich and poor in the US isn't lessening; that our disgraceful tax structure is probably less progressive, less fair than a decade ago; and that the boiling demand for increased social services (more police, more health care, better environment) is running short of funds.[48]

Compare this comment by a French observer on taxation in France:

> The state must not only protect the weak as a matter of priority but also correct the natural momentum that, if nothing is done about it, tends always towards an accumulation of wealth in the same hands.[49]

But the momentum by virtue of which the rich grow richer on the labour of the poor is not as 'natural' as some would have us believe. It is deliberately organized by powerful interests and their political representatives, whether through sordid motives or through conviction. Sordid motives? Control and supervision of the financial side of election campaigns would make it possible to eliminate the worst abuses, though without doing away altogether with trafficking in influence and corruption. Through conviction? But this is so often only a deceptive façade: we must encourage saving in order to stimulate investment. Sticking up for the Texas oilmen on the occasion already referred to, John Connally said straight out: 'What we have to concern ourselves with is who provides the jobs'—meaning in effect that the rich must be granted tax privileges as if their first concern were not making a profit but making investments in such a way as to create jobs. Their real leverage rests in the fact that, if need be, they do not hesitate to make a profit by speculating against the national currency. A state that is less democratic than it appears then offers them the Pinay loan, which makes it possible to escape probate duty, grants them a tax amnesty so that they can repatriate their capital, invents fiscal credit, lowers the bank rate, etc.

But these privileges, based on ruthless economic violence, have their respectable side: the rich provide the poor with employment. The privileges of the feudal lord had another side too: in the event of war the peasants could take refuge within the castle wall . . .

Only abolition of the privileges of capital will allow human labour to rediscover its purpose, its deep meaning, and its dignity in terms of the conditions in which it takes place, the way in which it is remunerated, and the style of life it makes possible.

From constraint to rebellion

The first concern of the privileged is to defend their privileges—firstly by denying their very existence or by belittling them; secondly by justifying them in terms of the weight of responsibility that accompanies them, the training and skill that are indispensable to their exercise, and their usefulness to society; and finally by protecting them with the economic power those privileges themselves confer, with the political influence that stems from that power, and by means of categorically rejecting all demands or granting concessions to certain groups in order to divide and weaken the enemy front.

The struggle between the forces of 'resistance' and the forces of 'movement' is an unequal one: on the one side the power of money, the larger wheels of government, the greater part of the mass communications media, all the resources of advertising, the machinery for the maintenance of order, and the support of that section of the population that sees or thinks it sees its personal advantage under the wing of power, the servants and vassals of lords often unknown to the public at large; on the other side the strength of numbers, the men and women who have nothing but their labour to live by and withholding that labour to protest by, nothing but their ballot to express the aspirations left unsatisfied by a semi-paralysed democratic regime and the street demonstration to back their basic claims—but it is a strength more theoretical than real for this mass is weakened by the numbers of the indifferent and the resigned, by political and ideological divisions, and by vested interests.

Yet the powerful know that this mass is difficult to handle, contain, and control. They offer it all the mirages of affluence and increasing consumption, but at the same time they harry the political opposition, the trade-unions, and all the voices of protest. Whether in the United States or in Italy, in France or in Germany, the forces of resistance to change see in discontent and agitation not a vital reaction against a situation they have themselves created but proof of a 'conspiracy'. On both sides of the Atlantic prison mutinies are denounced as the outcome of subversive manoeuvres. Americans who campaign for peace, like the Berrigan brothers, are accused of having plotted to kidnap Henry

Kissinger and blow up the Pentagon. The French authorities saw the influence of Peking behind the popular agitation of May 1968, and the Minister of the Interior accused Cuba of having inveigled young Parisians into waging urban guerilla warfare. Italy has its assassinations, attempted murders, and bomb attacks to create the right atmosphere. In West Germany Alfred Grosser sees 'a kind of defensive reflex common to the two big parties and directed against an enemy within, whose offensive has got to be stopped'. He adds that 'the decision taken by the states' Ministries of the Interior to fight in all spheres of public life, including education, against the presence of Communists is evidence of a new state of mind that some see as a resurgence of an attitude that was widespread in the West in the early fifties.'[50] Throughout the West every rebel is immediately presumed to be either a potential criminal or a subversive agent in the pay of a foreign power.

The rebels who are prepared to take action are only a minority. The vast mass, wholly taken up with the need to meet the demands of everyday existence, is aware of the injustices it suffers but, because it understands little of the complexities of society, sometimes underestimates the extent of those injustices and is not always up to analysing the causes and mechanisms that lie behind them. But it only needs some mysterious switch to be thrown and that mass is out in the streets, shoulder to shoulder with the rebels.

Why rebellion? Because trade-union action, for all its successes, cannot smash the system that secretes the inequalities the unions spend all their time fighting; because political action is unable to re-establish greater equity by means of compensating interventions. In the United States the most violent race riots broke out at a time when blacks had been granted their full legal rights but those rights were still restricted in practice. In Europe agitation has developed side by side with rising consumption, the spread of education, and increasing leisure time and holidays. The indignation behind it stems from the gulf between the hopes aroused and the reality of everyday existence, between the possibilities of technology and the human mind and the relative backwardness of society.

But that gap is not enough in itself to make such rebellion and indignation assume violent form. The temptation to violence, the last resort, arises out of a powerlessness to bring peaceful, democratic structures adequately to bear. All violence is deplorable and to be condemned because it constitutes an admission of paralysis in the institutions designed to ensure progress by peaceful means. But what do we mean by violence? Only the kind that comes out in assassinations, physical brutalities, bomb attacks, sabotage, and kidnappings? Or do we also mean the violence that uses legal means to maintain injustice, condemns men to a 'worsening of working conditions'[51] and, by virtue of the scale of remunerations and the structure of taxation, deprives them of a large part of the fruit of their efforts.

The violence of protesters, writes Jacques Fauvet, 'is often only the bitter fruit of another kind of moral or even physical violence, more underhand but just as serious, perpetrated against individuals or social or ethnic minorities, a violence that is too often wrapped in the cloak of legality or national sovereignty.'[52] It was Georges Bernanos who wrote: 'There are more human lives inside a millionaire's safes than even a monarch rules, but the millionaire's power is like that of idols, having neither ears nor eyes. He can kill just like that, without even knowing he is doing so. Perhaps this is the privilege of devils too.'[53]

This legal violence is first of all economic. By virtue of the organization of production, conditions of work, the hierarchy of wages, and taxation it condemns human beings to accept work that future generations will judge as unacceptable as child labour in the nineteenth-century mines. Manual and semi-skilled workers, some ten million foreign workers in Europe, some thirty million blacks, Puerto Ricans, and Mexicans in the United States—these are the principal victims of a society that would wish perhaps to stand in the service of man but in fact directs its energies towards beating its own production, consumption, export, and profit records.

This thirst for power has another class of victim whose labour it exploits—women. In the United States 43 per cent of adult women (31·5 million) have a job. Most of them are mothers. Congress did pass a programme for setting up day-nurseries but the project foundered on the presidential veto in December 1971. Some 600,000 children whose mothers go out to work are left to their own devices during the day. Avoiding this situation means that other women cannot work. Yet the hierarchy of qualifications and wages is such that only when both parents work is it possible for lower income bracket families to stay above the threshold of poverty.[54]

The 31 million American women who go out to work are a source of considerable profit to their employers. The table overleaf shows some examples of comparative average incomes (in dollars).[55]

According to the French Ministry of Labour the difference between wages per hour for men and women stood at 10·1 per cent in 1966, at

	Men	Women
Technicians	10,516	5,244
Teachers	9,415	5,812
Office staff	6,804	3,603
Sales staff	6,829	1,241
Workers	6,536	3,287
Waiters/Waitresses	3,684	1,497

7·3 per cent in 1968, and at 7 per cent in 1972. In fact the gap between the two, with overtime and bonuses included, is very much greater, although it has diminished slightly since the Grenelle agreements of May 1968: it has been reduced from 29 to 25 per cent for middle-management staff, from 24 to 23 per cent for office staff, and from 22 to 20 per cent for workers.[56]

The difficulties facing working women are well known and the problems have been sufficiently studied for a solution to be overdue. In no country in the West do men and women get the same rate for the same job. The organization of part-time work is everywhere inadequate despite the fact that in France there are 1,180,000 salaried women working less than a 39-hour week and 300,000 working between 15 and 34 hours. Women who work at home (as dressmakers, for example) are open to even more systematic exploitation in terms of both working hours and pay.

If so many workers—men and women, nationals and aliens—are exploited, can we still talk of a mere 'blot' on a system that has at least proved its efficiency and will one day, with improved efficiency, succeed in correcting its own mistakes? The rate of inflation and the high numbers of unemployed on both sides of the Atlantic would seem to put this in doubt. The monetary crisis has brought to light an even deeper fault. But even functional efficiency itself is coming to seem more and more a myth.

Under the title 'America the Inefficient', *Time* magazine drew up a pretty depressing balance-sheet of American efficiency—'around the world a by-word; at home, close to being a religion.'[57]

The magazine examined in considerable detail the difficulties every American encounters in trying to get his car, washing-machine, or television set repaired. It talked about congestion on the roads, at airports, and on telephone wires; the great blackout that paralysed the north-eastern United States in 1965, jamming lifts in skyscrapers and putting the subway and the air-conditioners out of action; government inefficiency with regard to 'urban renewal', subsidies to agriculture, and the F-111 project; the deficits run up by the railways and the airline companies; the time when the first two storeys of 'Big John', the 100-storey skyscraper project in Chicago, started sinking into the ground; big-store delivery times; postal delays, etc.

Time commented:

> For the sake of efficiency, US citizens have long been willing to give up many of the amenities of life that are common in less complex and slower-paced societies (. . .). Until recently, most felt satisfied with the bargain. But now that the US industrial and social system (. . .) no longer seems to be supplying the compensating efficiency, many Americans feel they have been swindled in the trade-off.

The verdict goes for industrial production, where American prices are becoming less and less competitive and the chief innovations have come from small firms. It also goes for the political authorities and social organization, particularly as regards race relations. And at a time when Americans are themselves beginning to question it, Europe is still dreaming of achieving the efficiency of the United States, pushing forward with the process of concentrating industry in vast and supposedly powerful agglomerations. But as *Time* rightly recalls: 'The giant company tends to become a political structure in which executives invest considerable time campaigning for higher office and protecting their flanks by rigidly following fixed procedures (. . .). These corporate rules are designed to promote efficiency but actually work against innovation.'

The pleasure a man may find in his work—or at least the concern to keep unpleasantness to a minimum—has gone by the board in this quest for a dubious efficiency. The inefficiency of modern society is above all apparent in its powerlessness to give a meaning to human activity in work and social life. A man can accept the harshest constraints when he can see their usefulness for himself or for those around him. Once he comes to doubt that usefulness, he rebels. Whereupon the privileged and the upholders of the status quo raise the banner of 'law and order': they have right and power on their side; they have the police and the courts, and they have the approval of all 'right-thinking'

7*

(for which read: unthinking) people. The constraints become harsher, and 'legal' violence makes the violence of the rebellion look pitiful.

'A guy has to be a political idiot to say all power comes out of the barrel of a gun when the other side has the guns,' says Saul Alinsky, one of the leading figures in the theory and practice of protest in the United States.[58] But would it be any less 'foolish' to drive citizens to violent rebellion? And if the violence of the system's victims is without hope, has the system itself any greater hope of surviving?

To combat this rebellion, whether violent or not, the guardians of order can employ a judicious combination of legal violence against their most determined opponents and concessions to certain interest groups in order to neutralize them or win their active sympathy. But there is one weapon they will never be able to use: the one that consists in thinking that social justice and a betterment of the quality of life will be effects of another cause than unlimited growth. Yet only when this dogma is abandoned will it be possible to change in depth the methods of production and conditions of work in the sectors where these are least human. But such a reversal of the trend presupposes an overthrow of received ideas and of the habits of consumption. Above all it presupposes the abolition of the economic privileges enjoyed by those who draw the greater part of their income either from their capital or from some independent activity and are thereby favoured by taxation: for the guardians of order it would be tantamount to suicide. Finally such a reversal would presuppose the abolition of the privileges of all who, without being holders of capital, draw high salaries, even if they are heavily taxed: the middle- and upper-management executives who are indispensable to the functioning of the system and who by education, standard of living, life-style, and place of residence live apart from the victims of the system, the poor and the oppressed. But the guardians of order can hardly agree to this renunciation, for it would isolate them by turning over to the enemy the things they cannot do without. Occasionally a *local* conflict evinces a short-lived solidarity between white-collar employees and the most exploited workers. Such solidarity however, is neither general nor lasting.

If the designated defenders of the order in the West are so powerless to instigate any real change, are their critics any better placed? They can open a few breaches in the defences, particularly by nationalizing certain sectors of the economy and radically altering the tax structure. But such reforms, however important, are not going to make much difference to the daily round of the tens of millions of manual and semi-skilled workers, underpaid women, foreign workers, and members of ethnic minorities. To offer these groups more human working conditions means cutting production rhythms and substantially increasing wages. Any change—whether by way of nationalization, worker-management, taxation, or whatever—that fails to achieve this goal will merely be perpetuating the underlying injustice and, by the same token, the crisis of civilization, possibly camouflaged behind fresh constraints. But an upheaval on this sort of scale presupposes a recasting of the price structure and some considerable closing up of the income range—all incomes, not just dividends, not just professional fees, but the highest salaries as well. There seem to be plenty of executives in the groups and political formations challenging the way the industrialized West is organized. They talk readily in terms of nationalizing certain sectors of the capitalist economy, introducing worker-management, and so on, while keeping quiet about their own privileges.

If the West is indeed undergoing not only a crisis of adjustment but a crisis of civilization, mere structural modifications are not going to settle anything for any length of time. If the West is in search of a new way of life, a new meaning in life, its only way out of the crisis will be by sacrificing all privileges both great and small and aiming at more equality, more justice—and an authentic democracy whose primary aim on the economic level will be a humanization of labour, with production designed not to secure a maximum of profit and power, but to give man the means of satisfying needs that are not exclusively of an economic order.

References

1 Quoted in the *New Yorker*, 19 December 1970.
2 Jean-Denis Bredin, professor of law; statement to the 'Comité d'études pour un nouveau contrat social'.
3 The *New Yorker*, 19 December 1970.
4 The *New Republic*, 1–8 January 1972.
5 Daniel Bell, *The End of Ideology*, The Free Press of Glencoe, Illinois, 1960.
6 Cf. Claude Julien, *Inquiète Amérique*, article V, 'Les colonnes du temple', in *Le Monde*, 2 February 1971.
7 Alfred Grosser, 'Le malaise allemand et l'opposition', in *Le Monde*, 14 March 1972.
8 François Perroux, *Economie et Société*, Presses universitaires françaises, 1960.
9 Pierre Drouin, 'La peur de l'an 2000', in *Le Monde*, 29 March 1972.

[10] Paul Fabra, 'Stopper la croissance?', in *Le Monde*, 6 April 1972.

[11] Dennis Meadows and an MIT team, *The Limits to Growth*, Universe Books, New York, 1972.

[12] Cf. Claude Julien, 'L'explosion des mythes', in *Le Monde*, 30 January 1971.

[13] Valéry Giscard d'Estaing, in *Preuves*, April 1972.

[14] Claude Julien, *l'Empire américain*, Grasset, Paris, 1968.

[15] John K. Galbraith, *The Affluent Society*, Hamish Hamilton, 1958.

[16] Pierre Drouin, 'La peur de l'an 2000', *op. cit.*

[17] 'Blueprint for Survival', in *The Ecologist*, January 1972; among the signatories were Sir Julian Huxley, C. H. Waddington, and Peter Scott.

[18] *Statistical Abstract of the United States*, 1971, p. 229.

[19] Jacques de Chalendar, *l'Amenagement du temps*, Desclée de Brouwer, Paris, 1971.

[20] Andrew Hacker, *The End of the American Era*, Atheneum, New York, 1970, p. 50.

[21] Andrew Hacker, *op. cit.*, p. 16.

[22] Cf. Claude Julien, 'l'Explosion des mythes', *op. cit.*

[23] Cf. Claude Julien, 'La renaissance du rêve', in *Le Monde*, 29 January 1971.

[24] *Idem.*

[25] Cf. Claude Julien, 'l'Explosion des mythes', *op. cit.*

[26] Claude Roy, *Nous: essai d'autobiographie*, Gallimard, Paris, 1972, pp. 159–60.

[27] Andrew Hacker, *op. cit.*, p. 52.

[28] *Idem.*, p. 43.

[29] Aneurin Bevan, *In Place of Fear*, MacGibbon and Kee, 1961, pp. 58–9.

[30] Cf. Claude Julien, 'Quartiers d'ombre', in *Le Monde*, 31 January–1 February 1971.

[31] *US News and World Report*, 11 November 1968.

[32] *Statistical Abstract of the United States*, 1971, pp. 309, 317.

[33] Cf. *Le Monde*, 29 December 1971.

[34] *Statistical Abstract of the United States*, *op. cit.*, p. 316.

[35] Cf. Gilbert Mathieu in *Le Monde*, 10 March 1972.

[36] Pierre Uri, 'L'impot et l'épargne', in *Le Monde*, 16 February 1972.

[37] Maurice Duverger, 'Petits et grands scandales', in *Le Monde*, 9 February 1972.

[38] Gilbert Mathieu, in *Le Monde*, 7 March 1972.

[39] Maurice Duverger, *op. cit.*

[40] Jean Cosson, *Les industriels de la fraude fiscale*, du Seuil, Paris, 1971.

[41] *Le Monde*, 7 March 1972.

[42] Melville J. Ulmer, in the *New Republic*, 7 November 1970.

[43] Glenn D. Morrow, in the *National Tax Journal*, September 1963.

[44] September 1970.

[45] *Congressional Record*, 27 October 1971.

[46] *Statistical Abstract of the United States*, 1971, pp. 472 and 379.

[47] *Idem.*, pp. 373–4.

48 The *New Republic*, 11 December 1971.

49 Pierre Drouin, in *Le Monde*, 11 February 1972.

50 Alfred Grosser, *op. cit.*

51 Christian Poncelet, UDR *député* for the Vosges, in *Le Monde*, 7 March 1972.

52 Jacques Fauvet, 'Ordre et contradiction', in *Le Monde*, 14 March 1972.

53 Georges Bernanos, *Journal d'un curé de campagne*.

54 Naturally women, like all exploited groups, are under-represented politically: none in the Supreme Court, 12 out of 434 in the House of Representatives, 1 out of 100 in the Senate, 1·3 per cent of the mayors of towns of more than 25,000 inhabitants.

55 *Statistical Abstract of the United States*, 1971, p. 229.

56 See Nicole Bernheim, in *Le Monde*, 12–13 March 1972.

57 *Time*, 23 March 1970.

58 See Claude Julien, 'Les colonnes du temple', *op. cit.*

CHAPTER FIVE

Violence and Freedom

- Priority to production
- Force in the service of law
- Violence in the service of the state
- Threatened freedoms
- Racialism and democracy
- Religion and democracy

Every customer who deposits $1,800 at the International Bank of Dallas for two and a half years receives a present of a revolver, complete with ammunition.[1] Dallas, of course, is in Texas. In other American cities more pacifically inclined banks reward a similar deposit with a mere toaster or radio set. But all over the United States several tens of thousands of sets of 'A Game for All Families' were sold for Christmas. In this new version of 'Monopoly' players compete for possession not only of houses, hotels, and stations but also of the city's various rackets: gambling, contraband, extortionate money-lending, housebreaking gangs, specialists in armed assault, etc.[2] A player can be wounded, but he never goes to prison—which is bringing fiction pretty close to reality. The *Wall Street Journal* and the *New York Times* refused to carry advertisements extolling the new game's 'educational' properties. Despite this boycott it appears to have enjoyed even greater success and made its promoters even more money than the miniature guillotine a toy-manufacturer recently launched in France.

Anger and madness can drive people to murder but if the 'crime of passion' still exists it is becoming more and more rare in a civilization that regards passion as a sign of psychological maladjustment or poor education. Violence and money, on the other hand, are progressing side by side, and often in step: between 1960 and 1969 the number of firearms sold on the American market annually increased from 2,163,000 to 6,180,000,[3] meaning big profits for manufacturers and dealers. Altogether some 45 million Americans are armed, and between them they possess between 100 and 200 million firearms. According to General Kane, the former leader of the local battalion of the National Guard, the inhabitants of Chicago can lay their hands on more individual light armaments than the entire regular army of the United States.

In June 1968 Lyndon Johnson, in order to limit what he referred to as a 'delirious traffic in arms', suggested compulsory declaration of all firearms held by private citizens. A public-opinion poll conducted in April of the same year had shown that 71 per cent of Americans were in favour of this kind of control. Yet the project was never adopted, and its defeat is attributed essentially to the National Rifle Association's efforts. When a pressure group with the powerful backing of manufacturers, dealers, and their customers can block a government proposal that is supported by almost three-quarters of the population, there are grounds for believing that democracy has ceased to function. This particular pressure group is neither more nor less contemptible than all bodies that, whatever their sphere of activity, force the majority to bow to the will of a minority. The case of the NRA merely happens to be more shocking because it leads directly to bloodshed. But other lobbies, as we shall see, are even more murderous in their effects, and they all, in the last analysis, strike at the very principle of democracy. The problem is an old one: it is more than thirty years since Attorney-General H. Cummings said: 'Show me the man who doesn't want his gun registered, and I will show you a man who shouldn't have a gun.'

It is not with impunity that profits are made out of the propagation of instruments of violence: the number of persons murdered increased from 8,464 in 1960 to 14,480 in 1969—65·4 per cent of them with firearms. Crime in all its forms cost the United States $20,980 million in 1965,[4] that is to say, more than car sales brought in for the same year. When it comes to doing away with human lives, however, cars have a coefficient of efficiency twice that of firearms: there are twice as many of them and they cause four times as many deaths.

Like the United States, Europe continues to increase the number of cars on the road. Unlike the United States, it regulates and controls the sale and carriage of firearms. A European runs less risk than an American of getting murdered: he runs just as great a risk of getting killed on the road, with 16,200 road deaths in France in 1971 and four times that number in the United States, with four times the population. Public opinion is slightly roused but not much, and in any case quickly reassures itself with talk of 'accidents', i.e. events that are both fortuitous and fated. On the other hand the public is quick to let conservative elements mobilize it under the banner of 'law and order' against all instigators of disorder—among whom it fails to include commercial and industrial 'dealers in violence'. Thirty-seven policemen were murdered in the United States in 1961, eighty-six in 1969, and police-force budgets more than doubled over the same period from $2,030 million to $4,430 million. The highway budget increased sharply too, but failed to prevent an increase in the number of traffic victims, just as bumping up the 'law and order' budget fails to stem an alarming rise in the crime rate.

Men and things

To death by murder, road accident, or illness the industrialized societies of the West react in one and the same way: they place their hope in an increase in the amount of money devoted to limiting the damage. Money will settle everything. Certainly money is necessary, but it is only really effective in a single sphere—namely in medical research, for prevention, cure, and the postponing of death through illness. This does not alter the fact that throughout the West less money is assigned to medical research than is put into the police and traffic control, where money may be indispensable but does not manage to do anything about reducing the death rate.

By investing money in this way, then, the West is breaking one of the basic rules of capitalism, which is to give priority to investment in those areas that give the best returns. In relation to requirements and efficiency, it invests less in public health or education than it does in the maintenance of order or in the motor car, less in combating pollution than in the activities that engender pollution. Ultimately it devotes more money to things than it does to men, in the hope that those things will improve the quality of life. Private and public expenditure on health in the United States went up from $26,000 million to $67,000 million between 1960 and 1970; expenditure on primary and secondary education went up $18,000 million to $32,000 million. But the purchase and upkeep of cars, the petrol they used, the insurance they required, the roads they drove on, and the accidents they caused absorbed ten times as much. In 1971 the administration of justice cost the federal government $148 million, while the cosmetics industry spent $323·5 million on advertising alone.

The judicial apparatus, public health, education, etc. continue to lag behind requirements while the number of people coming before the courts, the number of people requiring medical attention, and the number of young people starting school continue to go up. The critical overloading of these sectors adds to the discontent of a section of public opinion, offering a prime field of activity to all who challenge the established order and contest the order of priorities. Yet these sectors are among those that most directly concern man, his everyday existence, and his future.

In the societies of the West, Lucien Goldmann observes, the concern to produce has been increasingly giving way to a passive attitude centred on consumption, both material and cultural.[5] But does man consume what he most needs to consume? He has made the wrong choices, opting for things instead of what might help him towards more justice, better health, a broadening of culture, and increased freedom. True, man is not free in making these choices; he is conditioned by advertising, fashion, fads, his desire to show off, to conform to the prevailing trend, or perhaps again to distinguish himself from it. Some people think that possessing the rarer and more expensive things, always having the *de luxe* models, etc. puts them a cut above the majority; others drop out of the mainstream by refusing to abide by its norms, putting themselves on the fringe of society, identifying with an anti-fashion that very soon becomes just another fashion or with a counter-culture that is still at the inarticulate stage. Lucien Goldmann's remark holds true of both cases: the human being is 'entirely dominated and ultimately effaced by inanimate objects, which now occupy the foreground and are becoming the true active elements of this world.'

These 'inanimate objects' would appear to have created links between men: everyone can buy the same clothes, the same cars, and watch the same television programmes. But in fact, although most Westerners consume the same products, whether material or cultural, they are becoming more and more isolated in their cars and in front of their television sets, living in a sealed-off universe without any communication. Modern societies have achieved the miracle of bringing the communications media to an extraordinary peak of perfection and at the same time reinforcing the anonymity that makes communication of any kind virtually impossible. The fact that men 'can no longer carry on authentic dialogue', Martin Buber has written, is 'the most acute symptom of the pathology of our time'.

Yet the need to communicate is essential to man and he tries desperately to satisfy it by plunging into pseudo-communication. Having been at it longer, so to speak, American society offers more frequently than European the spectacle of individuals, for example in aeroplanes or restaurants, confiding to total strangers 'things they once wouldn't have confessed to a priest, a doctor or a close friend: their cruelest fears; their most shameful inadequacies; their maddest fantasies'.[6] There are no risks attached to a dialogue with a stranger one will never see again. The only trouble is that it is not a proper dialogue.

Private industry spotted this irresistible need to communicate very early on and discovered a highly profitable way of putting over an ersatz product on a virtually unlimited clientele. News-stands throughout the West are flooded with magazines whose columns are full of false confessions, phoney confidences, and apparent revelations about the private lives of the famous, but also with letters from readers telling of their problems and their frustrated hopes. This industry—for surely no one would dignify these tons of print with the name of 'press'—has a bigger clientele than the trade in pornographic books and magazines, which have after all found relatively few fans. It is to all appearances decent, even in the lies it spreads, and the question has never been raised whether it ought not, in the general interest, to be not so much censored as banned outright. Not because of the dangerous effects of this kind of opium on some people's minds but quite simply to cut down the waste of a scarce and valuable product—paper.[7] The growing success of this type of publication shows the extent of the loneliness experienced by tens of millions of individuals and of the emotional frustration secreted by the West. Private industry, always faithful to itself, has hit upon a thing that claims to meet a human need and is at the same time commercially profitable.

Desperately lonely in the crowd, the individual yearns to communicate. Totally anonymous in a society that cultivates the mythology of stardom, he wants his own personality to be recognized. Imprisoned in a narrowly specialized job, he dreams of wider horizons and of a destiny more amply human. How can he help being frustrated? He can seek satisfaction in what society offers him: consuming more and more material goods, asserting his personality by means of a car more powerful than the rest, identifying for a while with some film or television 'hero', looking for fresh sensations in drugs, risking his own and others' lives. Yves Charrier and Jacques Ellul, studying juvenile delinquency in France, have described a game played by one group of young people: a kind of 'Russian roulette' in which one motor-cyclist races round in tight circles that another motor-cyclist has to cross[8]—but the behaviour of many adults on the roads is not so very different. The same authors took the 'blousons noirs' and analysed their desire to break things and their thirst for noise, which reveal their disgust with society and a wish to drown the senses. They were followed by the 'cheveux longs' who, say the authors, 'want nothing to do with this society, which they judge and despise but are incapable of attacking'. Then came the 'minets' with their desire to mark themselves off from the adult world by their dress—outsiders too, but gentle, refined, allergic both to violence and to politics. Lastly there are the more lively-minded youngsters who go around looking tough, helmeted and sheathed in black leather: one of these, with the help of his friends, staged his own kidnapping in order to get ransom money out of his father. It is well-known what panic such gangs have sown in the United States.

These youngsters are not the only representatives of modern society. They bear more resemblance than they realize to the large numbers of adults who, like them, can only live in a context of noise, have trouble in expressing themselves, want to 'smash everything' but are kept from doing so by economic constraints, reject society but do not know where to start attacking it, seek escape from an existence in which they feel alienated, are prepared to do anything to make themselves conspicuous and attract the glances that even then do not see them, and lastly refuse to ask themselves too many questions, letting themselves be carried along by the current.

This form of society is taking its toll throughout the West: the number of people suffering from some form of mental disorder is steadily on the increase. In the United States 1,675,000 were treated in hospital or at home in 1955 and 3,381,000 in 1968. In France the annual figures for disablement through mental disorder quadrupled between 1950 and 1970, and in the Paris region they account for 24 per cent of all cases of disablement. Psychiatrists disagree among themselves as to the explanation of this phenomenon, but 'it would be difficult not to see this increase as reflecting people's maladjustment to certain aspects of present-day civilization.'[9]

It is the very spirit of that civilization that is in question. No one has dreamt of putting forward a strictly economico-political explanation of the great wave of agitation that began in the United States and reached Europe three years later, in 1968. It really was and is a crisis of civilization, affecting man in the very depths of his being, even if economic measures (such as the 1968 Grenelle Agreements in France or a modest effort on behalf of blacks in the United States) and political measures (President Johnson's departure, elections in France and the United States, prosecutions) have quieted the turmoil without, however, removing its causes. A 'civilization' that has chosen to sacrifice vital aspirations of mankind on the altar of economics and politics creates tensions that can make a sizeable minority succumb to mental illness while the majority, though not showing signs of any serious disorder, nevertheless remains deeply dissatisfied.

People experience varying degrees of inability or difficulty in facing up to 'the conditions of present-day existence, particularly in cities, the rules of community life, the solicitations of the mass media, or the methods of mass education'. Every city-dweller in the West is forced to react to 'the more or less restrictive character of the environment created by family, social, or educational requirements' and to defend himself against 'the vexations and insecurity of city life, community constraints, and the incessant call on his capacities of adjustment and competition'.[10] The West does not even have the resource of commiserating with the victims of a form of industrial civilization that otherwise blesses a contented majority with equality of justice and an unalloyed happiness: the law of the survival of the fittest can also operate against the majority.

The form industrial civilization has taken has provided man with material assets to which he is very much more attached than he would be prepared to admit. On the other hand it has deprived him of other assets whose worth he failed to realize: a more human pace of existence, the possibility of finding refuge in calm and silence, of 'whiling away' an hour in the company of friends, and of cultivating disinterested contacts. He is aware of being diminished in his humanity at a time when the prospect opened up by science appears to be virtually limitless; he knows he is less than he would like to be, and even less than the things he is asked to consume. The 'future shock'[11] ahead makes him want not to go backwards but to rearrange this order of things that he has himself created, find a new arrangement in which he will no longer be 'dominated . . . effaced by inanimate objects' but will once again have pride of place, no longer needing a firearm or a murderous vehicle in order to assert himself.

The difference is a minor one between the criminal who delights in seeing his name in the paper and the fool who asserts his superiority by driving a car in defiance of all the rules of safety: both are anti-social beings. But does Western civilization promote social integration? Or does it instead, by giving priority to economic power and expansion and inviting man to bend all his energies to the acquisition of material commodities and ever greater profits, finish up by setting man against man?

Jacques Fauvet has written:

By breaking man's ties with natural communities on a human scale present-day society has isolated the individual in an artificial environment and made all relationships relationships of force. Where there might have been understanding and emotional warmth there is only ignorance of one's fellow, hostility, and hatred. For proof (. . .) one need only look at two drivers face to face or two citizens on either side of a barrier or counter.[12]

All political parties, whether in power or in opposition, promise to change society in such a way as to make it more human and more just. 'We have to find a different kind of life,' says François Mitterand. We want a 'new society,' says Jacques Chaban-Delmas. 'Let us raise our spirits,' says Richard Nixon, 'let us raise our sights, let all of us contribute all we can to this great and good country that has contributed so much to the progress of mankind. Let us revitalize that faith in ourselves that built a great nation in the past and that will shape the world of the future.'[13]

There will be no new society without a reversal of the order of priorities. 'This world is upside-down,' says the French Communist party; 'we have to turn it the right way up' in order that we may 'live better (. . .) both materially and morally in a society that makes for a true flowering of the human personality.' Speaking of the necessity for reforming the American legal system, Chief Justice Warren E. Burger of the Supreme Court said that the solution did not lie simply in 'more money and more judges' but made the following remark, which goes for all the countries of the West and shows just how far the industrial societies have gone wrong in their choice of investment priorities:

The changes and improvements we need are long overdue. They will call for a very great effort, and they may cost money. But if there are to be higher costs, they will still be only a small fraction, for example, of the $200 million cost of one C-5A airplane, since the entire cost of the federal judicial system for one year, for the next year, is less than one of those planes. Military aircraft are of course important, essential in this uncertain world. But so is adequate support for the judicial branch.[14]

Since Judge Burger made his speech the federal justice budget has been increased from $128 million to $143 million, but for the year 1972-3 alone the government asked for an extra $6,000 million for the military budget, and the space ferry project will cost $5,000 million spread over several years.

'The President spends billions on defence,' Edward Kennedy has said in this connection, 'whereas what we need is billions spent on schools, construction, and health.' The criticism is pertinent to all of the West.

But it is not just the government's fault. The order of priorities will never be changed without powerful pressure from public opinion, and in the United States as in Europe public opinion has for a long time tolerated a distribution of public money that gives rise to social instability, tensions, frustrations, and the alienation of the individual. It is private citizens who continue to spend on firearms, cosmetics, and motor cars the resources so badly needed in the fields of education, public health, and the administration of justice. The state naturally behaves no differently. It comes under criticism from a minority, but its budgetary choices roughly correspond to the majority's order of priorities. And when yesterday's minority becomes today's government it introduces a few minor alterations in the budget without effectively changing that order of priorities.

An academic with a penchant for realism, Henry Kissinger wrote before his access to power:

> The modern bureaucratic state, for all its panoply of strength, often finds itself shaken to its foundations by seemingly trivial causes. Its brittleness and the worldwide revolution of youth (. . .) suggest a spiritual void, an almost metaphysical boredom with a political environment that increasingly emphasizes bureaucratic challenges and is dedicated to no greater purpose than material comfort.[15]

If 'material comfort' is not an adequate objective for a modern society, if it leaves a human 'void' and a deep 'boredom', then there is nothing 'trivial' about the forces that occasionally shake the system. On the contrary they go to the very heart of the matter. But if Henry Kissinger and with him the men in power throughout the West think this, what is preventing them from offering society a different objective, one that would fill that void and dispel that boredom? What counter-force stops them making that objective explicit and, by reversing the order of priorities that has brought Western civilization to the point of crisis, mobilizing the resources, both budgetary and otherwise, that would make it possible of achievement?

The 'panoply' of modern states is more suited to administration along traditional lines than to government by innovation—better at destroying than at creating. And clashing with the impotence of the state is another kind of impotence: that of isolated individuals and scattered groups, institutions that are themselves victims of a society founded on money, and a diffuse current of opinion that, in a society devoted to human anonymity, never succeeds in crystallizing. These two kinds of impotence leave the field free for a mastering force—money. When someone spots a new way of increasing a firm's profits or economic power, relatively little time goes by between the conception of the project and its carrying into effect. When on the other hand it is a question of a new way of serving mankind, the delay between idea and realization sometimes extends to decades.

One example is the administration of justice, the current resources of which are hopelessly over-taxed both in Europe and in the United States. In the speech already quoted, Warren E. Burger recalled what had been said sixty-four years earlier—in 1906—by Roscoe Pound, future Dean of the Harvard law faculty. The courts, Pound said, cannot operate in the twentieth century with the methods, machinery, and means of the nineteenth century. And Burger added: 'Judges and lawyers did not heed Pound's warning. And today, in the final third of this century, we are still trying to operate the courts with fundamentally the same basic methods, the same procedures and the same machinery that he said were not good enough in 1906.'

The Chief Justice of the Supreme Court also recalled that the population of the United States had meanwhile gone from 76 million to 205 million, that society's forms and norms had undergone complete upheaval, that there had been an enormous increase in legislation, that trials lasted longer, etc. He went on to trace the necessary reforms in broad outline and added: 'The addition of sixty-one new federal judgeships (. . .) by the Congress within recent weeks, bringing the total to 401 for the whole country, is the result of efforts that began five years ago. Since it will take time to fill these important positions —and new judges do not reach their peak of efficiency at once—the full impact of these new men will not be felt for a long time. We see, therefore, that the additional judges needed in 1965 were not authorized until 1970. We cannot solve our problems in the courts by meeting needs five or more years after they arise.'[16] To say nothing of the more basic reforms called for at the beginning of the century.

What is true of the administration of justice is true of all spheres in which the citizen ought to be considered in his capacity as a human being and not merely as a consumer contributing to this or that firm's profits. In principle the master of the apparatus of production he has himself created, man has relinquished his mastery to things, to the objects of production. This and only this is the source of the malaise and frustration of the individual today and of the crisis of civilization.

Violence and profit

A certain amount of force has always been present in human relationships, but modern means of production, mass communication, and so on have brought methods of coercion to a degree of perfection undreamt of at the beginning of the century. The feudal lord enjoyed more extensive rights than an oil company but his real powers were infinitely less. The late nineteenth-century cavalry charge against demonstrators was very much less dangerous than the tear-gas, laughing-gas, and other disabling chemicals used nowadays. A hundred years ago the means available for conditioning people's minds were laughably primitive, and detectives had neither the wire taps nor all the other gadgets for recording and photographing people unawares with which to invade the privacy of the individual.

By and large the individual today is slowly growing accustomed to these constraints wielded against him by the agents of economic, political, and police power. And since he is subject to forcible constraints, when he becomes aware of his own weakness he can see no other means of freeing himself than by force. But he is no match for them. He dreams of acquiring sufficient power himself to slip the chains that bind him. More ambitiously, he dreams of liberating by force a society in thrall to the power of money.

The world's biggest fortunes have not been amassed without violence. For the founder of the Rockefeller dynasty there was the economic violence of dumping to ruin rival oil concerns and the physical violence of massacring the miners on strike at Ludlow. For the Carnegies, the violence of the Pinkerton detectives against striking steelworkers. Violence against blacks in the plantations before the abolition of slavery and in the factories after it. Violence against trade unionists in the steel industry, mining, textiles, etc. in every country in Europe. Violence in the countries directly colonized by Europe or the United States or subject to more subtle forms of economic dominion, with the 'national' government taking upon itself to put down peasants' revolts and workers' strikes on the neo-colonizer's behalf. Historically such violence has always called forth violent reactions on the part of the oppressed: pitchforks, iron bars, shotguns, and Molotov cocktails against the most modern weapons of the period.

This kind of spectacular violence is becoming increasingly difficult to employ. Yet in its bloodiest form it still remains a source of profit. The three major television networks in the United States vie with one another in producing programmes of a more and more brutal and violent nature. Justifications are plentiful: 'Violence is acceptable. It's what the people want,' said one Chicago showman.[17] It is doubtless not enough in itself to ensure a show's commercial success but how many films have come out in the last quarter of a century under the slogan: 'Never before has such violence been seen on the screen.' And indeed each one goes a little further. 'There's a sense of imminent disaster when you're in an audience that's grooving on ultra-violence, and you're tempted to say that things can't go on this way too much longer. They can, of course, and probably will. Today's ultra-violent films will be tomorrow's "Wednesday Night at the Movies" on TV,' writes Joseph Morgenstern.[18]

The television networks have no alternative but to continue to outdo one another. They need their advertisers' contracts if they are to exist, and those contracts are based on each network's audience ratings. The public, young and old, likes violent programmes. The networks give them satisfaction, and violence pays off: the law of profit takes a lot of getting round. What is happening in the United States concerns Europe directly: a recent BBC investigation showed that American films put out on British television contained twice as many scenes of violence as British productions. The cinema too recognizes no frontiers: American producers were surprised to find Italian 'westerns' more violent than their American prototypes.

The television networks know what they are doing. They realize that in transmitting scenes of violence they are not merely satisfying the public's taste but influencing it. They are not interested in whether or not that influence is harmful: violence brings them viewers, and viewers bring them advertising contracts. Accused of cultivating the taste for violence, they have borrowed this defensive argument from elementary psychology: by a process of catharsis the viewer who watches a scene of violence is freed of his own murderous instincts. Humorists have replied that according to this hypothesis a commercial extolling the merits of an electric tin-opener or a convertible would free viewers of the need to purchase the object in question.

But the debate became more serious when, in 1969, after a particularly violent year, Senator John Pastore launched an investigation into the effects of violence on television. The investigation took two years, and at the beginning of 1972 the *New York Times* was able to summarize the report's conclusions as follows: 'Violence in television programming does not have an adverse effect on the majority of the nation's youth but may influence small groups of youngsters predisposed by many factors to aggressive behaviour.' So all was clearly for the best, etc., and the television networks handed out photocopies of the *New York Times* article by the thousand.

It was then that the scandal broke: the *New York Times* article was faithful to the official summary of the investigation, but that summary itself represented a distortion of the conclusions that emerged from the five fat volumes containing the observations gathered during the two years' research. How did it happen? The study had been entrusted to some forty qualified investigators working under the supervision of a twelve-man committee. The NBC and ABC networks objected to seven of the people approached to sit on this committee: they were known in advance to be critical. Two members of the committee were NBC and CBS men and three others were academics working for television. The psychologists and sociologists who had taken part in the investigation accused these five men of having 'managed to obfuscate and dilute most key findings that were detrimental to television's image'.[19]

Three methods were used to accomplish this. Firstly a specious argument: television is progress, and one does not criticize progress, whatever use is made of it. Secondly some astute editing: the CBS representative managed to sprinkle the conclusions with a lot of 'howevers' and 'nevertheless' that toned down all the unfavourable observations. Finally a political argument: Vice-President Spiro Agnew had been vigorously criticizing the mass-communications media in his most demagogic speeches, and who wants to carry water to that reactionary's mill, etc.

The television industry's ploy to prevent the findings of the investigation from becoming known in fact boomeranged. The investigation itself showed that scenes of violence developed aggression in more than 50 per cent of children, that youngsters regard such programmes not as fiction but as something more realistic than documentaries, that there is a direct link between the violence a child sees and the violence he subsequently perpetrates, and that the development of aggression in a child is proportional to the amount of time that child has spent watching scenes of violence.

Which is precisely what the heads of the television networks wanted to conceal from the public. The networks perform a kind of *public* service in that they provide viewers with news and entertainment. But they are *private* concerns and as such they are governed by the law of profit and competition, exploiting even that which is potentially harmful to the public. It is desirable that a public service should be able to pay for itself, but such a service cannot fulfil its mission if it is subject to the double necessity of competing commercially and of making a profit.

In some of its programmes American television has filled an essential role in placing before the public documents that it alone can present more effectively than the printed press: reports on the various aspects of the racial problem, on the links between the Pentagon and industry, on the Vietnam war, and on the conquest of the moon, political debates, 'cultural' programmes, sports coverage, etc. Commercial competition has driven the principal networks further and further in this direction and they have had some spectacular successes. But it has also driven American television to exploit and cultivate the violence that is latent in every society. This is a high price to pay for a freedom that is based on access to advertising income.

The public is profoundly shaken when violence leaves the sphere of fiction and becomes reality. But the reaction is short-lived. In 1968, following the assassinations of Robert Kennedy and Martin Luther King, an American film actor specializing in cowboy parts announced that he was hanging up his six-shooters for ever. Since then violence has been taken further and further, not only in mediocre films but also in very sophisticated ones. As *Newsweek*'s Joseph Morgenstern wrote of *A Clockwork Orange*: 'Moviemakers have found ultra-violence ultra-profitable, the mass audience has found it enjoyable—and an influential majority of reviewers has found it intellectually attractive and artistically valid.'

An audience of New York high-school students watched Roman Polanski's *Macbeth* dispatch his victims with considerable virtuosity and then screamed in horrified delight when, Macbeth having been himself decapitated, his hands groped for his own head . . . Long prohibited in public—and the West is unanimous in its indignation at public hangings in Iraq and Guinea—capital punishment as a spectacle has through the cinema become available to vast crowds who would never have got into the prison courtyard where the guillotine or the gallows was set up. How is one to interpret the coincidence whereby the act of execution is so ingeniously filmed just when the nations of the West are legally abolishing or in practice abandoning capital punishment?

The best producers and directors have arguments readily available to justify scenes of brutality. They say their art denounces the violence inherent in modern society, offers a dark parody of it, or prophesies a black future, inviting man to think again. Continually improved techniques lend power and beauty to ghastly images that lead the spectator to meditate on mankind, on the meaning of existence, and on society. Directors claim to be doing with their cameras what Goya did in *The Disasters of War* or Picasso in *Guernica*. But the effect is closer to that described by Joseph Morgenstern:

> They lend distance, but they also dehumanize victims in the way that high-fashion photography dehumanizes models (. . .). The Vietnamese war could look lovely in slow motion—Skyraiders floating in for the kill like seagulls, fragmentation bombs opening like anemones. But the horror would still be horror, with nothing added but technique (. . .). It becomes clear that *Bonnie and Clyde* was both watershed and quicksand. It used technique within a humanistic design and shocked us awake to violence. Now anti-humanists are using the same technique to lull us into dulcet dreams of death. Purveyors of the new violence can tell themselves and their critics that they're involved in a programme of character building, public service and ethical culture, but a few visits to neighbourhood theatres suggest that a large part of the mass audience simply loves the violence as violence.'

If the investigation launched by Senator Pastore in the United States showed that scenes of violence develop aggression in children, what is the effect on adults—is it the same? So far no scientific study has provided an answer to this question. Scenes of cruelty filmed in Vietnam initially provoked a wave of indignation in the United States that contributed greatly to President Johnson's unpopularity. The American army, emanation of the American nation, appeared in a guise in which the nation was reluctant to recognize itself. It was to avoid a similar reaction that the French government so jealously guarded films shot in Indo-China and Algeria. No doubt it was wrong to violate in this way the democratic principle of the right to the truth. But it seems to have been wrong above all in employing secrecy in the name of reasons of state. Because the public can get used to anything, even violence, as long as it is not itself the victim. American opinion grew accustomed to the prolongation of the war and to the televized pictures of that war that once so disturbed the peace of its living-rooms. Perhaps we do not even need to know whether scenes of violence stimulate aggression in adults: it is bad enough that they inure them to horror.

The revelation of the massacre that Lieutenant Calley and his men committed at My Lai in March 1968 jolted the American conscience. Three years later an opinion poll showed that 67 per cent of Americans would have done as Calley did. Only 19 per cent of those interviewed replied: 'We would refuse to kill civilians.'[20] Violence is becoming acceptable. Extremists of both camps lay claim to it as a means of action while between them most people tend to regard it as an unpleasant but unavoidable fact.

The resigned, just because they are so numerous, constitute a greater danger than the enthusiastic advocates of violence. Assassinations, bomb attacks, kidnappings, and other acts of sabotage have caused victims in the United States, France, West Germany, and Italy (with sixteen dead in Milan on 12 December 1969). And every time, in every country, as Arthur Schlesinger observed of the United States after the assassinations of the Kennedy brothers and Martin Luther King: 'While each of these murders produced a genuine season of national mourning, none has produced a sustained season of national questioning. In every case, remorse has seemed to end not as an incitement to self-examination but as an escape from it.'[21]

Controlling firearms, strengthening police forces, and tightening legal sanctions are perhaps relatively useful ways of stemming violence. But the most effective way is to examine the roots of the hatred, frustration, and despair that drive minorities to resort to violence. No less essential is to examine the reasons why the great mass of the public, initially shattered by an assassination or other violent crime, quickly banishes all disturbing facts from its mind: poverty, injustice, individual or collective acts of violence.

Andrew Hacker offers for the United States an explanation that holds true of all the industrialized nations:

> What was once a nation has become simply an agglomeration of self-concerned individuals; men and women who were once citizens are now merely residents of bounded terrain where birth happens to have placed them (. . .). The American people will of course survive;

and the majority will continue to exist quite comfortably, at least in the confines of their private lives. But the ties that make them a society will grow more tenuous with each passing year. There will be undercurrents of tension and turmoil, and the only remaining option will be to learn to live with these disorders.[22]

A 'lonely crowd', an agglomerate of individuals lacking any inter-personal ties, the anonymity of major urban concentrations—all very far from what one might regard as a living society. If there are those who reject such a caricature, does that make them anti-social? Turned in upon themselves, the masses of the resigned can only accelerate the trends that are steadily unravelling the fabric of society. The rebels, especially the violent ones, provoke a reaction of fear and shrinking repugnance. With a big dose of optimism one may perhaps hope they have a chance of shaking awake a society in process of decomposition.

Violence and the state

The mass-communications media and the individuals who make a profit out of marketing scenes of violence or the machinery of death are less influential than the state when, in its impotence, it employs, excuses, or otherwise countenances violence. Hardly had Lieutenant Calley been condemned for the My Lai massacre when President Nixon told him he could serve his sentence at home. In France the newspapers that denounced the tortures being practised in Indo-China and Algeria were either confiscated or prosecuted. The men who prac-tised torture in Algeria have never been brought to justice; successive governments strenuously denied facts that were clearly established and that General Massu admitted fourteen years later in seeking to justify them. In Northern Ireland the British army has been accused of seri-ously maltreating internees. In Germany Chancellor Brandt's gesture in kneeling at the monument erected to commemorate the victims of Auschwitz was bitterly criticized.

Anxious not to clash with other public authorities or to 'divide the nation', governments play down responsibilities and either keep pro-secutions to a minimum or decline to prosecute at all: they know their own guilt. Lieutenant Calley's trial was not a courageous act of justice but a parody of ritual sacrifice making it possible to clear his superiors. The trials that have never taken place regarding French torturers in Algeria would have been fully meaningful only if the courts had been able to trace the thread of responsibility right to the top. In Germany the zeal evinced in the prosecution of certain Nazis has been tempered by political considerations or by instances of complicity or indifference, enabling some of those responsible to escape prosecution altogether. Taking advantage of a solidarity based on the struggle against Communism and subversion, General Gehlen's secret service continued its activities in the Federal Republic on CIA money, and former policemen recently in the pay of Latin-American dictatorships now exercise their functions in European democracies, where it is their job to keep an eye on immigrants.

The files on torture will never be closed, nor will any amount of outlawing eliminate it. Here time bears nothing away, and the impunity enjoyed by yesterday's torturers paves the way for the torturers of tomorrow. A minority is aware of this, a minority drawn from all spheres of life in both America and Europe, while the majority reacts with no more than the occasional spasm of indignation that does not lead to any lasting action.

No revelations regarding the systematic employment of torture in Algeria, notes Pierre Sorlin, 'arouse any real emotion; the government and public opinion know the truth but absorb it almost as something fated; to change police methods would mean fully controlling the apparatus of administration, which is something neither an enfeebled government wishes to do nor a resigned society to be done; the weight of the state has become such that a shrinking of the traditional freedoms is accepted without resistance.'[23]

But the power of the state is more apparent than real. It hesitates to clash with the forces of order and their chiefs. Why should it do so when, with the exception of a handful of citizens, society itself gives its tacit consent to acts that will nevertheless one day redound against it? In the United States it was the identical scientific research that led to the discovery of the gases used against American demonstrators and to the chemical weapons used in Vietnam; the men who torture or countenance torture 'overseas' are one day going to come home. 'From the policeman who tortured to the judge who admitted the results of such an interrogation and to the President of the Council who lied or kept quiet, piece by piece an entire apparatus of deception was built up,' writes Pierre Vidal-Naquet.[24] But he spreads the net of liability even wider by recalling that the young soldiers sent off to Algeria had received 'no preventive education' from the trade unions, political parties, and churches. The same analysis holds good of the Americans

drafted into the Vietnam war. Nothing had prepared them for a situation
in which the most atrocious acts of violence were perpetrated in the
name of military necessity and on orders from above. It took months,
even years for the massacres and the 'tiger cages' to come out, carefully
concealed as they were by that same 'apparatus of deception'.

A society balks any examination obliging it to compare its principles
and such of its methods as violate the spirit of those principles. Solidarity has its limits: it did not extend to Jews and Communists in Nazi
Germany, nor does it extend to blacks in the United States or to colonized peoples. Yet solidarity as a fact is very much more extensive than
those who would wish to escape it suspect. Nazism collapsed, but its
methods have spread throughout the world. Police brutalities are
directed not at blacks alone but at whites of good family who militate
for racial integration, for peace, and for every cause that conforms to
the democratic ideal. The colonies have provided the testing-ground
for all the violations of law perpetrated in the mother countries.

It is no accident if, when a serious prison mutiny breaks out in France,
it is discovered that the governor of the prison made his military debut
in Algeria. But the virus of violence and illegality is not only passed on
from person to person: the contagion is in the air. Martin Luther King
drew a direct link between the violence unleashed by the United States
government in Vietnam and the consequent upsurge of violence in
American society. When the state gives its blessing to coercive interrogation and physical elimination, when research and industry devote
their talents and resources to ingenious fragmentation bombs and tiny
projectiles that no surgeon can remove from the human body, it is the
dominant forces of the societies of the West that are themselves creating
a climate of violence.

No moralizing speeches are going to stop a chain reaction. Blacks,
workers, young people turn against the established order with the
same violence that whites, the rich, and adults use against them. Like
them they place more faith in coercion than in persuasion. If reasons of
state, the need to keep order, and the national interest justify illegality,
the taking of hostages, false patriotism, lying, and slaughter, the same
methods will be used against the state, against the established order, and
against phoney definitions of the national interest.

'The violence that oppresses silently and insidiously and tends to
destroy man's dignity is worse than physical violence. It can only
arouse two kinds of reaction: apathy or the use of force.' These remarks
apply to all societies. Yet they were made in connexion with a very

particular kind of society that few citizens ever anticipate belonging to: they were made by Pastor Amedro, Protestant chaplain of Toul prison.[25]

The origins of violence are complex and its sociological workings obscure. Yet it proceeds from those in authority and power whenever they place that authority at the service of privilege and use that power to disguise their own weakness. At every level of the social hierarchy there are men, drunk with the powers they wield, who behave like those policemen who, in the words of one French divisional super-intendent, have 'an arrogant bearing, an abrupt and imperious tone of voice, a manifest belief in their own superiority, and a mode of speech that borders on vulgarity, all of which of course upsets members of the public.'[26]

From violence of manner and speech to actual brutality is but a step. The 'age of contempt' is paving the way for the 'concentration-camp world'. The French National Union of Police Officers declares in a memorandum it has made public that instances of violence are 'the exception, contrary to the generally held opinion'. But the rights of man, justice, freedom—these admit of no exceptions: it is always for oneself that the bell tolls. At the onset of the disease the cancerous cells are few in number, yet the entire organism is threatened with death. So is the social body in danger when it is subject to 'exceptional' occur-rences that the same police organization represents in the following terms: 'Clearly if, when a demonstrator or other individual is lying on the floor of a van or police station, members of the force go for him with truncheons, fists, or their feet, the procedure is inadmissible and must be stopped (. . .). Several men going for a single, defenceless man —what is usually known and denounced as the *"passage à tabac"*—not only shows little courage but smacks of totalitarian methods unworthy of a democracy and must be condemned without reserve.'[27]

There is a touch of stylistic facility about denouncing such methods as 'unworthy of democracy'. At a pinch society can swallow for a while methods that are 'unworthy' of its declared principles. It stands con-demned when it countenances more and more frequently and over longer and longer periods of time methods that strike at those principles, undermine public confidence, and whittle away the authority of governments that penalize them too rarely or too leniently.

Another policeman, Gérard Monate, general secretary of the Indepen-dent National Union of Police Officers, does not consider this process of decay as an unforeseen mishap. He recalls the part played by those policemen in the Resistance during the Nazi occupation who 'preserved the honour of a profession that a minority was sullying'. Actually a minority would never have been up to all the rounding-up of Jews that went on—or else it was a very large minority. At any rate it was sufficiently influential after 1944 to run an effective 'organized drive against militant trade-unionists and former members of the Resistance under the pretext of an anti-Communist offensive,conducted in Paris by a Prefect of Police who was himself an ex-trade-unionist, while at the same time various "eloignés de la Libération" were fully reinstated.'[28]

It was all done quite openly, government, parliament, press, and public being kept fully informed, if occasionally somewhat after the event. There was no conspiracy, no shady machinations, no surprise—and yet neither was there effective protest, nor control, nor veto. Not just the police are to blame but the country as a whole and in particular its elected representatives. The latter cannot plead ignorance. Is one then to assume that they were not free to act? Or that they lacked the courage? But then what were they afraid of? Victimization by the police? Were they, for all their self-assurance, vulnerable?

At any rate no one is surprised to find another policeman speaking of the 'seditious groups' that have gangrened the forces responsible for keeping the peace. 'The situation is even more serious,' writes Roger Daurelle, recently dismissed by the Minister of the Interior, 'if they are going to keep on the force seditious groups whose existence has been known of for a long time and who are far from observing the neutrality that is incumbent on a public service.'[29]

Excessive brutality, elimination of former members of the Resistance and progressive elements, reinstatement of former collaborators, official encouragement of 'seditious groups'—all this was bad enough,yet it was still not enough: it is understood that the so-called 'parallel police' do not exist—but then who are the authors of the acts of which they are accused? What is the explanation behind the impunity they enjoy?

It is easy to make a scapegoat of the police. But it is not autonomous and it does not, whatever anyone says, constitute a state within the state. It is in the service of the state, and the state occasionally takes punitive action when policemen threaten to occupy Matignon and the Ministry of Finance. It is a police in the image of the state—which gives priority to the maintenance of an order it claims is threatened by subversion from the Left and extreme Left. It reflects the dominant ideology.

Governments and the majority of the population throughout the West are tolerant of extreme right-wing factions, seeing danger only from the Left. Martin Luther King accused J. Edgar Hoover, FBI chief for half a century, of mobilizing his forces more readily against progressive groups than for unmasking the bosses of organized crime or the champions of white racialism. In California the Oakland police had the reputation of being one of the most brutal in the country, taking a particular interest in students, blacks, and pacifists. In 1968 its new chief started taking measures to 'limit the arbitrary use of police power', prohibit policemen from firing 'unless human lives were deemed in imminent danger', and 'give the highest priority to insuring your citizens their constitutional rights'. The Oakland police was on the way to becoming a 'near paragon of police virtue'. In a referendum organized by their union in November 1971, however, more than half the city's policemen, reflecting public opinion, accused their chief of 'jeopardizing the morale and safety' of the force.[30] Boston's black district of Roxbury contains only 14 per cent of the population but in 1971 it accounted for 36 murders out of a total of 114 for the city as a whole, 95 out of 303 rapes, and a third of all thefts and break-ins. Gangs operate quite openly, and it appears that 'at least some policemen are downright corrupt'. Finally, for their own protection, black associations managed to get a special thirty-four-man patrol set up that registered 'a phenomenal success' in the space of a few weeks. The Boston (white) policemen's union, however, demanded the dissolution of this special patrol on the grounds that, consisting as it did exclusively of blacks, it violated the 1964 civil rights bill.[31] In Philadelphia the former chief of police, a man noted for his toughness, got himself elected mayor by promising among other things to recruit two thousand more policemen.[32] In Baton Rouge, La., police broke up a meeting of two hundred blacks: two policemen and two blacks were killed, all four of them by police bullets.[33] In New York two policemen spent three years trying to alert Mayor Lindsay to the corruption rife among the city's 31,000 policemen. Having failed, they told their story to the *New York Times*, which published it in January 1970. Mayor Lindsay immediately set up a commission of inquiry into police corruption, a few people were prosecuted, but the papers continued to ask the embarrassing question: why did the mayor wait so long before taking action?[34] In January 1970 the Detroit police set up a special squad that earned the reputation in slum quarters of shooting first and asking questions afterwards. (It did in fact kill twelve people in fourteen months.) One day in March 1972 the squad saw an armed black man entering a building. They followed him to a flat in which four men were playing cards. Again they shot first, killing one of the blacks and wounding the other three. No member of the squad was wounded, but the four victims turned out to be black policemen. The superintendent defended his squad by saying that it 'behaved in a way the public expects police officers to'.[35]

The American press has always shown the greatest vigilance with regard to police brutality and corruption—without, however, succeeding in getting the competent authorities to proceed to the necessary weeding-out and reorganization. The American public has even given up protesting: it has become resigned to a state of affairs that, having been exposed and vainly denounced for so long, ends up seeming normal and inevitable.

In Western Europe, despite admitted exceptions, corruption and brutality are very much less extensive. Police are more carefully recruited, better trained, and more disciplined. When in the autumn of 1971 mutinies broke out within a few days of one another in prisons in Attica, New York, and Clairvaux, France, police intervened to restore order: forty-two men died at Attica, two at Clairvaux. In the course of a single demonstration at Kent State University the National Guard killed four students: it would have caused wholesale slaughter in the Latin Quarter of Paris in May 1968 where, notwithstanding undeniable brutalities, the French police did not kill a single demonstrator.[36]

Yet the situation in Europe has been worsening for some years and might look even darker if the European press were as active as the American in the matter of tracking down and exposing abuses. Will it one day be as bad as it is in America? Probably not—provided that the authorities responsible show no weakness and the crime rate does not reach American proportions. But comparison between Europe and the United States does show one thing: for all the stir it has aroused, the scandal of the American police is tolerated by a resigned society. If it is to be effective, the public must react at a very early stage—before the evil has spread to the point where it can no longer be eradicated. American society offers a tragic example of the weakness of a democracy in the face of a problem that nevertheless concerns people's safety and basic civil rights.

The Italian film *Investigation of a Citizen above Suspicion* depicted a character and situations that could come as a surprise to no one in Europe. The behaviour of the police is always one of the best indications of the feebleness or vitality of democratic institutions. The

proceedings instituted against the Milan anarchist Pietro Valpreda followed classic Western lines: the accused was charged with a serious
crime although, as Jacques Nobécourt observed, 'simple logic showed
that the only people who could possibly benefit from the disorder were
the extreme Right: even in Rome it was thought that the investigation
would take that direction, yet when it began it was directed uniquely
against anarchist circles (. . .) The Valpreda case is slowly disappearing
behind the mystery surrounding the machinations that are said to have
been aiming since 1968 at provoking a swing to the Right by subversive
and violent means. The advocates of Valpreda's and his friends' conviction are driven by the idea that a possible miscarriage of justice is
better than revolution.'[37]

In the absence of any coherent policy the temptation to stampede
opinion by exploiting a criminal affair becomes virtually irresistible.
The pseudo assassination attempt against François Mitterand in the
Jardins de l'Observatoire in Paris, the alleged 'Pigeon Plot' attributed to
Jacques Duclos, the proceedings instigated against some Black Panthers
in New York in 1970–71, with the only prosecution witness being an
FBI agent who had infiltrated their group, the arrest of Fr. Philip
Berrigan and six other militant pacifists on the evidence of an extremely
dubious informer who, together with the FBI, staged what has been
described as a 'sinister farce'[38]—none of these scandals equals the horror
of the Dreyfus case or the executions of Sacco and Vanzetti and Julius
and Ethel Rosenberg. Nevertheless they all stem from a kind of veiled
McCarthyism, a political tactics based on the exploitation of fear. In
late May and early June 1968 the police officers of Paris' Latin Quarter
admitted that the majority of the demonstrators' they were arresting
were in fact young plain-clothes policemen: it was a question of keeping the agitation going in order to foster a better climate for the elections. At a time when the entire West is susceptible to the 'law and
order' slogan, police infiltration of subversive groups does, on the
short-term view, pay off politically. In the United States certain Black
Panther cells have been created from scratch by the FBI, whose members once provided so many 'supporters' of the Communist party. Such
methods have solved nothing.

The disease has even struck at that model of all police forces, London's
Metropolitan Police Force, Scotland Yard. The number of policemen
molested went up by 25 per cent between 1965 and 1970 to reach the
unprecedented figure of 8,000 incidents. Eleven policemen have been
killed in ten years—an extremely low figure as compared with the

United States but unbelievably high for Britain. No longer is the 'bobby' quite the familiar, universally loved figure he used to be. In August 1971, following the murder of a police superintendent in Blackpool, *The Times* published an interview with an anonymous Scotland Yard man who accused the British legal system of coddling criminals. He also demanded the abolition of bail in cases of crimes of violence, longer working-hours for prisoners, and the banning of radio and television sets in prisons, and insisted on the need for greater firmness to stop the rising crime rate. The author of these statements was Peter Brodie, deputy director of the Yard.

Was he hoping to be appointed director in April 1972? The fact remains that the job went to Robert Mark and Brodie tendered his resignation the day before Mark took over; he considered Mark a 'moderate'. Yet Mark had long been calling for an important change in legal procedure whereby juries need no longer be unanimous but could return a majority verdict—a suggestion that was finally adopted by the courts in 1967. He also wants to do away with the obligation on policemen to warn suspects that they do not have to answer questions if their answers could incriminate them. In the face of increases in crime there is inevitably a growing current in favour of limiting the traditional guarantees. Citizens always see this as a means of protecting themselves better against dangerous elements, never for a moment thinking that such reforms might one day turn against themselves, if they ever came to be questioned as suspects. The rights of the individual are fragile, however, and it is easier to restrict than reinforce them.

And then on 31 December 1971 a top Scotland Yard official, Inspector of Constabularies Frank Williamson, resigned from office eleven years before retiring age on the grounds that he had not received the co-operation he needed in his investigation into police corruption. Two inspectors have been indicted on charges of corruption, and various investigations into corruption are currently in progress.

Police forces throughout the West are coming to be regarded with growing mistrust. Their reputations are tarnished by the activities of a minority and a rising crime rate calls their efficiency into question. In the United States an estimated nine million 'serious crimes' are committed annually; only half become known to the police, 12 per cent result in the arrest of a suspect, 6 per cent in a conviction, and 1·5 per cent in a prison sentence. In spite of these ridiculous percentages, prisons are overcrowded and the numbers of recidivists show that they are veritable 'colleges of crime' rather than re-education centres designed to

8*

reintegrate prisoners into society. Between 1956 and 1970 234 race riots caused fewer than 200 deaths while common-law crimes ran into one million cases of bodily harm and 50,000 homicides. Yet it is political and racial disorders that the 'law and order' school invoke in support of their demands for more policemen, fewer rights for prisoners, and heavier penalties.

Growing police powers have not managed to stop the rising crime rate. The murder of René-Pierre Overney at the Renault works on February 1972 raised a question that is still unanswered: how many armed 'vigiles' are there in France? The industrialized countries are coming to rely increasingly on private protection personnel. In Detroit there are 107 agencies supplying businessmen, tradesmen, and private individuals with more guards than the city's 5,200 policemen; to be authorized to carry a gun they merely have to prove they have no prison record. In Atlanta the number of private guards has increased by 2,000 over the last four years. The turnover of one Chicago protection agency increased by 40 per cent between 1969 and 1971. Another agency for private protection personnel in New York presents an annual balance-sheet of $134 million. But the graph of thefts and murders continues to rise.

Europe is not America, or at least is trying to persuade itself it is not. Yet 'European crime is evolving and tending to model itself on American crime', writes Jean Pinatel, professor of applied criminology at Paris University.[39] In Britain the number of offences leading to legal proceedings increased from 78,000 in 1938 to 182,000 in 1961;[40] serious offences known to the police increased by 43 per cent between 1958 and 1962. In France the number of convictions passed by assize courts increased from 914 to 1,329 between 1960 and 1968, while the number of convictions passed by courts of summary jurisdiction increased from 212,595 to 293,930.[41] Even Sweden, which has the lowest crime rate, has seen a slight increase in homicides; the figure rose from 170 in 1965 to 184 in 1967.

Obviously Swedish socialism does not eliminate crime any more than any other socio-economic system. Nevertheless Sweden's crime rate is three or four times lower than those of other European countries, which are in turn very much lower than that of the United States. Admittedly social structure cannot alone explain the behaviour of the individuals it conditions. But, as Jean Pinatel rightly remarks, growth in economic activity 'provides supplementary opportunities for crime by multiplying the number of interest relationships'.[42] Car thefts and shop-lifting in supermarkets and department stores offer the simplest illustration. High urban concentration in association with a particular form of industrialization has clearly increased the number of offences committed by real-estate firms while multiplying and aggravating cases of social maladjustment. This is why Denis Szabo advocates increased social facilities in the big cities of Europe if they are to avoid ending up 'in twenty-five or thirty years' time' in the situation of American cities today.[43] Jean Pinatel also sees a cause of social maladjustment in the gap between culture and traditional behaviour on the one hand and the style of life and the problems arising out of technological progress on the other. The tensions and frustrations of modern life lead not only to mental disorders but also to forms of delinquency expressive either of rejection of society or, on the contrary, a wish to become integrated in society by the criminal acquisition of the commodities that the consumer society holds to be indispensable to human happiness.

If the 'technetronic society' analysed in the United States by Zbigniev Brezinski is the normal outcome of progress in technology and electronics and if it inevitably involves fragmentation of human groups and accounts for 'the tensions and violence of today', then Europe has no choice: in following the way of 'progress' it will achieve the crime rate that the United States has now. If on the other hand American society is the outcome of a complex but continuous process of evolution that has harnessed technological and electronic progress in the service of a particular concept of economic and political power, in the service of a pattern of development that increases the profits of the rich, aggravates injustices and tensions, and adds to the difficulties of adjustment, then that society need not be surprised to find itself 'criminogenous', fostering in the individual the tendencies that drive him to rebel against a particular order, break certain laws, and reject certain 'values'.

There is no shortage of moralists to deplore the decay of 'principles' and of a 'conscience' they decline to examine more closely. They are the spiritual heirs of the middle-class French *députés* who, as bachelors or fathers of only one child, passed the 1920 law banning the advertisement of contraceptives and dragging performers of and accessories to abortions before the courts.[44] The supporters of that law, aiming for a high birth rate, preached to the working classes a 'morality' they were careful not to practise themselves in order not to dissipate the family fortune. Addressing himself to industrialists at the time, Dr Jacques Bertillon drew a clear connexion between economics and 'morality' when he wrote: 'A rise in the birth rate would have immediate advantages for you: nothing would do more towards preventing political strikes or unjustified stoppages. In nine cases out of ten trouble-makers and fomenters of strikes are bachelors or men with no children, and the majority of those who heed them are in the same position. Fathers of large families will not go on strike without imperative reasons and it is unusual for them not to be prepared to accept a reasonable settlement.'[45]

Half a century later the connexion between economics and 'morality' has undergone some evolution but is none the less strong. The holders of economic power have raised profit to a civil virtue on the grounds that it leads to investment, which leads to jobs, but in doing so they abandon millions of human beings to the destitution of low wages or unemployment. Through the medium of advertising they lend glamour to the objects that fill the shop-windows but that millions of people cannot afford and occasionally venture to steal. They market air-conditioners and swimming-pools while exploiting black labour that is accommodated in stifling ghettos where there are no green spaces and where the heat is conducive to race riots. They make money by the sale of weapons and alcoholic drinks, both of which push up the crime statistics. They impose inhuman production quotas and the hectic life of the megalopolis and live in fear lest some nervous wreck run amok and murder their families. They rule by coercion, have the police protect them, and make a fuss when the tables of violence are occasionally turned. They 'legally' make profits that the Inland Revenue is indulgent towards but pack off to prison the man who steals their car. They make money out of the production of instruments of wholesale destruction and condemn armed assault. They invest in 'respectable' enterprises the money gained by the sale of drugs, and proceed ruthlessly against the addict who snatches a handbag or wallet to cover his next fix. They promise, through growth, a paradise of affluence, but one to which too many can only accede by the method of breaking and entering—if, that is, they do not confine their attentions to breaking.

It is no longer the fathers of large families that hesitate before coming out on strike or are prepared to accept a 'reasonable settlement' but wage-earners who have to pay the instalments on the house, the refrigerator, the television, and the car at the end of the month. It is no longer a 'rise in the birth rate' but an increase in consumption that is of 'immediate advantage' to industrialists in bringing to their senses workers who, if they are not in debt, are on a very tight budget and can give up neither their purchases on credit nor their holidays.

Economic power radiates its own 'values': they are as alienating as the traditional 'morality' whose decay so saddens the Pharisees.

Freedom in jeopardy

In a democratic society technological progress stands in the service of man—that is a dogma. Only a perverted ideology can use it against citizens. In a windowless room in Washington two electronic machines can pull out in a matter of seconds any one of 754,000 cards containing confidential information about prominent citizens: anonymous denunciations, scraps of gossip, unconfirmed reports of various kinds. These cards are available to the Internal Security Committee of the House of Representatives, which made a name for itself at the time of the McCarthy witch-hunt. The Committee has an administrative staff of fifty-eight and the House gives it an annual budget of $525,000. McCarthyism is dead, but its instruments are kept in good working order against the next favourable opportunity, when all the resources of electronics will be at its service. The House of Representatives could have cut the Committee's budget; most of its members do not dare to do so for fear of being accused of being 'soft on Communism'.

The possibilities of electronics have only been partially exploited as yet. That is why in 1966 a Budget Bureau task force recommended the setting up of a National Data Center to collect in one place all the information held by various government bodies—from the Internal Revenue Service to the FBI—about American citizens. An electronic brain would ensure rapid handling of the three thousand million documents involved. Congress was hesitant about the project but did vote money for it to be partially carried into effect in a number of states, notably in California. The insurance companies have already fed into a computer all the information they have about some eleven million citizens. The association of firms issuing credit cards has done the same for one hundred million.

Time magazine has suggested what might—'in the interests of national efficiency'—be the advantages of assembling in a single electronic centre all the personal information in the possession of schools, hospitals, courts, insurance companies, banks, civil and military authorities, etc. The result no doubt would be increased efficiency on the part of tax and social-security departments, the police, and so on. But, as *Time* adds, it would constitute the 'greatest threat' ever to the rights of the individual. Because 'although a developing body of law has begun to establish the rights and wrongs of wiretapping and bugging, modern technology provides Government agencies and others with ever more subtle and delicate means of surveillance (. . .). People have become much too indifferent about protecting personal facts that once were considered nobody's business (. . .). Americans, in their blithe acceptance of technological inevitability, have failed to consider the broader implications of allowing information about themselves to accumulate so easily.'[46]

The risks are all the more real for the fact that the Internal Security Committee is still active and the Internal Security Division of the Department of Justice, set up in 1954 at the height of the McCarthyist hysteria, is enjoying a new lease of life. Since the autumn of 1970 it has been in special charge of 'harrying the Left' under the direction of Robert Mardian, formerly Goldwater's campaign organizer for the West in 1964, then at the Office of Education in charge of bending the rules regarding racial integration, and finally head of a group presided over by Spiro Agnew to help schools in the South fight court orders imposing desegregation.

In 'harrying the Left' or alleged supporters of it the Internal Security Division has at its disposal a formidable weapon, which proved its effectiveness in the days of McCarthyism. The law allows it to summon as a 'witness' a suspect before a grand jury; if he refuses to testify—if, for example, he refuses to give names of 'subversive' elements—he can be charged. The 'witness' is not entitled to the services of a lawyer, and the grand jury sits in secret. Alain Clément condemns in severe terms this 'perverted institution' that was originally designed to protect the accused against possibly arbitrary justice but 'is now little more, both at federal and state level, than a recording instance for prosecutions decided on by the district attorney. The latter lays down the law there, is the only one to call witnesses (prosecution witnesses, naturally), and interrogates them as he wishes, while neither the virtual accused nor the defence have access to the proceedings.'[47]

Following publication by the *New York Times* of the Pentagon's 'secret papers' on the Vietnam war, grand juries harried not only Daniel Ellsberg, who had handed over the documents, but also Professor Richard Falk (Princeton) and Professor Noam Chomsky (MIT) as well as the journalist David Halberstam. The grand jury procedure has been sharply criticized by such eminent jurists as William Howard Taft, Roscoe Pound, Felix Frankfurter, Herbert Packer, and Martin Levine, but it remains a favourite weapon against people whose guilt has been decided on in advance. Abolished in England in 1933, this inquisitorial institution could only be done away with in the United States by the complicated expedient of a constitutional amendment—which no member of Congress has yet initiated.[48]

The verdict of a grand jury can be challenged in the courts but it is an expensive business, and the judges then find themselves dealing with 'testimony' that the grand jury may have extracted by intimidation. The whole judicial system—overloaded and under-equipped—is going through a serious crisis. When Earl Warren was Chief Justice, the Supreme Court, guardian of the constitution, became the favourite target of the most reactionary groups, who disliked its liberal attitude with regard to blacks and human rights in general. President Nixon seizes every opportunity of modifying its composition in a more conservative direction. He nominated Clement Haynsworth and Harold Carswell, both of whom the Senate refused to confirm in an appointment that counts for so much in the general orientation of the country, and then William Rehnquist, who had supported Carswell's candidacy by writing, in a letter to the *Washington Post*, that 'further expansion of constitutional recognition of civil rights (. . .) logically brings in train (. . .) further expansion of the constitutional right of criminal defendants, of pornographers and of demonstrators.'[49]

The argument finds a large audience both in the United States and in Europe: to combat the crime wave more effectively it is necessary to limit the rights of the individual and the safeguards offered the accused. Since every accused person is presumed innocent, it is in fact the rights and safeguards of all citizens that would be dangerously restricted in this way: those of the assassin and the political opponent, those of the drug pusher and the pamphleteer.

In France, when the Minister of the Interior asked in April 1971 for an extension of the period of detention without trial ('garde à vue') for certain categories of offender, the French Law Association expressed its 'deep concern' and the Keeper of the Seals voiced his hostility to such a project, which appealed, he said, to 'a number of good people of a somewhat impatient nature'. He added: 'My job is to see that the law is respected, and the law must contain safeguards for *every* accused, no matter who he is.' This did not stop the Minister from taking the matter up again in March 1972. And the congress of the Union of Police Superintendents approved a report along the same lines, taking its stand on an argument calculated to appeal to the public at large: 'It must be pointed out that the "garde à vue" is not a police privilege but a safeguard for society, allowing justice to be done in the best possible conditions (. . .) Further it exists under various names in virtually every country in the world.'[50]

Privileges are only ever justified in terms of the advantages they bring not only to those to whom they are conceded but to society as a whole. In reality the 'garde à vue' is practised without effective supervision, it constitutes a serious infringement of the liberties of the individual, it is too often an occasion for brutality, and it can be renewed almost automatically. The fact that it is practised in a variety of countries is not necessarily an argument in its favour. One might as well suggest that Europe as a whole adopt a procedure that works wonders in Portugal: in pursuance of 'security measures' a convict can be reimprisoned as soon as his sentence expires. No one has ventured to put forward such a suggestion, but neither has anyone thought of introducing the Anglo-Saxon practice of habeas corpus into countries that do not have it. Worse still, France has not ratified the European Human Rights Convention, which offers citizens the opportunity of appeal, if necessary against the state itself, to a European commission and a European court.

Extremists of Right and Left are not the only ones to denounce the violation of civil rights and the liberties of the individual. 'Telephone conversations, particularly those of politicians and journalists, are increasingly subject to tapping,' wrote Michel Poniatowski in a question addressed to the Prime Minister. At the same time he called for regulations to be laid down to protect the privacy of the citizen.[51]

The US Justice Department fiercely defends its right to use telephone tapping in investigations into groups 'committed to the use of illegal methods to bring about changes in our form of government'. The Supreme Court has been asked to pronounce on the subject four times since 1969: on two occasions it upheld the Attorney General and on two occasions the plaintiff. The government justifies telephone tapping by citing reasons of national security. Its plea before the Supreme Court was to the effect that the activities of controversial groups were 'interrelated' with security threats from abroad. It added that if each case had to be brought up before a judge for authorization to tap a particular line, 'the Government would have to disclose sensitive and highly secret information'. Furthermore the judge is not qualified to discern the 'subtle inferences' that the Attorney General may extract from each case. Of course, admitted the Solicitor General in making his plea before the Supreme Court, the Attorney General could abuse this power, but that was 'not a valid basis for denying (him) the authority' to tap telephones without court authorization. Furthermore the prosecutor is not obliged to tell the accused what information has been obtained through tapping.[52]

Despite the fact that the majority of citizens remains unaware of or indifferent to the problem, there are people throughout the West who denounce the dangers threatening the liberties of the individual. Former US Supreme Court justice Abe Fortas has written: 'Clearly the time had come for the law to be available-in-fact to all, white, black, rich or poor (. . .). And clearly, I believe, the time had come for the magical phrases of equal protection and due process to acquire a new and additional dimension.'[53]

Continually improving methods of investigation have not found their counterpart in a strengthening of civil rights. In fact the rights of the citizen are on the wane, notably because they have never been re-defined in the light of contemporary problems and because the expense and protractedness of judicial proceedings are such that recourse to the law is not available to everyone in equal measure. The evolution of law and the legal system is lagging behind in relation to the evolution of society and the means the state has at its disposal for restricting freedoms it in fact theoretically guarantees to all. This lag impairs the equality of citizens before the law and strikes at the very foundations of a democratic society.

The malaise is an old one and it is getting worse as time goes on. One cannot reread without a shock of fear this sentence written more than sixty years ago by one of the most eminent figures of the legal world, Louis D. Brandeis:

> In view of the unrest in this country, in view of the widespread feeling that the law is something different for the rich than for the poor, it is of the utmost importance that men should not trifle with the law . . . that they should recognize that the law is supreme over man, and in this republic exists for all men alike.

The liberties of all citizens are threatened when, on the government's initiative or with its tacit approval, the safeguards offered by the law are in practice refused to national or immigrant minorities, to political groups, no matter how small, and to particular categories of citizen on the grounds of their professional activities or social condition.

An English lawyer, Anthony Lester, has cited three cases in which public opinion is either actively or passively an accessory to this trend:

Northern Ireland is as much a part of the United Kingdom as Mississippi is a part of the United States. The Ulster legislature (unlike the rest of Britain) enjoys considerable autonomy from the central government; and (unhappily, like other parts of Britain) a substantial minority of the people of Ulster are victims of deepseated prejudice and discrimination. For fifty years, local democracy has failed to protect the Catholics there, just as for centuries it failed the black people of Mississippi. But our Courts are literally impotent to deal with the problem.[54]

Which is how a failure of democracy, tolerated for generations by an indifferent or complacent majority, leads to civil war.

Anthony Lester's second example is liable to be quoted as a precedent one day:

In 1968, Parliament surrendered to popular prejudice against coloured immigration from the Commonwealth, and deprived 200,000 United Kingdom citizens of Asian descent of their right to enter and live in Britain. They possess British passports and have no right to live anywhere else. (. . .) No court can scrutinize the actions of the government.'

The societies of the West show themselves too easily resigned to the fact that the very principles of democracy can be 'democratically' violated. The Nazis came to power by legal means; the Vichy regime was set up with the dubious backing of a parliamentary division; racial segregation was legal in the United States until 1954; McCarthyism legally withdrew the passports of American nationals; French law refuses foreign workers the trade-union rights it grants to French workers. The old conflict between the legal character and the legitimacy of certain measures is unresolved. Contradicting as they do the very spirit of democracy, social and economic injustices of the most serious kind are none the less legal. Those who protest do so as much against the legality of such injustices as against the injustices themselves. Unable to appeal to any court, they resort to 'agitation' that will be countered by fresh restrictions on the liberties of the individual.

Anthony Lester mentions a final example. Every Western country is familiar with the art of drawing constituency boundaries in such a way as to benefit the majority while breaking up the strongholds of the opposition and submerging the fragments in new units favourable to the regime in power. Internal migration and developing urban concentration call for periodic revision of the electoral map. When the

British parliament entrusted an independent commission with this task, the commission's conclusions were rejected by the Wilson government. 'There is no judicial power to enable the electors to vote on equal terms,' Anthony Lester points out, concluding: 'There is (in Britain) mounting pressure for stronger legal safeguards of individual rights and liberties.'[55]

The 'legal safeguards' are indeed inadequate. *De jure* or *de facto* the powers of the state have been reinforced while the rights and liberties of citizens remain stuck with their old definitions. Moreover the legal system itself rarely enjoys the kind of trust it would have to have if citizens were to see in it a guarantee of equality. When the new general secretary of France's UDR, barely in office, publicly criticized the Bench he raised a first-class storm of indignant protest. Yet how many judges, having taken their oath to Vichy, judged the same regime's collaborators or, having condemned Algerians and their friends, found members of the opposite camp being brought before them? How many demanded to be 'covered' in writing before instituting proceedings? The judges whose careers bear witness to complete independence know how badly the reputation of the profession has been tarnished by certain members who have sought too keenly the approval of the regime.

Those countries that have known Fascism, Nazism, or foreign occupation have still not shaken off a past heavy with compromise and blameworthy caution. But are judges any more independent in other countries? Philip B. Kurland, Professor of Law at the University of Chicago and editor of the *Supreme Court Review*, writes:

> Whether elected or appointed, the great majority of American judges have their posts because—and only because—of prior services rendered to the dominant political party (. . .). State judgeships are usually regarded as sinecures awarded loyal lawyers for helping garner votes for successful elected officials. This is not to say, of course, that there are no judges of real talent on our courts (. . .). But they are few and far between (. . .). The resulting evils are not merely the incapacity to keep up with the ever-growing volume of business. The results include an incapacity to provide principled resolutions of difficult legal questions. More important, the results include a contempt for the judicial process, displayed no less by Governors and Congressmen than by ordinary litigants and the man in the street.[56]

Threatened by institutions whose inquisitorial zeal may be unleashed in a climate of hysteria or panic, insidiously nibbled at by electronic

devices that pierce the walls of private life, daily assaulted by new cru-
saders in the war on crime and subversion, unequally guaranteed to
different categories of citizens, impaired by strong yet impotent states
that dream of acquiring even greater powers, fragile because defined in
ways that the evolution of society and custom has made obsolete,
frankly encroached on by certain legal decisions, more or less well
served by a hopelessly overloaded legal system, the freedom enjoyed by
Westerners may yet appear enviable to those who lack it. And indeed
it is something enviable. The liberties it ensures are more than mere
formalities: it offers the practical, daily possibility of meeting and
speaking, criticizing and coming out on strike, denouncing abuses and
putting forward suggestions. But it is none the less fragile in the face of
bureaucratic power and undermined by the seditious elements that
abuse it, by the right-wing extremists who hold it responsible for every
disorder, and above all by the vast majority who take it too lightly and
too much for granted.

A freedom that is shrinking in areas regarded as secondary or that is
refused to individuals regarded as 'marginal', a freedom, above all, that
is stagnating instead of progressing and strengthening its foundations is
already a freedom exposed to 'rape by consent'. It is forty years since
the author of *Main Street* and *Babbitt* wrote *It Can't Happen Here*—a
title under which Sinclair Lewis pointed out that, contrary to general
opinion, *it* could happen here, *it* being Fascism. But without Mussolini's
absurd grandiloquence, without the raving 'magnetism' of the author
of *Mein Kampf*, without even the vulgar hysteria of Joseph McCarthy.
Without the uniforms, the flags, the monster parades; without the concentration camps, mysterious disappearances, public executions. Probably Fascism as history has known it will never conquer Europe or
North America. But the door is open to what Professor Bertram Gross
of Hunter College described in the *New York Times* as a 'friendly
fascism',[57] a society scientifically administered by a faceless bureaucracy,
repudiating all ideology the better to impose a 'technocratic ideology',
developing all the factors of alienation in modern societies and multiplying control networks by having them control one another.

Commerce and information

It makes little difference whether this dark prophecy comes true in
every detail: the combinations that can lead to the anaesthetization of
the liberties of the individual are infinitely variable. What is constant is

the fact that familiarity with certain forms of freedom makes it increasingly difficult clearly to discern their limits—limits that have a tendency to shrink. The development of mass-communications media, for example, goes hand in hand with a prodigious increase in the amount of information made available to the public and at the same time with a lessening of real freedom of information.

The most disturbing aspect of the slow erosion of the right to information lies in the ill-informedness of a public that is increasingly swamped with a flood of news, analysis, and comment from which the reader simply does not have time to extract the essential. It is the same with information as it is with money: inflation makes possible a measure of expansion but itself constitutes a danger that the 'consumer' is powerless to arrest. He simply cannot read several newspapers a day and pursue a systematic programme of research, comparison, and cross-checking in order to find out the facts governing the evolution of the world he lives in. No one expects him to read the *New York Times* or *Le Monde* from beginning to end—and even that would not exempt him from tackling a quantity of weeklies, monthlies, and specialized works to get hold of the necessary background knowledge.

Under the influence of technical developments, rising production and distribution costs, and the changing structure of commerce and advertising the freedom of the press has become a freedom to swamp the reader with masses of information that do not necessarily make a better-informed citizen of him. Overeating has never been synonymous with good health, nor does it necessarily provide the organism with the quality of nourishment it needs to lead a balanced existence.

The industrialized West has confused freedom of the press with the *commercial* freedom to publish newspapers and periodicals. Organs of information can respect the rules of sound management (which is not always the case) and yet stifle freedom of expression by suppressing facts or opinions offensive to a section of their readership and giving priority to the quest for profit and the desire to expand. Thus Daniel Morgaine has written: 'The publishing company producing the mass-circulation daily is, like every industry producing a commodity for mass consumption, in the service of its public.'[58]

It looks an attractive principle—and no doubt it would be if in a mass-consumption society the size of a firm's clientele were sufficient proof that the firm was genuinely in its service. The real situation is rather different. In the United States, for example, Andrew Hacker writes that 'the steel companies can be inefficient, and still be

profitable'.[59]Ralph Nader showed how the motor industry was marketing millions of vehicles that did not offer the public the safety it was
entitled to expect. The experience of every democratic government has
shown that, in the absence of stringent controls, industry is perfectly
capable of knowingly selling to a vast public foodstuffs and pharmaceutical and beauty products that are detrimental to health. Not every
industry producing commodities for mass consumption is necessarily
in the service of its public, even if that public supports it loyally: this is
as true of a brand of aperitif as it is of all the sob and scandal sheets or
quite simply the mediocre press.

Everything that goes into the composition of a newspaper, writes
Daniel Morgaine, must be designed 'to give the public what it wants'.
One thus arrives, in theory, at newspapers that are commercially prosperous—proof positive that they enjoy the favour of the public. Yet
history shows that the newspapers that have most indulged their
readers have not always been the most successful. Their public, however, was not disappointed: it learned that an enthusiastic crowd had
greeted Nungesser and Coli as they landed; it was moved by the
forged photograph of a sovereign on his death-bed and by the genuine
photograph, taken by someone who broke in on Charles Dullin's
death agony; it discovered that Thomas Dewey had beaten Harry
Truman in the contest for the White House, and in 1946 it learned
through the offices of the celebrated Walter Winchell that General de
Gaulle had been imprisoned 'in his own house in Paris by order of the
commie high command'.[60] Perhaps that really was what the public
wanted. . .

Since then this kind of news-mongering has been brought to a high
degree of perfection. Today's public knows all about Fabiola's difficult
pregnancies and about the loving care with which, on Onassis' island
and with the blessing of the late Pope John XXIII, Jacqueline Kennedy
continues to surround the former President of the United States—dis-
figured and robbed of his reason by the Dallas incident. The public
even knew about Maurice Chevalier's death in advance.

These are trifles. But the same public learns from an enormous head-
line in a mass-circulation daily that Egyptian tanks entered Israel in the
early hours of the Six-Day War. It knows that Mao is a sick man and
as good as dead, which will one day be confirmed. It learns after the
event that in 1962 President Kennedy asked the *New York Times* not to
publish information in its possession about the 'missile crisis', thus
making the discovery that the Cold War involved sufficient real

dangers to make the press both in Europe and in America careful not
to over-excite opinion and sharpen the atmosphere of crisis—despite
the fact that 'the public', it is said, loves sensation.

Almost every newspaper in the United States gave quite extraordinary publicity to the maddest pronouncements of Joseph McCarthy
without a word of qualification or warning, quoting 'objectively'
remarks of his to the effect that he had in his possession 'the list of 205 . . .
a list of names that were made known to the Secretary of State as being
members of the Communist party'. Next day those 205 Communists had
become 205 'bad security risks'. The day after there were only '57 card-
carrying Communists'. Eleven days later, before the Senate, the same
'list' contained 81 names. 'His charges,' wrote Jack Anderson and
Ronald W. May, 'made page 1 headlines in almost every newspaper in
the nation, and the name of Joe McCarthy was heard again in the
land.'[61] An irresponsible press, giving its public the expected daily dose
of anti-Communism, made the reputation of the 'witch-hunter' and
maintained a climate of suspicion and fear that was to shatter the careers
of reputable people, coarsen American politics, and ultimately turn
against the better newspapers—which then, belatedly, carried out a
disintoxication campaign.

A recent American study has shown how many newspapers, in order
to comply with what they assumed to be the wishes of readers they
were supposed to be informing, printed tendentious versions of the
Alger Hiss affair, the Rosenberg trial, the beginnings of the Vietnam
war, etc.[62] More recently a concern to please the public led *Life* magazine, which was then in a precarious financial situation, to pay a fortune
for the forged autobiography of the enigmatic Howard Hughes—a
guaranteed publishing success. After all it was only a repeat of the
profitable business of Khrushchev's 'Memoirs' a year before. 'Whether
true or not,' writes *Harper's*, 'it is widely believed inside Time Inc., as
outside, that not only the KGB but the CIA had a hand in the author-
ship of the Khrushchev transcripts, with material not only deleted but
added in the West. (. . .) Even the suspicion, combined with the known
and flagrant inaccuracies of the book—demonstrated by George Kennan
and by Svetlana, among others—makes clear that no fact whatever can
be established or even confirmed from *Khrushchev Remembers.*'[63]

Yet colossal sums are paid for this kind of material by dailies as well
as weeklies, both American and European, which then serialize it in
the hope of increasing their circulation. The authenticity of such documents is of minor importance: the public likes to be taken into the

confidence of the great of this world and share their secrets, whether true or false. It is the natural outcome of a competitive situation viewed first and foremost from the commercial standpoint.

Freedom of the press can only be safeguarded and the press can only truly serve the public on the condition that it does *not* indulge readers by giving them what it assumes they expect of it. By making newspapers into businesses the condition of whose existence is commercial success the West has impaired the freedom of its press. Britain has seen dailies with circulations of more than a million simply disappear from the scene; independent organs have been bought up by businessmen. In France the demise of Parisian dailies has gone hand in hand with a concentration of provincial papers. Of the fifteen dailies New York was publishing in 1900 only three are left. Commenting in 1967 on the disappearance of the *World Journal Tribune,* itself born of the fusion of three once prosperous newspapers eight months previously,[64] the *New York Times* wrote: 'But anyone coming into the New York market will have to be prepared to invest many millions of dollars—anywhere from $25 million to $50 million as a starter—and to run the gauntlet of 10 unions that still show no sign of having read any moral from all the tombstones in the journalistic cemetery.'[65]

Can newspapers that adopt the structure and aims of purely commercial enterprises still fulfil their role? Robert Hersant recalls how Edmond Michelet, 'whose record in the Resistance no one would argue with', handed over the *Courrier du Centre* to him in 1956, and how subsequently André Morice, whom no one would fête as a *résistant,* brought him *l'Eclair de l'Ouest.* The Gaullist Christian Democrat and the Radical editors were followed by Maurice Violette, who 'entrusted (to Robert Hersant) the fate' of *l'Action républicaine,* then by the Socialist Guy Mollet with *Nord-Matin,* General de Gaulle with *France-Antilles,* and the moderate *Le Havre-Press,* not to mention *Brive-Information,* the *Berry républicain,* the *Liberté du Morhiban,* and the *République des Pyrénées.*

All without the slightest spirit of partisanship: 'In every case and at all times,' writes Hersant, 'I have maintained the political line that was laid down for me; by keeping myself out of the picture I have safeguarded plurality of information.'[66] Pierre-René Wolf, editor of *Paris-Normandie,* replies: 'Although a *député* he flogs socialism here, radicalism there, and Gaullism somewhere else. Pluralism he calls it—but there are those who would say that as newspaper publishing it smacks more of opportunism.'[67]

In the United States as in Europe the majority of provincial towns have only one daily, which deprives the reader of any freedom of choice. When a town does have two they are often both owned by the same proprietor.

The television networks, despite some excellent programmes, are 'proof of a decadence, an escape from the realities of the world we live in,' said Edward R. Murrow—himself, among others, proof that quality does have a place on television. Walter Lippmann hit on the real problem when he wrote that there is 'something essentially wrong with the basic principles governing the exploitation of television'. He added that the *laisser-faire* attitude had made television 'the creature, the handmaid, and alas the prostitute of commercialization'.[68]

Walter Lippmann's verdict applies equally to many newspapers diverted from their role by the commercial game of pursuing new readers and advertisers. 'To enable existing newspapers to continue to exist and—which is a condition of their survival—to invest, and to make it possible for others to be born and thrive would require an extraordinary combination of circumstances and men of good-will,' writes Jacques Sauvageot.[69]

Those circumstances and those men of good-will have little chance of coming together as long as the press continues to be based on the commercial foundations of capitalist society. Hubert Beuve-Méry long ago put forward a formula that offers the best chance of safeguarding—or is it reconquering?—the freedom of the press. The founder of *Le Monde* realized how the commercial success of a newspaper or its unsuccessful search for such success can divert it from its role. He rejected for his newspaper two laws that are inherent in the capitalist system: the enrichment of shareholders as a result of commercial success and the devolution of such shares by way of inheritance. To keep those responsible for newspapers out of the temptation to make a profit at any cost he recommended that they be published by non-profit-making companies or by 'foundations'.

When the proprietor of *Paris-Jour* decided to wind up publication the reaction was one of astonishment from various quarters. Yet it is quite normal for a commercial enterprise, even if it happens to be a newspaper, to terminate its activities when those activities have ceased to pay. It is the law of such matters and there is therefore nothing scandalous about the disappearance of *Paris-Jour*. The only scandal—and it is a whopper—is that a private proprietor should for years have been able, simply and solely because he possessed the necessary capital, freely' to publish a newspaper and influence opinion in a way that was not open to citizens who lacked his financial resources. This privilege of capital is incompatible with a democracy that lays down as a matter of principle the political equality of all citizens. This relic from an era when democracy was identified with the rights of the owner class illustrates the fundamental weakness of the societies of the West: totally transformed in terms of social and economic structure, they have failed to bring about a parallel evolution in the institutions that are essential to the proper functioning of democracy. The technical possibilities of news transmission, printing, and distribution have progressed: the freedom of the press is stuck at the stage of the horse-drawn carriage and the carrier pigeon.

The enormous gap between the old definitions of our civil liberties and their clearer and more stringent perception in the future lies at the heart of the crisis facing the democracies of the West. The defenders of the established order rely on a simple and effective argument: those liberties, however anachronistically conceived, do not even exist under other regimes—so the West is still in the vanguard of democratic progress. A civilization is not judged by comparison with the systems or regimes with which it is at odds. Its only justification can lie in continued striving towards the goals it has set itself.

Men and institutions

The sickness of the West is not solely a matter of its institutions. These, even in their most inhuman form, have never become depersonalized: it is men that choose their member of parliament and their newspaper, adopt or reject opinions, and seek or avoid debate. The citizen cannot throw responsibility for his own malaise onto the structures of his society. Those structures do not exist as something apart from him, and deep down he does recognize himself in them, for they reflect an enlarged image of his indifference to others, his thirst for power, his improvidence, and his greed for gain. Democracy can be judged by its structures for they are a more or less faithful reflection of the attitudes of its citizens.

Institutions themselves may be slightly ahead of or slightly behind citizens: rarely do they stand in open contradiction to them. The House of Commons, in withdrawing the passports of British citizens of Asian origin, was *following* public opinion. When on the other hand the US Supreme Court ordered racial integration in public education in 1954 it was in advance of a public opinion that, two decades later, has still not evolved to the point of admitting that a principle should be applied in practice. The House of Commons capitulated to the racial prejudice of certain categories of voter. The US Supreme Court, however, and subsequently Congress in passing a number of civil rights bills, were fulfilling their normative function: laying down rules in full knowledge that they would be contested not only by a large section of public opinion but also by state legislatures, educational committees, courts, and finally the White House itself, which, under President Nixon, put a brake on the process of racial integration for electoral reasons.

Democracy cannot survive unless it applies the goals to be achieved to the whole of society. But the dialogue between institutions and public is down to its simplest expression, with the result that society can hardly rely on its elected representatives and its courts to translate its democratic aspirations into deeds. Progress is possible only at the price of citizens' associations putting constant pressure on institutions. All economic interests have their 'pressure groups', which seek to steer investment, legislation, taxation, or the appointment of officials in a direction favourable to themselves. Completely taken up as they are with electoral preoccupations, political parties are inadequate as 'pressure groups' to prompt the public authorities to defend interests of a non-economic nature. More than any other country in the West the United States has a wide variety of private associations campaigning for justice, for racial equality, for conservation, for consumer protection, etc. The recent development of clubs and local associations in Europe is evidence both of a certain awakening of opinion and of the short-comings of political parties.

This kind of initiative usually focuses round a local concern: building a recreation centre or zoning a green area, preventing the disfiguration of a particular quarter or the felling of some trees. Rarer are the private non-political organizations that devote their attention to more general and more disinterested objectives: support for ethnic minorities, justice for all, a quickening of cultural life, opinion campaigns, general orientations of society. The political effectiveness of such activities needs no further proof: in the United States the patient efforts of the National Association for the Advancement of Coloured People in securing lawyers for victims of racial discrimination have resulted in the removal of many legal obstacles to true equality. In France the activities of private groups resulted in the passage of the Neuwirth law on contraception.

Democracy is inconceivable without this kind of active participation of citizens in private organizations taking it upon themselves to study particular problems, alert public opinion, and make their presence felt in the administration, parliament, the press, and the unions. The schema whereby political parties constitute the only or at least the preferential channel for such activities is too simple; their political colouring divides citizens who may find themselves united around objectives of general interest. Any kind of 'participation' organized by the state will be suspect both as to intention and methods. If participation is not to be so suspect citizens must wrest it for themselves and not wait for it to be granted them.

Racialism and democracy

Illustrative of this point is the role of the anti-racialist associations that unite militants of widely differing political convictions in combating attitudes that are incompatible with the Western concept of man and democracy.

Of all the breaches of democratic principle in the West racialism is undeniably the most serious. Impediments to freedom of opinion and the various forms of pressure, perversion, and censorship of information do not prevent citizens from thinking, expressing themselves, and communicating with one another. Social and economic injustices can be fought by trade unions and political parties. Inadequacy of political institutions or opportunism in the men in power can be effectively denounced. But racialism penetrates to every part of society, even to certain unions, parties, and newspapers and into the fields of education, administration, and justice. The slightest encroachment on freedom of expression provokes a scandal; the daily manifestations of racialism give rise to only episodic protest. Yet they withhold from individuals not only essential freedoms but the right to recognition as human beings. To borrow the phrase of a former Secretary-General of the United Nations, racialism is a 'malignant tumour', and one that eats away at the entire social organism.

For a long time Europe was inclined to take an indulgent view of its own racialism and to extenuate it by reference to the more virulent and openly avowed racialism rampant in the United States. Following the collapse of Nazism, racialism ceased as it were to be respectable in Europe. The memory of the gas chambers drove the subject from the political arena. It was 'against the law', whereas in the United States it

was actually upheld by a carefully elaborated system of laws and prece-
dents. The contrast quieted Europeans' democratic conscience. But for
a number of years now both sides of the Atlantic have been in the same
situation: the United States has followed Europe in abolishing all
racialist legislation yet racialism is just as widespread on both continents. Even in the period when American racialism was backed up by a
whole complex of legislative and judicial decisions it set a smaller gap
between blacks and whites than existed between, for example, French
and Algerians (though the latter were 'citizens' of the French Republic)
as regards standard of living, education, or the right to vote. Even
England had its race riots. Too many incidents suggest that Europe
would adopt the attitude of the United States if its population included
the same percentage of coloured people. Even as its more shocking
public manifestations are being eliminated, racialism is making
inroads into minds that protest their devotion to democracy. Particularly at the time of the Six-Day War the most impassioned reactions to
the conflict in the Middle East were marked by the confrontation of
anti-Jewish and anti-Arab feelings, more or less effectively camouflaged
behind considerations of a politico-strategic nature.

Scrawled by hand on a poster put up in Lyon by a union wishing to
draw attention to the rights of immigrant workers: 'No jobs for wogs'
('Pas de travail pour les bicots'). A classified advertisement in a German
newspaper: 'For sale: farm in good condition with outbuildings. Suitable for horses and foreign workers.' There is a German law to the
effect that a sheep-dog must have fifteen square metres of living-space,
but Turkish workers can be crowded any number to the room. 'The
foreign workers are our Negroes,' a German journalist has said. The
'Bar américain' at Saint-Claude in the Jura refuses to serve Algerians, as
the 'Latin-Musique' in Paris' Boulevard Saint-Germain refuses to serve
blacks. The Prefect of the Rhône *département* has denounced the gangs
of youngsters who, using stolen cars, go round at night beating up
workers from North Africa and Portugal.[70] The Bishop of Dijon has
protested at the sale of caricature dolls manufactured in West Germany
and bearing the label: 'Jew: Fr. 23·50'.[71]

It would be nice to think that the churches and the public authorities
did everything in their power to combat racialism. Yet although it is
so widespread it is rare for the courts to penalize racial discrimination.
Victims of it do not always dare to bring charges, nor do they often
have the money to finance a trial. But above all employers are careful
to conceal the racial character of their decisions and leave no material

proof. The two firms fined Fr. 4,000 and Fr. 1,000 respectively for dismissing workers on the grounds of their ethnic origin are the exception.[72]

Furthermore, up until 1972 French law contained loop-holes allowing racialism to manifest itself with impunity. Refusal to serve a black man or an Algerian could be penalized as an infringement of commercial law but not as a crime of racial discrimination. France did in 1971 subscribe to the international convention for the abolition of racial discrimination, which provides that member states can be induced to take fresh legislative measures towards this end, but the preamble to the draft bill authorizing membership stated that 'French law is very largely in conformity with the convention (and) fresh legislative measures do not at the moment appear to be necessary to its application.'

Yet the laws in force make things pretty difficult for the private associations trying to bring cases of racial discrimination or insult before the courts. Several proposals to reinforce anti-racialist legislation have been tabled—by the Communists in 1968, by the Socialists in 1971. The government was planning as early as 1961 to place before parliament a project designed to stop the various forms of racial discrimination. The plan was not put into effect until 1970.

The passage of more effective legislation is important but not enough in itself. In the United States every possible step has been taken by Congress and the courts to put a stop to racial discrimination. *Time* writes: 'There has been no longer or more bitter social and political struggle in contemporary America than the eighteen-year fight to eliminate racially segregated schools.'[73] The battle has not produced the results that were legislated for: racial discrimination in schools will continue to be the rule as long as there is residential segregation. The progress of integration has whipped up racialist feelings to the point where they have become a major electoral consideration. The only possible confirmation of democracy is conformity of custom and law. The law in this respect has evolved in the direction of progress, but custom hinders its application.

In Paris on 27 November 1971 an Algerian worker named Cheik Bouabdelli was involved in a slight collision with another car. The two drivers were amiably settling their differences when a police car drove up and took the Algerian to the police station of the *5ᵉ arrondissement*. There policemen insulted him, forced him to drink wine and afterwards take the breathalyser test, and finally beat him up so badly that he had to be taken to hospital for surgical attention. Illegal, of course, but such things are done none the less.[74] At the beginning of October 1971 Gacem Ali, a father of four living in the Paris suburb of Boulogne-Billancourt, died of injuries inflicted by a group of young racialists.

These examples, chosen from among hundreds, are the natural upshot of the spread of racialist propaganda. The 'Ordre Nouveau' group exalts the defence of the 'white race'. An anonymous pamphlet published in Grenoble states: 'China and Japan are on the way to becoming giants thanks, among other things, to the absence of Jews from their lands, making true national union possible. The countries without Jews are on the way up, while the Jewish invasion is effecting the decay and disappearance of the countries they occupy.'[75] On the death of Xavier Vallat, former Commissioner for Jewish Affairs under the Vichy regime, *Minute* paid feeling tribute to his 'exemplary public life'. But it is a mass-circulation magazine that publishes readers' letters seeking to justify racialism in terms such as these: 'It only takes two or three generations to rot the host country; with our three million allogenous immigrants in France, conditions are ripe.'[76]

The private associations campaigning throughout the West against racialism in all its forms are doing society an irreplaceable service. Occasionally their activities receive the support of unions, political parties, the press, and the churches. But the battle only touches the surface, whereas racialism has penetrated every corner of our modern societies that keep their lowliest jobs for workers belonging to one or another ethnic minority. The West as a whole is no more racialist today than the Weimar Republic was, but it was not many years after the Weimar Republic that the gas chambers and crematoria started to operate the 'final solution'.

'The battleground, today, is in the trial courts, and especially the lower trial courts; because it is in these tribunals that legally approved racism and classism flourishes in its most virulent form,' says George W. Crockett, President of the American National Bar Association.[77] Of some 20,000 officiating judges in the United States, only 289 are black. White judges often reflect the dominant opinions of their own milieu and are harder on blacks than on whites. The same attitude operates in France against workers from North Africa. American anti-racialist organizations have launched a big drive to get more judges recruited from among the black population. But they insist over and over again that the fight against racialism can only be successful if it is fought with the active participation of the largest possible number of citizens.

In Europe as in America that fight can indeed only be won if it is

---

fought on all fronts—in schools, trade unions, and political parties, in the press and in the churches, at home, at work, and at play. A society that is content to satisfy the aspirations of the majority has given up the democratic struggle. At the very heart of the democratic principle is the obligation to safeguard the rights of the minority—and that includes minorities. Democracy denies itself when social and racial minorities are exploited and citizens fail to rise up in revolt. A minority that rebels in order to secure recognition of its rights is not working in its own interests alone: it is saving democracy itself by urging it to stay faithful to its obligations. The success of the black revolt in the United States is indispensable not only to the liberation of blacks but to the salvation of American democracy. The elimination of racialism in the West would secure justice for its 'allogenous' minorities and at the same time save the West's democracies by freeing them from the most serious of all the contradictions undermining their foundations.

The author of *The Legend of Tucker Caliban* wrote:

The whole white world (. . .) has to answer for centuries of wrongs, injustices, and racialism. All whites (. . .) are prisoners of the same illusion (. . .). They have no other alternative but (. . .) the verbal fantasies of an unreal commercial world and the violent cruelty with which they react when they temporarily wake up to all that threatens to thwart their puerile dream.[78]

That 'unreal commercial world' has based its affluence and expansion on 'areas of poverty' that can be topped up by immigration when required, on speculation of a kind that has led to monstrous urban agglomerations, and on the exploitation of unskilled workers. It has paralysed democratic institutions that, if allowed free play, would have shattered the system. Racial prejudice itself is not solely economic in origin, but the chief victims of that 'unreal commercial world' are racial minorities. Which led Thomas Merton to a conclusion that few Westerners will accept: 'The whites (. . .) cannot free the Negroes because they are incapable of freeing themselves (. . .). We need the Negroes to be free for our own good even more than for theirs.'[79]

From his Trappist monastery in Kentucky the monk Thomas Merton got to the heart of the 'crisis of civilization' affecting the West. He saw its economic and sociological causes, which in his view 'are the symptoms of a universal spiritual crisis that may soon reach apocalyptic proportions'—leaving us to remember Auschwitz, the race riots, Hiroshima . . .

The churches and democracy

Among the groups that have contributed to this 'universal spiritual crisis' and which supposedly have the mission of constantly reminding society to respect the persons that make it up, the churches ought in principle to occupy a special place. Thomas Merton, however, wrote·

> I question whether our claims to be the only sincere defenders of the person of man, his rights, his dignity, and his nobility as a creature made in the image of God (. . .) are justified by our deeds. It seems to me we have little more than slogans left, concepts void of all reality.[80]

The societies of the West are sick not only because they have sacrificed human aspirations to their will to power and to purely material aims but also because the groups (and they include the churches) that put themselves forward as champions of man have failed in this aspect of their mission. The Roman Catholic and Protestant churches are faced with the same fundamental question: what is their place and their role in the context of the materialist societies that have emerged in the democratic and traditionally Christian West?

Statistics alone cannot account for the crisis the churches are going through. The acute shortage of priests[81] and the disaffection of the faithful do not give an adequate indication of its extent. Indeed there is no evidence that the churches' influence on society was any greater or more beneficial in the days when parishes and seminaries were able to submit satisfactory statistics. It was even during that period of apparent vitality that all the elements of the crisis to come were distilled. Carried along by momentum and force of habit a political party, a regime, an educational system, a newspaper, or a church can survive for a long time after the onset of sclerosis or decay.

For all its divine institution a church is nevertheless made up of human beings and as such is subject to the same sociological laws as govern all societies. It is in this respect that the churches are involved in the malaise of the West. When Cardinal Alfrink, Archbishop of Utrecht, asks whether the Roman Catholic church is 'entirely credible',[82] the answer can be provided neither by the Vatican nor by any committee of theologians but only by the attitudes of the believers and non-believers who watch it at work.

When the American bishops arrived at the conclusion more than ten years ago that the 'national ideal' of the United States 'no longer rests upon the foundations of broad and solid popular morality', they quoted by way of proof circumstances that are incompatible with democracy: 'the sensational treatment of violence', 'the disclosures of greed and cynicism in government, labour, and business', 'race prejudice and injustice', and 'a disregard of the sacredness of human life'.[83]

The bishops, however, did not ask whether they were 'credible': had they not themselves contributed to destroying the principles whose demise they deplored? If some small Roman Catholic groups, notably around the Jesuit John Lafarge, had taken up the battle against racialism long before and if one or two bishops did very slightly anticipate the action of the Supreme Court in this field (1954), the vast majority of the episcopate was content merely to follow once the trend had become irreversible. And if we assume that the investments of the Roman Catholic church, which are kept secret, fall into more or less the same pattern as those of the Protestant churches, then the bishops had done their bit to promote the greed, cynicism, and violence they denounced. For ten Protestant churches, several of which have come out against the Vietnam war and one of which is avowedly pacifist, have invested in twenty-nine firms working for the Pentagon more than $200 million, which in 1970 brought them in some $6·2 million in interest.[84]

To cease to be 'credible' it is not even necessary for a church modestly to avert its gaze for generations from what was after all virulent racialism or discreetly to make a profit out of activities it deplores. It is enough if its voice is no longer heard, and how far that voice carries depends neither on the size of the clergy nor on the numerical strength of the faithful. During the Nazi occupation the lone, broken voice of Cardinal Saliège was heard when he denounced the persecution of the Jews. In liberated France the episcopal voices that ought to have denounced such anti-Christian and anti-democratic practices as racial discrimination and the torture used in Indo-China and subsequently in Algeria were both tardy and unobtrusive. It is hardly surprising that racialism is so widespread in Christian circles (so influential in the West) in its most virulent as in its most subtle form—i.e. when its victims are unaware. On the other hand the episcopate was right in 1971 when it described the arms race as 'an intolerable evil from which the first to suffer are the poor' and denounced 'the traffic in arms that fosters war and aggravates oppression'. But did their protest touch the consciences —whether Christian or not—to which it was addressed? In a democratic society as in a strongly hierarchical church, the laying-down of a principle is not enough to alter attitudes: it only becomes meaningful when it is lived in practice.

In this respect the churches, in spite of all that distinguishes them from other organizations, are up against the same difficulties as all citizens who are concerned to convince others and change the course of history. The church, writes Monsignor Huyghe, Bishop of Arras, wants 'the values of justice, freedom, and peace that the Lord came to win us for to be propagated and increased'. This is one of the aims of democracy too. But those values are widely ignored or thwarted and the church, in defending them, accepts that it will be 'criticized by those who, whether members of the church or not, profit by the misfortune of their brethren'. In fact it is very much less criticized than it thinks, because in the last analysis it does little enough about effectively reducing injustice. Monsignor Huyghe is one of the few bishops to have spoken up on behalf of the victims of the injustices of democratic society: the 'unskilled workers with no professional body to defend them', who are subject to a 'modern form of slavery' and who are in addition 'condemned to silence'. For his pains the Bishop of Arras has been accused of 'meddling in politics', and he does not duck the charge: 'To speak up is certainly a political act. But what about keeping silent? Whether it is the silence of prudence or of fear, it too is a political act.'[85] Its silences more than its words reproach the church, especially since too many of its words have not been attended by any tangible results.

The churches' official publications testify to their devotion to truth, justice, and human brotherhood, and their opposition to hatred, contempt for human life, violence, and racialism. Men who have nothing to do with the churches are no less devoted to the same values. Yet the form of industrial civilization that has developed in the West is characterized by injustice and oppression, lies and distortions of the truth, contempt for the individual and racial prejudice. It is admittedly not the churches' mission to organize temporal society but to impregnate it with the values they preach. They do so hardly or not at all. Because they have not dared to preach in fair weather and in foul? Because their faith is not deep enough to find living expression in deeds? Because, having eternity before them, they set too much store by patience? Because Christians have failed to have any effect on the temporal sphere assigned to them? Because their principles do not inform their social, professional, and political lives?

There is no shortage of cases of grave surrender of principle and blatant contradiction between words and deeds, but they do not explain everything. When Cardinal Spellman publicly consorted with Senator Joe McCarthy and later with the supporters of escalation in Vietnam he was doing a poor service both to his church and to American democracy. But the silence of the rest of the episcopate lies even more heavily on the American conscience. When in February 1972 Cardinal Pellegrino forbade priests to collaborate with the police in supplying the personnel department of the Fiat works with information regarding their parishioners he exposed an astonishing practice that does not, however, in itself account for the malaise.

The churches' powerlessness in the face of a society whose tendencies dismay them has very much deeper roots. It has a lot to do with the kind of education Christians receive. The number of Roman Catholics in the United States rose from 28 million in 1950 to 42 million in 1960, and then to 48 million in 1970—i.e. an increase of 14 million in the period 1950–60 and of only six million in the period 1960–70. But these figures are less revealing than the results of an investigation carried out in 1965. At that time a bare 53 per cent of Roman Catholic students regarded love of one's neighbour as being more important than the obligation—soon to be abolished—to fast on Fridays. Only 55 per cent thought that 'the heart of the race question is moral and religious'. Finally, asked to choose between 'a comfortable life' and 'a job which enabled you to do good to others', 77 per cent of Roman Catholic students opted for a comfortable existence.[86]

More recent studies have confirmed this tendency to put 'social morality' in second place. Whether the Roman Catholic church grows rapidly as it did in the decade 1950–60 or more slowly as it did in the following decade is consequently a matter of only minor importance to American democracy when such a vast proportion of Roman Catholic students shows so little desire to serve its neighbour, racial minorities, and society as a whole. These choices—not of course the monopoly of Roman Catholics—dictate the very form of a civilization that places the individual interest above the collective, the white race above the black, and material profit above the dignity of labour. A similar investigation among Roman Catholic or Protestant students in Europe would not produce appreciably different results. The only possible conclusion is that the churches have not, in the training they endeavour to give so many young people and adults, placed sufficient emphasis on the principles whose rejection or neglect contribute to the malaise of the industrial West.

The churches, as is hardly surprising, are somewhat disturbed to find certain of their own shortcomings in this modern society inhabited by so many tens of millions of believers on whom they have lavished their teachings. In America as in Europe both Roman Catholics and Protestants see in that society what the Italian bishops, for example, have denounced as 'various forms of injustice perpetrated at the expense of the weak', creating situations that bring out the 'temptation to react in almost desperate fashion to pressing problems that appear to be without solution'.[87] Pronouncements of this kind are plentiful. In a much-discussed 'working document' the Protestant Federation of France has put this proposition to the churches: 'The churches are not properly questioning the broad options of contemporary society.'[88] This 'working document' has been sharply criticized by a number of prominent Protestants who nevertheless admit in a published statement that 'present-day French society, like every society, calls for a sustained effort on the part of Christians to reform it.'[89]

Over and above differences of political opinion and confessional allegiance, then, the Christian churches broadly agree that Western society needs to be transformed. It is not being transformed. Thirty-four European and American Roman Catholic theologians think they know why: 'The authority of the church,' they write, 'which at the time of the Council dared to face old and new problems with astonishing boldness, no longer seems (. . .) capable of achieving positive results in such important and urgent domains as justice and peace in the world and the crisis of the ministry.' They decline to look for the 'fundamental causes' of this situation in the 'ill-will' of certain leading personalities, preferring to put the blame on the form of power in the church: 'an absolute power (. . .) that is behind the times.'[90]

This being 'behind the times' would appear to be a constant of the church. Apart from one or two prophets—and is it not their role to cry in the wilderness?—the church began to take an interest in the working class at a time when it had already been won for Marxism; it discovered colonialism when colonialism was on its last legs; it became concerned about the problems of the young after having smashed the Roman Catholic youth movements; it got worked up about anti-Semitism after six million Jews had been exterminated and—one racialism behind the way some army officers are one war behind—put up no resistance to anti-Arab prejudice; it waited for the Synod of 1971 to study the question of justice in the world; it told Christians some time after they had stopped asking that not everything about socialism was wrong; it is behind the times with regard to psychoanalysis, sexual and social morality, and the traffic in armaments; the Vatican will undoubtedly be the last state represented in Formosa; it anathematizes, excommunicates, and silences less contemptuously than it once did but it remains intolerant of freedom of research and expression although nothing can stop these now.

This dilatoriness is the fault not just of the Vatican or of particular bishops or theologians but of multitudes of Christian men and women. It is not unrelieved: on the contrary isolated voices—bishops, theologians, priests, laymen—have in every case been raised at the right time. But they have gone unheard—sometimes tolerated with a bad grace, often forced publicly to retract their words, even banished underground as Teilhard de Chardin was during his lifetime.

The phenomenon is understandable, however, and cannot in itself be criticized. Indeed it stems from the very structure of the Roman Catholic church and from that 'absolute power' to which it remains stubbornly attached in a world in which men's yearning is for a more authentic democracy. The thirty-four theologians quoted above write further: 'The Pope and the bishops, who are in fact the absolute masters of the church, hold all legislative, executive, and judiciary power in their hands without any effective control.' There is so such thing as a 'good' monarch or an 'enlightened' despotism. 'Wrapped in its own self-sufficiency,' writes Henri Fesquet, 'the church scorned, insulted, and condemned modern man. Modern man has repaid it in kind.'[91] Absolute power is absolutely evil. Certain bishops are not unaware of this: 'In the church,' says Cardinal Marty, 'the head is Christ. Neither the bishops nor the first among them (the Pope) is the head.'[92] But the church hangs onto its monarchical form—a rigid pyramid whose summit occasionally consults the odd representative carefully chosen from the base, an archaic structure in which life and truth have little room to move, an anachronistic conception of authority that is in flat contradiction to the realities of modern society.

The church neither accepts nor understands such criticism. Replying to the statement of the thirty-four theologians through the pen of Cardinal Garrone, the Vatican began like any temporal head by conceding that things are not of course perfect. 'The church,' wrote the Cardinal, 'needs continually to be reforming itself; it has no right to put up with its faults any more than with its slowness when these can be avoided.' So it looks as if it might be possible and even desirable to draw the church's attention to such faults and instances of slowness, to look into their causes, and to engage those concerned in discussion. But no. 'There would be little hope for the church,' Cardinal Garrone went on, 'if the will of the faithful alone or even of a body of theologians could lay down the requirements of doctrinal fidelity on the basis of numbers or demagogic pressure.' The argument is decisive: intervention goes unheard if it is unobtrusive and if it creates a bit of a stir is equated with 'demagogic pressure' applied not to put across a point of view but to 'lay down' the direction to be followed. It only remains for theologians to keep their mouths shut. You must, the Cardinal told them, 'have a great deal of presumption to believe (yourselves) the authentic witnesses of the Gospel against those responsible for the faith'.[93] But who are 'those responsible for the faith'? They presume nothing: they *know* that they are the 'authentic witnesses of the Gospel'.

This kind of attitude cannot possibly help Christians to conduct themselves either in the church or in temporal society as responsible people alive to what is going on in the world, aware of the kind of problems that arise, and prepared to look for possible solutions. Right across the political spectrum only a minority of Christians is actively involved in the life of society: verbally the church encourages them to be so but without preparing them for the task, instead bogging most of them down in a contradiction between the habit of obedience to the absolute power it wields and the invitation to commitment that it holds out to them. 'Can a Christian remain inactive,' asks Monsignor Huyghe, 'when he sees injustice and violence proliferate?' The facts show that the majority of Christians do indeed remain inactive. Used as they are to an absolute authority within the church, there is every chance that they will take no initiative in social, economic, political, and cultural life. Yet, said Paul VI in his closing speech at the Council, 'we more than anyone exalt man; the church revolves around man; the Catholic religion is for humanity; in a sense it is the life of humanity.'[94] Humanity is not convinced.

For the churches as for the democratic societies of the West, man is tending to become an abstraction. The victims of drugs, of road accidents, of murder—these are abstractions: only the peddlers' profits, the driver's rash conceit, the murderer's madness are real. The exploited workers, the bludgeoned demonstrators, the public steeped in scenes of violence—these are abstractions: only the firm's balance-sheet, the order maintained or restored, the film or television company's receipts are real. The citizens whose cards are computer analysed, whose telephone conversations are tapped, whose private lives are subjected to every kind of invasion—these are abstractions: only efficiency, the police, public security are real. Abstract too is the reader of a newspaper regarded as a commercial undertaking: only the advertising receipts are real. Abstract the victims of racialism and the truths preached from the pulpit: real only the power of the white man and the authority of the hierarchy.

It is not easy to 'obliterate' man, as Lucien Goldmann puts it, without a good deal of violence. Thomas Merton wrote: 'Clearly a system of defence that leads to the destruction of millions of innocent human beings and a severe curtailment of liberties (. . .) can be regarded as legitimate when it is a question of defending another *system* or an organization.' But, he added, it was obviously not 'a means of protecting the *person* and his rights since (the system) sacrifices them to what it believes to be its own interests.' And he concluded: 'It is not the human being and his rights that are considered first of all but the system. It is not a question of flesh and blood but of an abstraction.'[95] The churches are an integral part of that system.

Further on Thomas Merton wrote:

When we speak of ourselves as the 'free world' we are speaking above all of a world in which *business* is free. The liberty of the individual only comes afterwards, because we see it as depending on money (. . .). Consequently the most essential freedom is the freedom to make money (. . .). Our society is mainly organized for business, and every time we have to make a choice between the rights of the human being and the advantage of a profit-making organization, the former have a job getting a hearing. Profits first, people second.[96]

The physical violence, legal or otherwise, that maintains this state of affairs would be as nothing without the implicit violence of the values from which it stems and that it seeks to protect—even, if need be, against man himself.

References

1 *Time*, 20 December 1971.
2 *Newsweek*, 20 December 1971.
3 *Statistical Abstract of the United States*, 1971, p. 144.
4 *Idem.*, p. 147.

5 Lucien Goldmann, *La création culturelle dans la société moderne*, Denoël-Gonthier, Paris, 1971.

6 Melvin Maddocks, 'In Praise of Reticence', in *Time*, 23 November 1970.

7 Between 1950 and 1970 paper consumption doubled in the United States and quadrupled in Western Europe. Even with used-paper recovery it exceeds the annual growth rate of forests: the West is becoming deforested.

8 Yves Charrier and Jacques Ellul, *Jeunesse délinquante*, Mercure de France, Paris, 1971.

9 Dr Escoffier-Lambiotte, 'L'origine des troubles mentaux', in *Le Monde*, 9 February 1972.

10 *Idem.*

11 Alvin Toffler, *Future Shock*, Random House, New York, 1970.

12 Jacques Fauvet, 'Ordre et contradiction', in *Le Monde*, 14 March 1972.

13 Speech of 15 August 1971.

14 Speech on the state of federal justice, given at St Louis, Missouri, on 10 May 1970; printed in full in *US News and World Report*, 24 August 1970.

15 Henry Kissinger, in *Agenda for the Nation*, Brookings Institution, 1968.

16 *US News and World Report*, 24 August 1970.

17 *Newsweek*, 17 February 1972.

18 *Idem.*

19 *Newsweek*, 6 March 1972.

20 *Le Monde*, 30 December 1971.

21 Arthur Schlesinger Jr., *The Crisis of Confidence*, André Deutsch, 1969.

22 Andrew Hacker, *The End of the American Era*, op. cit., pp. 226 and 230.

23 Pierre Sorlin, *La Société française*, vol. II, Arthaud, 1971.

24 Pierre Vidal-Naquet, *La Torture dans la République. Essai d'histoire et de politique contemporaines*, Editions de Minuit, Paris, 1972.

25 *Le Monde*, 16 December 1971.

26 Fernand Cathala, honorary divisional superintendent of police, *Cette police si décriée*, Editions du Champ-de-Mars, Paris, 1971.

27 *Les problèmes de la police*, memorandum of the 'Syndicat national des officiers de police', 1972.

28 Gérard Monate, *La Police, pour qui? avec qui?*, Editions de l'Epi, Paris, 1972.

29 Roger Daurelle, president of the Independent Federation of Police Unions and general secretary of the National Union of Uniformed Police, 'Pour une police républicaine', in *Preuves*, 1st quarter, 1972.

30 *Newsweek*, 27 December 1971.

31 *Newsweek*, 3 January 1972.

32 The *New Republic*, 13 November 1971.

33 *Newsweek*, 24 January 1972.

34 *Time*, 3 January 1972; *Newsweek*, 3 January 1972.

35 *Newsweek*, 20 March 1972.

[36] A number of trials have still not isolated the person or persons responsible for those deaths at Kent State University. See *Time*, 20 December 1971.

[37] Jacques Nobécourt, 'Les juges de l'affaire Valpreda vont devoir s'interroger sur l'existence d'une machination politique', in *Le Monde*, 23 February 1972.

[38] Alain Clément, in *Le Monde*, 23 February 1972; see also *Newsweek*, 31 January and 14 February 1972.

[39] Jean Pinatel, *La Société criminogène*, Calmann-Lévy, Paris, 1971.

[40] John Barron Mays, *Crime and the Social Structure*, Faber & Faber, 1963.

[41] The population index increased from 100 to 112 between 1960 and 1968, the index of convictions from 100 to 145 for the assize courts and from 100 to 138 for courts of summary jurisdiction.

[42] Jean Pinatel, *op. cit.*, p. 91.

[43] Denis Szabo, 'Urbanisation et criminalité', in *Chronique sociale de France*, July 1969.

[44] Roger-Henri Guerrand, *La Libre Maternité*, Casterman, 1971.

[45] *Idem.*, p. 77.

[46] *Time*, 16 February 1970.

[47] Alain Clément, in *Le Monde*, 29 February 1972.

[48] See 'Judging the Grand Jury', in *Time*, 7 February 1972.

[49] *Washington Post*, 14 February 1970.

[50] *Le Monde*, 21 March 1972.

[51] *Le Monde*, 1 March 1972.

[52] See 'Turmoil on Taps', in *Time*, 6 March 1972.

[53] Abe Fortas, 'The Law: Time for Change', in the *New York Times*, 12 December 1970.

[54] Anthony Lester, 'The Supreme Court—For Export?', in the *New York Times*, 12 December 1970.

[55] *Idem.*

[56] Philip B. Kurland, 'The Judicial Process: It Needs More Able Judges to Resolve Tough Legal Questions', in the *New York Times*, 12 December 1970.

[57] Bertram Gross, 'Can It Happen Here?', in the *New York Times*, 4 January 1971.

[58] Daniel Morgaine, *Dix ans pour survivre: Un quotidien grand public en 1980*, foreword by Pierre Lazareff, Hachette, Paris, 1972.

[59] Andrew Hacker, *op. cit.*, p. 44.

[60] See 'The Great WW', in *Newsweek*, 6 March 1972.

[61] Jack Anderson and Ronald W. May, *McCarthy*, The Beacon Press, Boston, 1952, p. 174.

[62] James Aronson, *The Press and the Cold War*, Bobbs-Merrill, 1971; see also John Hohenberg, *Free Press, Free People: The Best Cause*, Columbia University Press, 1971.

[63] Bucinator, 'Counterfeit News', in *Harper's Magaziine*, May 1972, p. 34.

[64] The three newspapers were the *Journal American*, founded in 1937 with the

amalgamation of *The Journal* and *The American*; the *Herald Tribune*, outcome of the 1924 merger of four dailies published in 1900; and the *World Telegram and Sun*, heir to seven newspapers in 1950 after a series of mergers.

65 'A Newspaper Dies', in the *New York Times*, international edition, 8 May 1967.

66 Robert Hersant, letter to *Paris-Normandie*; quoted in *Le Journaliste*, August–September–October 1971.

67 *Le Journaliste, op. cit.*

68 Edward Murrow and Walter Lippmann quoted in Claude Julien, *Le nouveau Nouveau Monde*, Julliard, 1960, pp. 281–3.

69 Jacques Sauvageot, 'Les quotidiens en péril', in *Le Monde*, 27 October 1971.

70 See *Le Monde*, 2 December 1971.

71 See *Le Monde*, 8 March 1972.

72 See *Le Monde*, 16 March 1972.

73 *Time*, 6 March 1972.

74 See *Droit et Liberté*, organ of the MRAP, January 1972.

75 *Idem.*

76 *Lecture pour tous*, December 1971.

77 Quoted by Marquita Pool, 'Black Judges', in *Essence*, November 1971.

78 Thomas Merton, *The Black Revolution II: The Legend of Tucker Caliban*, 1963.

79 *Idem.*

80 *Idem.*

81 Between 1965 and 1970 the number of ordinations of secular priests fell from 646 to 284 in France, from 473 to 277 in West Germany, and from 80 to 4 in Holland; in the United States the number of seminarists fell from 48,046 to 23,822. Italy had one priest to every 350 inhabitants at the beginning of the century and has one for every 1,900 now. 8,287 priests were released from their vows between 1 January 1963 and 31 March 1969, and another 3,350 in 1970 alone. A further 3,000 are estimated to have given up their ministry without asking for dispensation (*Informations Catholiques Internationales*, 15 September 1971).

82 Statement of 6 February 1972.

83 Statement of 19 November 1961.

84 See 'Pacifist Portfolios?', in *Time*, 17 January 1972.

85 Monsignor Huyghe, Bishop of Arras, 'L'Eglise fait de la politique', in *Informations Catholiques Internationales*, 1 April 1972.

86 See *Newsweek*, 3 May 1965.

87 Statement by the Italian episcopate; see *Le Monde*, 2 March 1972.

88 Fédération Protestante de France, *Eglise et Pouvoirs*, p. 23.

89 See *Le Monde*, 9 February 1972.

90 'La résignation dans l'Eglise', in *Informations Catholiques Internationales*, 15 April 1972.

91 Henri Fesquet, *La foi toute nue*, Grasset, Paris, 1972, p. 17.
92 See *Le Monde*, 4 July 1971.
93 Cardinal Garrone, in the *Osservatore Romano*.
94 Paul VI, speech given on 6 December 1965.
95 Thomas Merton, *op. cit.*, p. 34.
96 *Idem.*

CONCLUSION

Hope or Annihilation

Notwithstanding the enormous progress they have brought their citizens the democracies of the West have failed to achieve their aims. This is in itself no condemnation for it is rare enough for human endeavours to be wholly crowned with success. But have the democracies mobilized all available resources to realize their declared ambitions? A review of the situation in Western Europe and North America suggests a pessimistic answer: the industrialized societies appear to have sacrificed their properly democratic objectives to other preoccupations. Without openly repudiating them, they have pushed them into the background—sometimes to the point of losing sight of them altogether.

Indeed the pursuit of wealth and power seems to have become their prime concern. But other, non-democratic states or states answering to different definitions of democracy are also, with varying degrees of success, pursuing the same goals. If it is to be democratic increasing affluence evidently presupposes an equitable distribution: the fruits of expansion, however, are most inequitably distributed and certain social categories, if they are not passed over altogether, receive only crumbs, while a minority helps itself to the lion's share. Economic power can set man free by relieving him of worry about his means of livelihood: when seized by a small group, however, it imposes other forms of alienation upon a majority that is coerced into forms of labour it has not chosen, a style of life in which it is more or less ill at ease, and a bondage it has no chance of escaping. Similarly, political power is indispensable to any democracy in so far as it provides a means of restraining or breaking the power of modern feudalisms: it becomes intolerable when instead it makes itself their ally or vassal.

Wealth and power are among the aims of every human society, but they can never be the primary aims of a democratic society. For a democratic society the primary aims are and will remain liberty, equality, justice, and fraternity—and these will never be mere by-products of economic expansion. Since the beginning of this century the West has radically transformed its apparatus of production, vastly increased its wealth, pushed up its level of consumption, and completely changed its way of life. It has freed millions of men and women from poverty, sickness, and ignorance and has whisked them—to take only one example—from the horse and cart to the supersonic airliner. But have liberty, equality, and justice progressed as rapidly? No—their progress has been extremely slow, continually coming up against the privileges of money or of a particular class, against prejudice, sectarianism, and the paralysis of thought. The humblest strata of society are on the threshold of secondary education and the private car at a time when the class whose privileges these once were has reached the stage of highly specialized education and the private aeroplane. Wealth and power have enormously boosted the general level of society and yet failed to make society truly democratic. The poor are less poor but inequalities are as great; their ignorance has been lessened but without putting them in possession of the knowledge of humanity indispensable to the exercise of power; their comfort has been increased but without making the relative luxuries of the rich any less offensive; they raise their voices but make less noise than the megaphone men of the mass media and the advertising industry. Their only weapons are what they were at the beginning of the century—their vote and the withholding of their labour, while the instruments at the disposal of the economically and politically powerful have been perfected by every resource of science and technology. Wealth and power could have brought democracy to manhood: they have assiduously maintained it in infancy.

Over the ruins of autocratic and feudal regimes the democracies once promised man freedom: they have left him in the grip of faceless bureaucracies, powerless and ill-informed with regard to decisions in whose making he has no hand, and finally subject to a new absolutism —that of a conception of 'progress' arbitrarily identified with the categorical obligation to continue—in the name of survival—to push the production-consumption rate higher and higher and pay any price for expansion.

The democracies once promised equality—a difficult commodity to secure. But the privileges of wealth and culture remain solidly grounded in a discriminatory system of education, even in countries where education is highly developed, in the inequitable remuneration of capital and labour, and in the structure of taxation. In the age of affluence poverty is an accident neither for southern Italy nor for the unemployed of the Milan region, any more than it is for 24 million white and black Americans, for the West's unskilled workers, for the 10 million migrant workers in Europe, for the old people reduced to the subsistence level, and above all for the children of poor families.

For modern man the social and economic equality proclaimed by the democracies was to be a form of everyday justice that he would achieve by his labour and by his own sustained endeavours. He knew it would never be perfect, but great things could be hoped for because rich and poor had identical rights in the voting-booth. Universal suffrage, the source of the new power, would give the underprivileged a decisive say in government. With numbers on their side they would be able to correct politically the most serious economic abuses and prevent the powerful from crushing the weak. The sovereignty of the people would usher in a new and genuine order based not on oppression but on solidarity. Utopia? All those ballots have not succeeded in getting the better of the power of money. The rich man's vote carries more weight than the poor man's for the simple reason that the whole story is not told in the voting-booth. It takes a great deal of money to finance an election campaign, pay for propaganda, or run a newspaper. And democracy, in abandoning its efforts to secure political equality of citizens, has stopped halfway.

Economic and social justice was to be backed up and reinforced by the justice the courts would administer in the name of the sovereign people. But here too men's hopes have been disappointed. When Ramsay Clark, former US Attorney-General, published his book *Crime in America*, *Life* magazine, hardly a subversive organ, wrote: '(This is) a book that could stir people of conscience to demolish the courts, the prisons, and police networks and replace them with a system that is decent.'[1] With the crime rate so much higher in the United States than it is in Europe, a former member of the American government could even say: 'What we have is a non-system in which the police don't catch the criminals, the courts don't try them, and the prisons don't reform them.'[2] Europe, following in America's footsteps, knows its justice is not the same for all. The black man and the Puerto Rican in the United States, the Algerian and the Portuguese in France, the West Indian in Britain, and the poor and under-educated everywhere know that they are dealing with a fallible judicial system—permanently overloaded because it is under-equipped, and too often marked by incomprehension and the prejudices of education and class.

The old words have become worn for not finding expression in deeds. Can one still write them without fear of ridicule? Liberty, equality, justice—even more than these democracy bred the hope of a fraternal society. Yet the societies of the West are marked by surliness, resignation, and opportunism—all of which presuppose either indifference or greed, leaving no room for fraternity. Fraternity, however, is born again with every spark of confidence in the future. Whenever there is a fresh surge of hope, whether real or fallacious, as in Paris at the time of the Liberation and then again in May 1968, or as in the United States in the wake of Roosevelt despite the economic crisis, in Adlai Stevenson's entourage despite the Korean war, in Eugene McCarthy's despite the Vietnam war—each time the crowds rediscover the spirit of fraternity, spreading alarm among the adherents of the *status quo*. 'Another and much more drastic result of shattered hope is destructiveness and violence,' writes Erich Fromm.[3]

For encroachments on freedom, social inequalities, and 'economic frustration'—to quote Fromm further—can irritate and anger but are not enough to drive a person to 'hatred and violence'. To get that far he must also have lost all hope of changing the order of things. 'There is little doubt,' Fromm adds, 'that groups which are so deprived and mistreated that they cannot even be hopeless because they have no vision of hope are less violent than those who see the possibility of hope and yet recognize at the same time that the circumstances make the realization of their hopes impossible.' That is why the sub-proletariat is less rebellious than the students. This will to hope and fraternity has been interpreted as a play urge, a 'ludic tendency'. A spontaneous popular fête followed the fall of the Bastille and recurs whenever, in Washington, Paris, or Rome, an aberrant power looks to be on the verge of tottering. Once dashed, that hope gives way to a gloomy resignation on the part of the majority and, on the part of the few, to the destructive instinct, the thirst for violence. In neither case is there any room for fraternity.

Abandoning their great aims of increased liberty, fuller equality, more equitable justice, and the fraternity of communal endeavour, the democracies of the West have concentrated their energies and their resources on developing production and consumption at the same time as buttressing their security. The two spheres are inextricably bound up with one another: the apparatus of production must be protected against Communist 'subversion' during the Cold War and against 'Leftists' in time of peaceful coexistence. But security is also threatened from without, and on both sides of the Atlantic improvements in the machinery for maintaining order at home are accompanied by armaments pro-grammes that have the additional merit of stimulating production.

Asked to choose, large numbers of citizens opt for security rather than freedom. In the name of security, with the established order threatened by little but itself, they accept state secrecy, the violation of privacy, telephone tapping, police raids, the extension of pre-trial detention, the banning of demonstrations, and pressure—successful or not—on the press. 'Those who are attracted to the non-alive are the people who prefer "law and order" to living structure, bureaucratic to spontaneous methods, gadgets to living beings, repetition to originality, neatness to exuberance (. . .). They want to control life because they are afraid of its uncontrollable spontaneity.'

No one has given a better definition of the conservative attitude in the modern world: wedded to the 'law and order' slogan, it reinforces bureaucracy, rates organization above the individual and the material object above life, and thinks it can fulfil man's aspirations by fitting him out with gadgets and appliances. Thus the consumer society is born.

Other countries have developed bureaucratic regimes that do not give the individual the fun of fiddling around with gadgets and do not tolerate spontaneous reactions. Has their hostility towards the Western democracies become the chief justification of the sclerosis affecting the democratic spirit in the West? Will the West protect itself by promot-ing the freedom on which it is based or, as it is only too inclined to do, by tightening the controls imposed in the name of security?

Over against this curious yet powerful civilization a kind of 'counter-culture' is—hesitantly enough, it is true—taking shape: not 'law and order' but freedom; rather than the dominion of bureaucracy and organization, the spontaneity of the individual; instead of things and the consumption of things, life; not possessing or *having* more but *being* more fully oneself. For all its folkloristic aspects this counter-culture by no means rejects technology—only the ideology underlying it, according to which the tasks assigned to man are chosen not on the basis of his needs and desires but on the basis of what technology can and cannot do. When it stops being an instrument in the service of man, technology starts dictating norms: the machine can go faster, *ergo* it will go faster and the operator has no choice but to speed up his movements, however crazy the pace; it is possible to manufacture a fragmentation bomb, *ergo* industry produces it and the army uses it in Vietnam. In a study for the Massachusetts Institute of Technology a

management expert, Hasan Ozbekhan, criticizes this widespread intellectual attitude: 'Thus, feasibility, which is a strategic concept, becomes
elevated into a normative concept, with the result that whatever technological reality indicates we can do is taken as implying that we must
do it.'[4] The values have been reversed: ceasing to be man's instrument,
technology has come to impose its own requirements upon man.

The first country to enter the technological era, the United States is
also the first country effectively to have challenged this 'technological
ideology'. Under pressure of public opinion, the government had to
abandon construction of the SST supersonic aircraft, a costly project
that was scrapped in favour of projects of a less spectacular nature but
of more use to man. Lagging behind America as it does, Europe will
eventually come to see that it has taken a wrong turning: it is technically
possible to put more and more cars on the road every year, to produce
and consume ever greater quantities with ever increasing waste, and to
depopulate the countryside and pile everyone up in skyscrapers—but is
it *desirable*? That is the only question.

In his last book Lewis Mumford has supplied the 'counter-culture'
with the historical foundation it lacked and concludes:

> For its effective salvation mankind will replace the mechanical world
> picture with an organic world picture, and give to the human per-
> sonality, as the highest known manifestation of life, the precedence
> it now gives to its machines and computers.[5]

While crushing the individual between its wheels, a mechanical
world fulfils the dreams of the conservatives by enthroning the non-
alive. Only an organic world can respect life, open the way to human
progress, and resurrect hope.

In the West, but also in the rest of the world, technology can only
be salvaged as an instrument if it is made subject to a culture and choices
dictated by man. 'The way to escape the domination of the machine
over man is not by taking longer holidays far from a life dominated by
machines or an existence ruled by them,' wrote Bruno Bettelheim,
professor of psychology at the University of Chicago. 'It is a question of
finding a way of giving man dominion over machines while still allowing him to draw full benefit from their advantages.'[6] It is an old problem and one that is too often posed in abstract terms. For it is not
mechanism as such but the priority given to production that has cut off
man from man and mankind from nature.

Fromm, Ozbekhan, Mumford, Bettelheim, and many others do not reject technology but the domineering use that is made of it by the holders of economic and political power. It is in the name not of liberty but of security that the public authorities employ the resources of electronics to pierce the walls of private life. It is in the name not of economic equality but of profit that the captains of industry push ahead with automation. It is in the name not of the humanization of labour but of an abstract conception of returns and power that the state and industry develop the apparatus of bureaucracy and technology. It is the conceptions of those in power that stand accused by a form of civilization in which man feels robbed of his pride of place and ranked second to things, the non-alive.

Is their power democratic? Power is defined by the source from which it emanates, the controls to which it is subject, and the aims it sets itself. By these three criteria the undemocratic nature of power in private industry is beyond dispute. As for political power, it will never be truly democratic as long as election campaigns fail to offer the possibility of clear choice, as long as voters have no control over their members of parliament and members of parliament over the government, and as long as the broad lines of policy do not form the object of ample debate.

How has the prosperous and scientifically advanced West come to deny its democratic ambitions? Why poverty, injustice, and crippled freedoms? The holders of political and economic power appear to have believed that increased wealth—expansion—accompanied by one or two adjustments to compensate the least favoured would usher in an acceptable level of social equity. They have failed to see how growth causes fresh victims, or more exactly they have remained the willing prisoners of out-dated doctrines that provide comfortable alibis for hanging onto acquired interests and questionable or totally anachronistic privileges.

They thus cling obstinately to a 'culture' marked by an intolerance that has drained the life from it. Concepts, a language, and techniques that are inaccessible to the vast mass of the population mean that the powerful live in a world apart, a world that lacks any real communication with the rest of humanity. Why can they not break out of this tight circle? Believing in their specialness, which is often the negation of an authentic culture, they seek to condition opinion in order to impose their own conclusions rather than submit those conclusions to the people's judgement. This feeling of superiority frequently borders on the most insulting contempt, even—and especially—when the

cleverest of these mandarins try to cloak it in populist demagogy. They
have explained to workers the laws of productivity and to the Third
World—with notorious success—the stages of development. They have
the knowledge: why should the man in the street not trust them? Not
particularly democratic of course, but it works. It works so splendidly
that the world monetary system they have organized, the educational
system they have set up, and the urban life they have failed to control
are all of a sudden on the point of collapse.

The experts thought they knew and their failures have failed to dis-
courage them: mere 'blots', they say, written in the stars that govern
history and in the irrational behaviour of crowds but not the outcome
of their own mistaken ways. They have quite simply forgotten that
their 'culture' has degenerated for having been made the privilege of a
caste.

The gulf they have drawn between rich and poor within the industrial democracies they have drawn even deeper in the world. Neither
the World Bank, nor the United Nations, nor any government dares
to say that the gap between the West and the southern hemisphere can
be closed. The prosperity of Western Europe, like that of the American
empire, rests on an imbalance that 'nourishes their affluence' but 'at the
same time undermines their democratic principles'.[7] This link between
the prosperity of some and the poverty of others is coming to be more
and more widely admitted. The world economic system, writes Tibor
Mende, is indeed transforming the under-developed areas of the world,
but not in the direction of improving their lot. The change is one of
status, from 'recipients of aid' to 'suppliers of raw materials to the rich
world'. And he adds: 'No foreign-aid programme has much chance of
helping an under-developed country to achieve the given objective of
growth.'[8]

The poor of the West and the 'proletarian nations' of the Third
World are subject to the same exploitation. 'We poor peoples are sub-
sidising the prosperity of the rich peoples with our raw materials and
our labour,' said President Salvador Allende, opening the United
Nations Conference for Trade and Development in Santiago, Chile,
in the spring of 1972.[9] The labour of immigrant and manual workers
in Europe and of blacks in the United States is just as indispensable to
the comfort of the wealthy. For them as for the peoples of the Third
World, Péguy's words remain true today: 'The burden and irremedi-
able force of poverty is that it makes the poor irremediably weak.' It
will continue to do so as long as they remain in subjection to present-day

conceptions of power and to powers that are less democratic than they claim.

Whether it is a question of nationals, immigrant workers, or the peoples of distant lands, the exploited, as every government knows, are the victims of an injustice that threatens the powerful. This imbalance, both at home and abroad, is at the root of all the tensions and conflicts that threaten one day to swallow up not only the affluence of the West but also the freedoms to which it appeals without managing to ensure their full implementation. Why this helplessness? Those in power, however well-meaning, must one day come to understand that they are first and foremost the slaves of their own attitude and of the false values that have led them to reverse the hierarchy of priorities in giving production and money precedence over man. They will never find true freedom without first freeing themselves from their own intellectual limitations.

Meanwhile they struggle to understand a world that has them confused and is slipping through their fingers. Caught unawares by the student revolt, by wildcat strikes, by the Cuban Revolution, by Vietnamese resistance, and by the achievements of Red China, they seek assurance in telling themselves over and over again that they possess the material means to impose law and order—their law and their order—at home and in the world. The arsenals of the police have indeed reached a level no one could have anticipated a few years ago, and the arsenals of the army have swollen even further. Of course police and army can 'treat' the symptoms, but they will never get rid of the causes—unless they get rid of us all.

Since it does after all pay to play the democratic game and respect its rituals, governments emphasize that they only use force in the service of freedom. There is a whole rhetoric by means of which the Western democracies manage to clear their consciences in this way and keep up an appearance of liberalism. They tolerate, both at home and abroad, the odd outburst, that fringe of nonconformity—as long as their essential privileges remain unimpaired. They are fond of 'granting' a people its independence when that independence has been wrested by main force, of 'accepting' a freedom that is beyond being refused. All of which is a far cry from a living democracy as continuing process of creation. Mirabeau denounced this paternalist vocabulary almost two centuries ago: the attitudes it implies are 'tyrannical', he said, 'because the authority that tolerates might also not tolerate'. In a democracy, freedom dies if it is no more than tolerated. It has to be proclaimed—

and then persistently strengthened, upheld, and shielded against everything that threatens it.

Existing rights shackled with ancient definitions, liberties of the individual in an alarmingly frail condition, social justice inadequate and ill-assured, powerfully entrenched privileges—the balance-sheet is hardly up to democracy's promises. The gap between the hope and the reality is what is fostering the crisis of civilization that has hit the West. Other regimes are up against similar and even more serious difficulties and shortcomings. But what Westerners have a chance of rescuing and reforming is democracy such as it was conceived by their forefathers. Democracy cannot be content with surviving: it will last only on condition that it does everything in its power to grow and develop. Has it ever really tried?

Philip B. Kurland, Professor of Law at the University of Chicago and editor of the *Supreme Court Review*, in fact answers for the West as a whole when he says of the United States: 'For if, as a nation, we are guilty of failure, it is not the failure to attain the ideals that we profess, but the cynical failure to try.'[10]

Is there still time? If they wait too long the democracies of the West will destroy in their peoples that hope without which men are driven irresistibly to violence and annihilation.

July 1972

References

[1] *Life*; see also Claude Julien, 'Inquiète Amérique', in *Le Monde*, 2 February 1971.

[2] See 'Justice on Trial', in *Newsweek*, 8 March 1971.

[3] Erich Fromm, *The Revolution of Hope: Towards a Humanized Technology*, Harper and Row, New York, 1968.

[4] Hasan Ozbekhan, *The Triumph of Technology*, study for MIT; text reproduced by System Development Corporation, Santa Barbara, Ca.

[5] Lewis Mumford, *The Myth of the Machine: The Pentagon of Power*, Harcourt Brace Jovanovich, New York, 1970.

[6] Bruno Bettelheim, *The Informed Heart*, The Free Press, New York, 1960.

[7] See Claude Julien, *L'Empire américaine*, Grasset, 1968, p. 399.

[8] Tibor Mende, *De l'aide à la recolonisation: Les leçons d'un échec*, Editions du Seuil, 1972, pp. 175, 178.

[9] See *Le Monde*, 15 April 1972.

[10] Philip B. Kurland, 'The Judicial Process', in the *New York Times*, 12 December 1970.

BIBLIOGRAPHY

Of the many books consulted in the course of research for this book I
list below only those I have drawn on most directly.

ABEL-SMITH, BRIAN and TOWNSEND, PETER, *The Poor and the Poorest*, Bell,
London, 1965.

ANDERSON, JACK and MAY, RONALD W., *McCarthy*, The Beacon Press,
Boston, 1952.

ARONSON, JAMES, *The Press and the Cold War*, Bobbs-Merrill, New York,
1971.

BAGDIKIAN, BEN H., *In the Midst of Plenty: The Poor in America*, The
Beacon Press, Boston, 1964.

BELL, DANIEL, *The End of Ideology*, The Free Press of Glencoe, Illinois,
1960.

BETTELHEIM, BRUNO, *The Informed Heart*, The Free Press, New York,
1960.

BEVAN, ANEURIN, *In Place of Fear*, MacGibbon and Kee, London, 1961.

BIRNBAUM, NORMAN, *The Crisis of Industrial Society*, Oxford University
Press, New York, 1969.

BUTLER, DAVID and PINTO-DUSCHINSKY, MICHAEL, *The British General
Election of 1970*, Macmillan, London, 1971.

CATHALA, FERNAND, *Cette police si décriée*, Champ de Mars, Paris, 1971.

CHALENDAR, JACQUES DE, *L'Aménagement du temps*, Desclée de Brouwer,
Paris, 1971.

CHARRIER, YVES and ELLUL, JACQUES, *Jeunesse délinquante*, Mercure de
France, Paris, 1971.

CLUB JEAN MOULIN, *L'Etat et le citoyen*, le Seuil, Paris, 1961.

COATES, KEN and SILBURN, RICHARD, *Poverty: The Forgotten Englishman*,
Penguin Books, 1970.

COSSON, JEAN, *Les Industriels de la fraude ficale*, le Seuil, Paris, 1971.

EHRLICH, PAUL and ANNE, *Population, Resources, Environment: Issues in
Human Ecology*, Freeman, San Francisco, 1970.

FESQUET, HENRI, *La Foi toute nue*, Grasset, Paris, 1972.

FROMM, ERICH, *The Revolution of Hope: Toward a Humanized Technology*, Harper and Row, New York, 1968.

GALBRAITH, JOHN K., *The Affluent Society*, Hamish Hamilton, London, 1958.

GILMOUR, IAN, *The Body Politic*, Hutchinson, London, 1969.

GOLDMANN, LUCIEN, *La Création culturelle dans la société moderne*, Denoël-Gonthier, Paris, 1971.

GOTTMAN, JEAN, *Metropolis*, 20th Century Fund, New York, 1961.

GREER, SCOTT, *The Emerging City*, The Free Press, New York, 1962.

GUERRAND, ROGER-HENRI, *La Libre Maternité*, Casterman, Paris, 1971.

HACKER, ANDREW, *The End of the American Era*, Atheneum, New York, 1970.

HARRINGTON, MICHAEL, *The Other America: Poverty in the United States*, Macmillan, New York, 1962.

HOHENBERG, JOHN, *Free Press, Free People: The Best Cause*, Columbia University Press, New York, 1971.

JACOBS, JANE, *The Death and Life of Great American Cities*, Random House, New York, 1961.

JOHNSON, LYNDON B., *My Hope for America*, Random House, 1964.

JULIEN, CLAUDE, *Le nouveau Nouveau Monde*, Julliard, Paris, 1960.

JULIEN, CLAUDE, *L'Empire américaine*, Grasset, Paris, 1968.

KISSINGER, HENRY and others, *Agenda for a Nation*, The Brookings Institution, 1968.

KRUTCH, JOSEPH WOOD, *Human Nature and the Human Condition*, Random House, New York, 1959.

LA GORCE, PAUL-MARIE DE LA, *La France pauvre*, Grasset, Paris, 1965.

LERNER, MAX, *America as a Civilization*, Simon and Schuster, New York, 1957.

LYNCH, KEVIN, *The Image of the City*, The Technology Press and Harvard University, Cambridge, Mass., 1960.

MAYS, JOHN BARRON, *Crime and the Social Structure*, Faber and Faber, London, 1963.

MENDE, TIBOR, *De l'aide à la recolonisation: les leçons d'un échec*, le Seuil, Paris, 1972.

MERTON, THOMAS, *The Black Revolution*, 1963.

MILLS, C. WRIGHT, *White Collar*, Oxford University Press, New York, 1951.

MILLS, C. WRIGHT, *The Power Elite*, Oxford University Press, New York, 1956.

MONATE, GERARD, *La police: pour qui? avec qui?*, l'Epi, Paris, 1972.

MORGAINE, DANIEL, *Dix ans pour survivre: Un quotidien grand public en 1980*, foreword by Pierre Lazareff, Hachette, Paris, 1972.

MOSHER, FREDERICK C., *Democracy and the Public Service*, Oxford University Press, New York, 1968.

MUMFORD, LEWIS, *The Culture of Cities*, Harcourt Brace, New York, 1938.

MUMFORD, LEWIS, *From the Ground Up*, Harcourt Brace Jovanovich, New York, 1956.

MUMFORD, LEWIS, *The Myth of the Machine: The Pentagon of Power*, Harcourt Brace Jovanovich, New York, 1970.

PAHL, R. E., *Patterns of Urban Life: The Social Structure of Modern Britain*, Longmans Green and Co., London, 1971.

PERROUX, FRANCOIS, *Economie et Société*, Presses Universitarires Françaises, 1960.

PINATEL, JEAN, *La Société criminogène*, Calmann-Lévy, Paris, 1971.

RIESMAN, DAVID, *The Lonely Crowd*, Yale University Press, 1969.

ROMASCO, ALBERT U., *The Poverty of Abundance*, Oxford University Press, New York, 1965.

ROSSI, PETER and DENTLER, ROBERT, *The Politics of Urban Renewal*, The Free Press of Glencoe, Illinois, 1961.

ROTH, ANDREW, *Can Parliament Decide?*, Macmillan, London, 1971.

ROY, CLAUDE, *Nous: Essai autobiographique*, Gallimard, 1972.

SAINT MARC, PHILIPPE, *Socialisation de la nature*, Stock, Paris, 1971.

SCHLESINGER, ARTHUR JR., *The Crisis of Confidence*, André Deutsch, London, 1969.

SORLIN, PIERRE, *La Société française*, Arthaud, Paris, 1971.

TAMBOISE, MAURICE, *Le bruit: fléau social*, Hachette, Paris, 1965.

TOFFLER, ALVIN, *Future Shock*, Random House, New York, 1970.

VIDAL-NAQUET, PIERRE, *La Torture dans la République: Essai d'histoire et de politique contemporaines*, Editions de Minuit, 1972.

WARNER, SAM and others, *Planning for a Nation of Cities*, Harvard University Press, Cambridge, Mass., 1966.

WHITE, MORTON and LUCIA, *The Intellectual Versus the City*, Harvard University Press and MIT Press, Cambridge, Mass., 1962.

INDEX OF NAMES